ROUTLEDGE LIBRARY EDITIONS:
ECONOMICS AND SOCIETY

Volume 2

AN ECONOMIC HISTORY OF THE BRITISH BUILDING INDUSTRY 1815–1979

AN ECONOMIC HISTORY OF THE BRITISH BUILDING INDUSTRY 1815–1979

C. G. POWELL

Routledge
Taylor & Francis Group
LONDON AND NEW YORK

First published in 1980 by The Architectural Press Ltd.
First published as a University Paperback in 1982 by Methuen & Co. Ltd.

This edition first published in 2026
by Routledge
4 Park Square, Milton Park, Abingdon, Oxon OX14 4RN

and by Routledge
605 Third Avenue, New York, NY 10158

Routledge is an imprint of the Taylor & Francis Group, an informa business

British Library Cataloguing in Publication Data
A catalogue record for this book is available from the British Library

ISBN: 978-1-032-97576-4 (Set)
ISBN: 978-1-041-12872-4 (Volume 2) (hbk)
ISBN: 978-1-041-12882-3 (Volume 2) (pbk)
ISBN: 978-1-003-66705-6 (Volume 2) (ebk)

DOI: 10.4324/9781003667056

Publisher's Note
The publisher has gone to great lengths to ensure the quality of this reprint but points out that some imperfections in the original copies may be apparent.

Disclaimer
The publisher has made every effort to trace copyright holders and would welcome correspondence from those they have been unable to trace.

AN ECONOMIC HISTORY OF THE BRITISH BUILDING INDUSTRY 1815-1979

C. G. POWELL

Methuen
London and New York

To Pamela, Joanna and Alexander

First published in 1980 by The Architectural Press Ltd

First published as a University Paperback in 1982 by Methuen & Co. Ltd
11 New Fetter Lane, London EC4P 4EE

Published in the USA by
Methuen & Co.
in association with Methuen, Inc.
733 Third Avenue, New York, NY 10017

Printed in Great Britain at the University Press, Cambridge

British Library Cataloguing in Publication Data
Powell, C. G.
An economic history of the British building industry, 1815–1979. — (University paperbacks; 753)
1. Construction industry — Great Britain — History
I. Title
338.4'7690'0941 HD9715.G72

ISBN 0-416-32010-4

Contents

Acknowledgements

My debt to the many people whose efforts and ideas made this work possible in the first place, and who contributed in all sorts of ways as it proceeded, is gratefully acknowledged; to any whose names may have been overlooked here and in the references below I offer my apologies. I have been most fortunate in the help received from those who read, and often re-read, early drafts. Those who helped immeasurably by bearing the brunt of early efforts are David Anderson, Peter Coe of Bristol University Department of Architecture, and Peter Whiteley of the Department of the Environment, to all of whom I extend deeply felt thanks. I am indebted also, for help with particular parts of the manuscript, to Peter Brandon and Professor John Burnett, and to colleagues at the Welsh School of Architecture, prominent among whom were Dr Ian Cooper and Jeremy Lowe. Gratitude is due also to my wife for checking, and for patience in the face of adversity (much connected with very practical aspects of building activity!). A great deal of the labour was theirs, though lack of space sometimes prevented my taking full benefit of it; responsibility for errors and omissions remains my own.

Preface

This book sets out to describe a century-and-a-half of building activity, in context, seen both in finished buildings and in the means of their creation. Emphasis is placed on that which was typical since the exceptional, whether major works of architecture or advanced methods, hitherto has received greater attention. The scope of building activity is wide, but at the centre of the study is an attempt to examine the simple issues of who built, what they built, why and by which means. More particularly, there is consideration of change in the national stock of buildings, and agencies of provision of buildings, since the rise of industrial society. The main aspects discussed are the decision to build, additions to stock and losses from it, the physical form of buildings, the position of the building industry in the national economy, building professions, firms and labour, and materials and methods. Concentration on that which was commonplace often has precluded concern with pioneering examples and that which was unusual. Neither have the experiences of building occupants or civil engineering activity been included in the scope.

The study has dual origins: the first is connected with prevailing uncertainty in architectural circles, both with size of workload and, more theoretically, the basis of design. From uncertainty came a climate of introspection in which fundamentals and circumstances leading to the present position began to be re-examined. It appeared that there might be a part to play in this reassessment for a broad outline of building activity, set in historical perspective against the changing needs of society. The second origin lay in the opinion that economic and social influences on architecture too often suffered from the neglect accorded to Cinderella, being regarded as superficially decorative if one looked hard enough, but best kept in obscurity. Extending the analogy, it may be remarked that even where economic and social influences were recognised as significant, often they were treated as the ugly sisters, unattractive compared with more elegant and compelling sights nearby. The hope is that this introductory study may help to heighten appreciation of economic and social generalities as an aid to better understanding of other particularities and the overall position of building in society. Such an appreciation appears to be all the more important at a time when demand for buildings is changing and when resources for their provision are more than usually scarce.

The approach is a descriptive rather than analytical one, relying largely on secondary sources. The aim is to draw together in one volume disparate strands to give a single, more unified, picture. Those who would prefer greater depth are asked to bear in mind the breadth of the subject, the pitfalls associated with sectional views, and the pressing demands of space which enforced brevity and sometimes curtailed explanation and evidence. The structure is that of four pairs of chapters, the first pair dealing with the earlier nineteenth century and the second pair with the later. The third pair of chapters covers the inter-war period and the fourth covers events up to the early 1970s. The first of every pair considers the national stock of buildings and the second considers the building industry.

Throughout, the building costs quoted refer to finished buildings including profit but excluding land, except where otherwise stated. Units of cost, volume, area and so on have been retained in their original forms in order to avoid errors of interpretation. The term sponsor, by which is meant the person or organization with responsibility for initiating and paying for a building project, has been adopted for reasons of consistency, although equally suitable terms might have been client, customer, employer or owner. Statistics and generalizations refer to England and Wales, except where noted to the contrary, reference to Scotland being sacrificed with regret, here as often elsewhere, in interests of space.

I

Buildings in Coketown: 1815-50

'... a town of red brick, or of brick that would have been red if the smoke and ashes had allowed it ... of machinery and tall chimneys ... and vast piles of building full of windows where there was a rattling and a trembling all day long ... It contained several large streets all very like one another, and many small streets still more like one another ...'

(*Charles Dickens,* Hard Times, *1854*)

DECISION TO BUILD

Decisions and decision makers

Every building ever built arose from a carefully premeditated decision which was usually of the utmost importance to the person who made it. Accordingly, we begin at the beginning by looking at the people who decided to build, who they were, why they built, and how they set about the task. Their identity and motives often remain shadowy, particularly if they originated lesser and commonplace buildings which made up most of the national stock. A major reason for gaps in our understanding is the great variety of people and methods connected with building sponsorship and production. Sometimes the initial decision was to develop a site, without heed to the type of building to go on it, and at other times it was to erect a particular building without yet knowing its location. Landowner, sponsor, developer and builder may have been different or one and the same and, if different, their respective interests may have coincided or conflicted; practices changed over time and often varied from place to place. Decisions to build can seldom be pinned down to single persons or moments, rather each one occurred over a period of time and involved a variety of people.

Custom building and developers

The simplest decision to build was one in which an individual resolved to build on his own land using his own labour and materials. The example of a country landowner improving his estate by new building work was slightly complicated by the probable need to pay others for their labour and materials. A similar but more involved case was that requiring a land transaction; examples included a trader seeking to expand who acquired land for new premises, and an industrialist seeking to house his new workforce. Their decisions to build were related to a landowner's decision to develop or dispose of land and here another interest, that of the developer, was likely to be involved. The figure of the independent developer acting as intermediary between landowner and those with interests in finished buildings was well-established, having been prominent in London a century-and-a-half earlier, after the Great Fire. Developers ranged from such well-connected figures as the architect John Nash to a heterogeneous collection of rather less illustrious small building tradesmen, and retailers such as grocers. Their differences were more obvious than their similarities of which the most significant was a willingness to take financial risks. Large projects demanded large developers while small projects were within the means of correspondingly 'smaller' men. Many early nineteenth-century developers were fairly substantial middle-class men such as merchants, manufacturers, attorneys, architects, surveyors and builders. Usually they possessed considerable capital or access to credit and were attracted to development by potentially high profitability. Although developers were varied and the scale and complexity of their work increased with the years of the century, their essential function remained the same: to provide the organization and capital necessary to create buildings in return for profit. Both the case of country estate improver and expanding trader or industrialist, like projects initiated by the State, were examples of a decision to build made after demand for a building became evident. The resulting buildings were likely to be of higher quality and tailored closely to the specialized requirements of their particular sponsors, thereby reflecting their custom-built origins.

Speculative builders

The widely favoured alternative to custom-produced buildings was to put them up in advance of demand for disposal on the open market; in other words many buildings originated as speculation. In this case the decision to build was more complicated and events could take any one of a number of courses. Alternative procedures included that of the landowner acting as builder by employing his own labour or, instead, employing a builder under contract. Rather more common was the appearance of the developer to relieve the landowner of some risk and responsibility. Developers might either purchase land outright for development or lease it, in which case the landowner might impose controls on the nature of the building proposals.[1] Having secured the land, developers could proceed either to develop it themselves, sub-contract the work to others, or resell it. When building work began, if not before, several other interests became significant, one of which was the source of money reaching the builders to pay for materials and labour. Builders raised loans for this working capital where they could, which often meant a precarious hand-to-mouth existence under the anxious eyes of private creditors, materials suppliers and others. Another important financial interest was that of people and institutions who bought completed buildings for purposes of investment or occupation. At one extreme were widows, spinsters, small shopkeepers and so on, who owned a pair of cottages or small terraces and lived off the rents which they produced. At the other extreme were relatively wealthy and secure investors and bankers, and elsewhere again were building clubs and societies. These were of the terminating type, unlikely to have exceeded 1,500 in number at any one time, among whose members the lower middle class and artisans were well represented.[2, 3] Great and small investors alike were united in earnest expectation of safe reliable income from their property.

The roles of those who decided to build, whether landowner, developer, builder or investor, overlapped and merged so that within the tangle of aims and methods were great diversity and few universally recognized procedures. Nevertheless decisions taken and procedures followed at the earliest stage largely determined the ultimate use and physical form of buildings, and hence remained stamped on them for life. It is to the buildings themselves that consideration is now directed.

*Notes appear at the end of the book, on p. 187.

BUILDING STOCK IN 1815

Geographical distribution

A static view of the stock of buildings which existed in England and Wales in 1815, including those of every age, purpose, form and ownership, shows a range from dilapidated byres at one extreme to impressive new mills and country houses at the other. The geographical distribution of the stock reflected the predominantly rural population; with two-thirds or more of the people living in scattered villages, hamlets and farms, it followed that town buildings were the exception rather than the rule. Certainly the population of towns was increasing rapidly, but the early impact of this on building stock should not be overestimated since many migrants seem likely to have crowded into existing urban accommodation, rather than have been an immediate cause of new building. This being so, the building stock in 1815 would have reflected the geographical distribution of the population only within broad limits. Foremost among the fast-filling towns was London, shown in the 1821 census to have a population of 1.5m, vastly larger than its nearest rival. This was Liverpool with a population of 138,000, followed by Manchester (126,000), Birmingham (102,000), Bristol (85,000), and Leeds (84,000). After that, each with more than 40,000 were Sheffield, Plymouth, Norwich, Bath, Portsmouth, Hull, Newcastle-upon-Tyne and Nottingham.[4]

Houses and farms

Individual buildings in the stock were almost as diverse as the activities which they accommodated, but in quantitative terms it was housing which towered over all other types of building. In 1811 there were 1,798,000 houses recorded in the census in England and Wales, growing to 2,088,000 by 1821.[5] Houses were not only where people lived, but also where many worked; there was a multitude of domestic servants in the homes of the rich and of the emerging middle class and, in rather different circumstances, there were cottage industry outworkers making goods such as cloth, gloves, lace, nails and chairs. The second great category of buildings was in agriculture, although the distinction between this and housing was not always clear, with animals and humans mingling freely in the homes of the poor. The times generally were good for farmers, if not always for their labourers, since population growth stimulated demand for food. This encouraged land reclamation and enclosure and improved farming methods, all of which made building and re-building a major pre-occupation among farmers.[6]

Industrial buildings etc.

Manufacturing and processing of all kinds attracted great and ever growing attention, the reason for their appeal being more novelty than prominence, for the staple industries of the nineteenth century were still only in their infancy. The significance of the proud new mills of the textile industries was more as an economic portent than as an established major part of the building stock. If their numbers were relatively small, the size of some was the opposite, with mills already thirty years old insured for sums of the order of £12,000 or more.[7] The second staple, coal mining, was relatively unimportant as a source of demand for industrial buildings and, likewise, the iron industry did not directly require great numbers of buildings, although some here, too, were impressive in size and operation. The development of transport was in a lull, suspended between the near-completion of the canal system and the beginning of railway building, and with dock construction more in the field of civil engineering than building. A minor field was building provision for horse-drawn transport, required by the quickening pace of commerce, leading to improved roads and a range of small toll-houses, stables, coach-houses, provender stores and the like. Among less prominent industries building need came from breweries and maltings, tanneries, shipyards, potteries and glassworks. The building stock also included a wide assortment of structures required for purposes of commerce, health, worship, entertainment, national administration and defence. To list examples like market buildings, theatres, churches, schools and hospitals is far easier than to gauge their quantitative significance, but according to Chalklin[8] expenditure on such amenity buildings, in the eighteenth century at least, was not more than about 10 or 20% (at the most) of expenditure on housing.

Physical form

The stock was mainly of quite small buildings although there were exceptions, by any standards, in the cathedrals and houses of the aristocracy. Small institutions and small businesses operating in small towns had little need for much more than correspondingly small accommodation. Another feature of the stock was that buildings were less standardized than subsequently became common, apparently due to moderate rather than intense demand for buildings and to increments of growth often being small and unplanned. This led to a stock composed of a high proportion of unique buildings and correspondingly few groups of repetitive ones. Notable exceptions to the rules were the terraced houses of parts of Georgian London, Bath and to a lesser extent other towns.

While the physical form of most groups of buildings was heterogeneous, the degree of differentiation and specialization to shelter specific activities appears quite small. The modest scale of most commercial and industrial activities made it possible for many to be carried out in general purpose buildings; the example of cottage industry has already been noted. Only later, when the means of production became bigger and the division of labour had proceeded further, were more specialized buildings required. Something similar applied in the case of administrative buildings which as yet were undeveloped, but which were to blossom before long into various forms. Although relatively unspecialized in simple functional respects, part of the building stock prominently displayed a different kind of specialization, that of architectural symbolism and expression of desirable qualities. Among them were the high social standing and good taste of building owners and occupiers, whether rich families, their less powerful but respectable brethren, or the occasional institution.

Age and condition

The survival of old high-quality buildings was fairly extensive as a consequence of their durable nature and of the slow pace of social and economic change creating little obsolescence. In contrast, the survival of low quality buildings was poor because low incomes permitted only flimsy short-lived construction and materials. Dr Brunskill[9] has described this differential rate of survival between high and low quality pre-industrial buildings with examples high on the social scale surviving from an early period, from mid-scale surviving from more recent times, and from the bottom of the scale from yet more recent times. The physical condition of the stock generally was rather poor since low incomes enforced low maintenance standards and prohibited replacement and renewal unless essential. Contemporary descriptions of bad and downright appalling physical conditions are not difficult to find. This comment came from Dorset in the 1840s[10], but applies equally to earlier decades:

'. . . *I have often seen the springs bursting through the mud floor of some of the cottages, and little channels cut from the centre under the doorways to carry off the water* . . .'

It is well known that conditions were hardly any better in the industrial towns such as Manchester where cellar dwellings

'... consist of two rooms ... the back room ... has only one small window, which ... is often covered with boards or paper and in its best state is so much covered with mud as to admit little either of air or light ...'[11]

Neglect soon reduces any building, but never more rapidly than when it was inadequate when new; in 1815 conditions such as the foregoing were commonplace, making building replacements a perennial necessity.

Variety in construction and quality

The variety of different methods of construction embodied in the building stock was very considerable. First was variety with respect to the date of building; a relatively large number of ancient survivors meant that many obsolete methods of construction were still visible. Second was variety with respect to locality; the buildings of pre-industrial society reflected in their materials the geology, climate and prosperity of the area in which they were built. Vernacular patterns of building were approaching their twilight, with water-borne transport of materials opening new markets and breaking down local self-sufficiency. Nevertheless local building character had not been subject to erosion for very long and the local availability of brick earth or workable stone still left an unmistakable mark on commonplace buildings in less accessible places. The third aspect of variety was the range of quality between the most costly forms of building and the cheapest. Just as the difference in wealth between the richest and poorest people has diminished since 1815 so, too, has the corresponding difference between high building quality and low. Certainly the qualitative gulf in 1815 between large ornamented country houses and tiny turf huts is difficult to match in the new buildings of our own time.

ADDITIONS TO BUILDING STOCK

Increasing demand for buildings

Pre-industrial society had possessed a quite slow rate of economic and social change and was likely to have had a building stock which fitted fairly closely the demand for buildings. Annual alterations to the stock were limited mainly to that small proportion of buildings which wore out and had to be replaced by new ones meeting similar needs. The stock reflected, more or less, the social, economic and political structure of the society which created and occupied it. When society began to change more rapidly with the onset of industrialization, an effect on the building stock was soon evident. The hitherto close fit between stock and society altered to become more tight in some places and slack in others; this meant that over-use and stress developed in some parts of the stock and redundancy occurred in other parts. Some demand for new buildings went unmet for a while and some established demand for existing buildings melted away to leave them without their original purpose. The growing lag between changing demand and the condition of the building stock gave rise to various responses particularly evident from 1815. One which was appropriate in the short term was that of improvised alterations to existing buildings. Storage cellars were pressed into service as dwellings, handlooms were installed in former bedrooms and old merchants' houses were subdivided into multiple occupancies. The obvious longer term response to the mismatch between stock and society was a combination of new construction and demolition, of town growth and renewal. The provision of new buildings began to change from being primarily a means of conserving a near static building stock into becoming itself one of the agents of change in society.

Social need

The foregoing discussion of change in society and consequences for the building stock has been concerned only with *effective* demand. That is to say, the only buildings to be considered have been those which were both required and for which there was the capacity and will to pay. This is to disregard the existence of widespread and deep social need for buildings among those who could not afford them. An illustration of the distinction between social need and effective demand comes from the lethally overcrowded squalor of the slums where social need was demonstrably great, but low incomes prevented its translation into effective demand. This being so, the poor had little direct impact on building activity and the significance of social need still lay far in the future.

Growth of towns

The period was pre-eminently that of spectacular town growth in which the age-old numerical dominance of rural population over urban was challenged, despite some growth in the rural total. It followed that building activity was most heavily concentrated in the towns: in the inter-censal period 1821 to 1831, the population of Manchester and Leeds grew by as much as 47%. At the time of the 1851 census, the five largest towns in England and Wales, in descending order of size, were London, Liverpool, Manchester, Birmingham and Leeds.[12] The dominance of London was reinforced, with a population of 2,491,000, Liverpool had 376,000 and Manchester, 303,000. Other fast growing towns were Bradford, Sheffield, Salford, Newcastle-upon-Tyne, Preston and Brighton.

Growth and fluctuations

Population growth was closely associated with economic growth which raised the total gross national income in Great Britain at current prices from £291m in 1821 to £523m in 1851. Sustained growth occurred in all major sectors of the economy, particularly in mining, manufacturing and building, and trade and transport, on a sufficient scale to surpass the rate of population increase. The importance of building in this expansionary picture appeared to contemporaries to be fairly constant, at least until around the mid-1830s and probably later. Buildings were estimated to comprise about 15% of the national capital of Great Britain in 1812 and almost the same in 1832. Sometime thereafter the percentage appears to have begun to climb, to exceed 20% by 1885.[13]

The rate of building activity from year to year varied very widely so that it proceeded in a series of cycles of boom and slump about a rising trend. These fluctuations, which also occurred in the eighteenth century, have been the subject of much study[14] and debate. Their origins have been described memorably by Parry Lewis[15] in the words: '. . . population change, the credit situation, and stochastic events are the Punch, Judy and Hangman of our show.' Expressed in more mundane language what happened was that demand for buildings would increase with population growth, rising business confidence would make money for building purposes readily available so that more and more speculators would become ever more bold in their ventures, to the point of recklessness. Then, just as the market for buildings was replete, an externally administered shock, such as war or poor harvest would trigger a collapse. Working capital would dry up, completed buildings would become unsaleable, and incomplete buildings would be left as overstretched speculators failed. With an overprovision of buildings activity slumped until the population eventually increased to mop up the surplus stock. The growth part of the cycle would then restart, tentatively at first, then with increasing confidence. The pattern of cycles which took place after 1815[16] was that of a trough about 1816 leading to a peak of activity in 1819. A trough followed about 1821 and was succeeded by a period of intense activity, particularly in London, which included simple house building as well as many buildings of great size and cost. The boom petered out and the inevitable recession set in, reaching a trough in 1832, followed by more good years and another peak in 1836, succeeded by a trough in 1842 and the final peak in the first half of the century in 1847. This highly simplified account of fluctuations expresses national aggregate figures of activity which provide only one side of the picture. What remain concealed are the wide differences in building activity in different places at a given time; when one town (or trade) was up, another might well be down.

Housing: numbers

Houses continued to be quantitatively the most important buildings, although the exact proportion of all building activity represented by them is not known; even at its lowest in the 1840s, it appears to have been substantial. The increase in housing stock between 1821 and 1851 was 1,274,000, that is to say from 2,158,000 houses in 1821 to 3,432,000 in 1851. The increase was greatest in the middle of the period: in the decade starting 1821 it was 443,000; in the decade from 1831 it was 516,000; and in the following decade it was 315,000. However, these figures should be treated with caution for they refer to totals in existence in the year of the census, rather than to new houses built in the inter-censal period. A period of heavy demolition would give the impression that house building had been slack, which need not necessarily have been the case. Another reason for caution is that census enumerators had no clear definition of what constituted a house, with the probable result that a large house which counted as one in an early census might be counted as, say, six in the following one, if multiple occupation had occurred in the intervening period.

Housing: pace and variety

The rapidity of housebuilding is evident from the example of Liverpool[17] where, according to the census, there were about 16,000 houses standing in 1811, more than another 4,000 ten years later and 38,600 altogether in 1851. During a boom in the mid-1840s, set off by the prospect of higher costs likely to follow impending by-law legislation, new houses appeared in the town at a rate of over 3,500 a year. This equivalent to some sixty or seventy houses every week was impossible for contemporary observers to miss. Here is the Rev. J. R. Stevens commenting in 1849 on another northern boom town, Ashton-under-Lyne.[18]

'Within a narrow ring of what a few years ago was clay bed and moorland with a stretch of hill and a sweep of lovely dale, now swarm not less than a hundred thousand souls. Suddenly, as if by spell of fairy or fiend, stray hamlet scattered township and straggling parish have run together and have become one vast unbroken wilderness of mills and houses, a teeming town . . .'

Neither were the activities of 'fairy or fiend' confined to Lancashire. Those who witnessed the inexorable spread of London added astonishment at sheer size to their wonderment at the speed of growth. The *Morning Herald* saw the capital like this in 1848.[19]

'No one who has recently travelled with his eyes open . . . in the environs of this overgrown metropolis, can have failed to observe that houses are springing up in all quarters . . . Money is scarce; the whole nation is in difficulties; but houses spring up everywhere, as though capital were abundant – as though one-half of the world were on the look out for investments, and the other half continually in search of eligible family residencies, desirable villas, and aristocratic cottages . . .'

The *Morning Herald* seems to have been writing about houses intended for the middle class but there was a world of difference between their houses and the cheapest ones. Some of the very poorest examples were like those at Lye, between Stourbridge and Dudley. There, we are told,[20] Black Country nailers squatted in one-roomed huts made of fire clay mixed with straw and stubble, with thatched roofs, no windows, no gardens and with smoke issuing from the doors. These and others like them were part of the tail end of a long standing tradition of do-it-yourself housing which included flimsy agricultural 'cottages' built for as little as £5 or £10 in the 1840s. At the opposite extreme of quality were vast new country houses which, like the example of S. S. Teulon's Tortworth Court, Gloucestershire, cost as much as £45,000 in 1849, had accommodation on three major floors and thirty rooms on the ground floor alone. Between the standards at Lye and Tortworth was an infinitely varied gradation to suit all pockets: agricultural cottages of the 1840s frequently cost between £40 and £60 for two rooms and between £60 and £100 for four.[21] At the same time typical working-class houses in Sheffield, consisting of cellar, living room, bedroom, attic, privy and yard ranged from £60 to £75;[22] elsewhere in the remote Ebbw Vale ironworks colony in 1811 cottages cost £55 each, while better quality examples built thirty years later by Ashworth to serve his mill at Turton, Lancashire, cost £120 each.[23] The trend of unit building costs, at least for industrialists' cottages, appears to have been downward from about 3¾d per cub. ft around 1815, perhaps to 2½d by the 1830s and 2d at mid-century.[24] At about that time it was possible to build a terraced house for £200 with the following accommodation on ground floor: 218 sq ft parlour, 170 sq ft living room, 105 sq ft scullery, hall, pantry and privy. There were three bedrooms on the first floor and the front elevation was graced by an ornamental door surround, string course and plinth.[25] A considerable improvement on this was a parsonage costing £670 which appeared in a builders' pattern book of mid-century and offered on the ground floor a 208 sq ft drawing room, 195 sq ft dining room, 135 sq ft library, 151 sq ft kitchen, 95 sq ft scullery, pantry, china pantry, w.c., stable and gig house. Further up the social scale was a suitably ornate villa for £1,550, the ground floor accommodation of which included 388 sq ft drawing room, 352 sq ft dining room, breakfast room, kitchen, scullery, vestibule, cellars, larder, china pantry, coal store, two w.c.s, yard, stable and gig house.

It is apparent that the vast majority of houses cost less than £1,000 and that not very many exceeded £300, but the pattern of distribution by cost remains open to conjecture. It is evident that the number of working-class families increased very greatly between 1821 and 1851 and many required new houses in hitherto thinly populated districts. Equally, it is apparent that not very much of the great increase in national wealth trickled through to manual workers before mid-century, implying that the middle class received a disproportionately large number of the new houses. Flinn[26] has suggested that the increase in per capita income, together with a fairly constant average number of persons per inhabited house (5.76 in 1821, 5.46 in 1851), implied improved housing conditions at the upper end of the social scale and deteriorating ones at the lower end. If we tentatively translate this into terms of quality of houses built, then the emphasis clearly lay with superior houses. Yet generalizations are bedevilled (or enriched) by local exceptions and peculiarities; for example, house quality and cost in south London are unlikely to have resembled closely, except by accident, those in the pit villages of Co. Durham or the insalubrious courts of Leeds.

Industrial buildings

In the earlier decades of the century farming, although prosperous, was overhauled in economic importance by industry. Where economic strength moved, so the provision of buildings followed; the early staple industries of textiles, coal and iron all thrust ahead, not only requiring buildings directly in order to produce goods, but also generating wealth and stimulating the whole economy, becoming an ultimate source of demand for all sorts of buildings. Most evident was their effect on housing, both for the labour to operate new manufacturing concerns and as an investment outlet for newly created wealth. The textile and dress industries alone employed in 1851 no fewer than 10% of the total population and over 20% of the occupied population in Great Britain. The industry expanded from a United Kingdom real net output of 100 in the year 1800 to 127 in 1815 and 803 in 1852.[27] This greatly stimulated industrial building activity, both in total and in the size of its constituent parts. For example, Sedgwick Mill, Manchester, built in 1818, was eight storeys high, and Fishwick Mill, Preston, built about 1830 was seven storeys high and had forty-two bays. Traditionally constructed cotton factories of that time cost about 1/8d per sq ft although the most advanced iron-framed examples cost well over double that figure.[28] A similar pattern of expansion was shown by the coal industry which tripled United Kingdom annual output between 1816 and 1850, although here pit head capital investment in the form of engine houses and stores was overshadowed by engineering expenditure. Production of iron, the other staple, rose from 0.3m tons per year in about 1818 to 2.8m tons in the early 1850s, and the number of blast-furnaces erected in England and Wales during the boom years of the 1820s approached 100. As with coal mining, much investment was in engineering, but casting shops, engine houses and so on were also important.

A major new source of building demand came from railway construction in which the peak of activity occurred in the 1840s mania, when house building, it was noted, was quite light.

Route mileage more than tripled between 1843, when it was nearly 2,000 miles, and 1850. Again, much expenditure was on civil and mechanical engineering (itself a stimulus to accommodation for machinery making) but there was heavy investment also in building so that the field '... became an engineer's paradise – sometimes a megalomania – with elaborate stone-built bridges, stations, engine sheds ...'[29] Principal passenger termini were among the most impressive buildings and there appears to have been little hesitation in spending, say, £30,000 on the Liverpool Lime Street station of 1846. The South Eastern Railway terminus at Dover cost about the same in 1843, while a smaller installation at Windsor, designed by Tite in 1850, cost £7,000. Less impressive, but probably amounting to much more in total, were the large number of small wayside station buildings. Tender prices for the five intermediate stations on the twenty miles of line north of Bristol amounted to a total of £6,660 in 1843, although it may be relevant to add that the contractor for two of them, one George Hawkins, bankrupted himself,[30] perhaps by underestimating for the job.

Commercial buildings

Approximately in step with railway construction but not directly connected with it, emerged the commercial office as another new building type. Banks, insurance offices and allied business concerns increasingly built new premises in the City and leading provincial towns. As with many railway buildings, these manifestations of Victorian commercial spirit were often imposing and costly, expressing in architecture power, prestige and dependability. A leading example was Cockerell's four-storey Sun Assurance offices, Threadneedle Street, which cost £18,500 in the early 1840s, about the time when the same architect was responsible for the Bank of England branch at Liverpool costing £23,000. These big and costly buildings may be compared with much smaller examples of similar function built for less than £1,500 each. Other buildings of a broadly related type which appeared in response to industrialization included warehouses, shops and the occasional exchange and market building. The ranges of size and cost were wide and defy easy generalization: in 1850 £7,400 was enough to provide Northampton with a quite ambitious corn exchange, while another in Worksop which included assembly rooms and markets cost £2,500. Such buildings primarily served purposes of goods storage and movement, but increasing personal mobility also led to building provision exemplified here by new hotels such as the Regent, Leamington of 1817 and Royal Victoria, St Leonards of 1827.

Agricultural buildings

The rise of industry and commerce should not distract attention entirely from agriculture where landlords and their more progressive tenants were keenly interested in providing a variety of buildings. Among them were shelter for farm stock, machinery and crops, and accommodation for processes such as threshing corn, cider and butter making, chaff cutting and oil-cake breaking. A plan of 1843 for a small farmstead which was estimated to cost £230 included a barn bay, threshing floor, open shed, small fold, cart implement shed, stable, cow shed, pig bed and run, dairy, fuel store, brewery and small house complete with cellar. This was cheap compared with a mid-century figure of £770 for farm buildings and house near Grimsby, and no less than £2,300 for yet more ambitious proposals at Feltwell, Norfolk.

Buildings for social control, churches

It was the opinion of the *Builder* in 1843 that the distinguishing features of building operations were, in addition to housing, the construction of churches, workhouses, gaols and barracks. Runaway urbanization had led to a rather belated attempt by the State to equip the raw new towns with an apparatus of social control. It led to the provision of a range of buildings which, in view of the attitudes which prevailed towards public spending, is remarkable for size, variety, and high quality. Churches (a term used here to include all places of worship) were prominent among such provision and possessed importance in the economic sense in several ways. Being charged with religious and cultural significance, they had great care lavished on their design which meant, more often than not, that they were costly to erect. In terms of architectural style and perhaps quality of craftsmanship their influence on other building types was considerable: 'Churches are the main and engrossing feature of building operations now-a-days; churches are the determining influence in the question of taste in design, &c.'[31] The major spur to their provision came from the Church Building Act of 1818 which led within twelve years to completion of 134 'Commissioners' Churches' of an eventual total of 214[32] of what Cobbett characteristically (and unfairly) described as 'heaps of white rubbish that the parsons have lately stuck up.'[33] The Catholic Emancipation Act of 1829 also gave impulse to building activity consequent on the Catholic Relief Act of 1791. In addition there was intensive building by nonconformists with the result that at mid-century perhaps one half (less in Wales) of church seating capacity was in churches and the remainder in other places of worship. By that time the quantity of church building and restoration had reached remarkable proportions, but even before then there had been much activity. There were at least thirteen new churches in Manchester in the seven years before 1843, and in the Diocese of Salisbury were fifteen new churches, fourteen rebuilds and forty enlargements. Church building costs, as much as those of other buildings, varied depending on the availability of funds; twenty or so architecturally significant churches discussed by Hitchcock[34] show a range from £40,000 for the 2,500 places of St Luke's, Chelsea (J. Savage, 1819–1825) down to £1,450 for the 480 places of St Agatha's, Llanymynech, Shropshire (R. Kyrke Penson, 1842). The average cost in this sample was around £10,000 and the typical size was less than 1,000 places, although architecturally less distinguished churches (of the sort of only secondary interest to architectural historians) may be surmised to have cost less. An instance in which money seems not to have been plentiful, recorded by the *Builder* in the early 1840s, was at Penrhos, Caernarvon, where eighty sittings cost only £205.

Schools

Another key aspect of social control was education; school building, like church building, passed through a quantitative revolution as a consequence of urbanization. The first government grant for education was made in 1833,[35] and between 1839 and 1859 more than £1m was spent on building, enlarging, repairing and furnishing elementary schools. There was some activity before that time, on the part of the explicitly-named National Society for Promoting the Education of the Poor in the Principles of the Established Church. The Report of that body for 1816 indicated that the cost of some recently built schools[36] ranged from £122 for one with 120 places at Ightham, to £599 for one of two-thirds that number of places at North Creake. The average cost for nine schools was £258, compared with an average of £340 for ten larger schools referred to in a report of 1835. In that year the list ranged from £65 for a forty-place school at Tinwell up to £718 for a 640-place school at Burnley.

The customary space allowance was 6 sq ft per child and the average cost per place in the Durham area, at least, between 1832 and 1850 was about £2, rather more than the averages of the schools in lists referred to above. As with churches, the range of costs was a wide one: the 600 pupils of Hoxton Ragged School got their Tudor-style building for only £750, while the same number of pupils at Wicker Parish School, Sheffield, luxuriated in a building which cost £1,300.

Workhouses, gaols, asylums, etc.

Other recipients of heavy public expenditure were the workhouses which appeared as a result of the Poor Law Act of 1834, grouping parishes into unions for the purposes of dealing with the destitute. The buildings often were substantial, consisting of chapel, administrative block and several wings of accommodation, graced with the popular nickname 'bastilles'. In 1843 Liverpool planned to build one with a principal frontage of 800 ft for as much as £30,000. In Sculcoates, Hull, the lowest tender for a less dramatic building was £8,300, while the paupers of Bromley were to have to make do with a structure costing £5,800. Buildings such as these were not devoid of merit, judged on purely architectural rather than humanitarian criteria. The Liverpool and Bromley examples were both in an Elizabethan style, and no less a figure than Sir George Gilbert Scott designed more than fifty of the building type.

All too closely associated in the public mind with workhouses were lunatic asylums and gaols. Both were expensive buildings, with examples in Northampton costing £19,000 and at Reading (another Gilbert Scott job) £33,000 in 1843. Twenty years earlier a design by Richard Elsam for a county courthouse and prison was estimated at £70,000. The court buildings consisted of a large domed hall, civil and criminal courtrooms each measuring about 50 ft by 40 ft; jury, judges', and witnesses' rooms; clerk's offices and w.c.s. The adjoining prison accommodated 300 prisoners together with gaoler and turnkeys, and its cruciform plan had wings about 30 ft in breadth and almost 300 ft in length.[37] Among the more important prisons built towards mid-century were Holloway which cost £100,000, Pentonville and Wandsworth. Not all were as large as these however, for the charmingly-named Lincoln and Lincolnshire Penitent Females Home was the subject of tenders in 1850 which ranged down to as little as £1,770. Rather similar institutional accommodation was provided by the Lunacy Commissioners whose concerns in the 1840s ranged from a £200,000 asylum for 1,300 inmates at Colney Hatch[38] to one at Northampton for a paltry £1,500. Perhaps the bluntest of all instruments of social control were the barracks. One at Portsea was estimated at £35,000 in 1848 and another on a ten-acre site at Newport was estimated five years earlier at between £40,000 and £50,000.

Health, welfare, etc., buildings

Hospital building relied on philanthropy and appears to have been moderately large in volume. London, where the largest concentration existed, provided many examples including the West London Hospital, inaugurated in 1818, and University College and King's College teaching hospitals. The Royal Orthopaedic Hospital was founded in 1838 and the Hospital for Consumption and Diseases of the Chest in 1841, in addition were smaller examples such as the British Lying-in Hospital, Long Acre, which cost £5,200 in 1848. Another category of welfare buildings in the larger towns were public baths and wash-houses, the building of which was stimulated from 1846 by Local Bath and Wash Houses Boards. In 1850 Preston town council voted as much as £8,000 towards a building with 100 baths and 100 washing compartments, a little more than one in St. James's, Westminster, of about the same time. On the other hand, the great unwashed of Miles Platting were expected to make do with premises which were to cost only £2,000. The sheer diversity of minor building types inevitably renders impossible a comprehensive treatment of all parts of the national stock. Many buildings remain to be mentioned, among them clubs, museums and public houses, beyond which were an infinite variety of structures such as bandstands, greenhouses and the rest.

LOSSES FROM STOCK

Abandonment, dilapidation, obstruction

We have seen that the rapid growth of population and national economy led to heavy demand nearly everywhere for buildings for numerous purposes. When functional redundancy occurred, accommodation hunger meant that conversion and adaptation was far more attractive than abandonment. Among the few exceptions were buildings connected with declining trades such as handloom weaving which left ruins in, say, remote parts of Montgomeryshire. Buildings most liable to loss were of two main sorts, those which simply wore out and those which impeded opportunities for gain. Outworn buildings might well be ones for which there was demand, but which were beyond usefulness because of their physical condition. Structural instability and other serious defects existed readily in a society which had no authority much concerned with the danger posed by unsafe, let alone unhealthy, buildings. Survival was tolerated of buildings in the most advanced states of decreptitude due to extreme age and overuse, with the result that unexpected collapse of buildings took place from time to time. Engels[39] noted that some insubstantial working-mens' cottages lasted on average only forty years and many might be good for as little as twenty or thirty. As expiry of their leases approached such cottages were stripped of timber for firewood and metalwork for scrap, leaving only gaunt shells. By the time that they reverted to their landowners, they were reckoned to be worthless and must certainly count as losses to stock. Another category of loss which has left little physical presence today was the cabins and hovels of the poor, more likely to be found in country and suburb than town, and built (if that is the word) of the most short-lived of materials. Probably many had a life of years rather than decades and would have appeared and disappeared in some quantity during the period.

Buildings cleared because they impeded opportunities for gain may well have been comparatively few. Given the small size of towns and the existence of a land market free from planning restrictions, the incentive to expand on open sites rather than by redevelopment must have been strong. Redevelopment of residential sites with new buildings offering larger accommodation and commanding higher rents was not a very inviting prospect since the cost of buying out existing owners counted against redevelopment compared with building on green field sites. Another reason against redevelopment was connected with the separation of the social classes into middle class and working class quarters. The redevelopment of a poor area into a socially superior one was unlikely to attract occupants who could just as easily move to new and more socially secure developments elsewhere. On the other hand the redevelopment of old central areas was attractive financially where new offices, banks and exchanges were required. These were the sort of buildings which were tied to town centres for reasons of accessibility, incidentally a consideration which hardly applied to new mills and factories. Just as residential districts became increasingly differentiated by social class and house value, so central area business districts began to emerge as distinct from other urban land uses. This segregation was as much advanced by demolition of non-conforming types of buildings as it was by the erection of new buildings.

Railway demolitions

Perhaps the most potent single cause of building loss, at least towards the middle of the century, was that which stemmed from the railways. The construction of new termini near large town centres was the cause of much demolition and the railway companies possessed a commercially understandable preference for old slum areas rather than more costly residential or commercial ones. This kept to a minimum both their expenditure on land and resistance to their plans from owners and occupiers. In other words, the disturbance costs of the poor were less than those of others, and they suffered accordingly. Kellet[40] noted the example of the Manchester site required for the terminus of the Manchester, Sheffield and Lincolnshire Railway which was occupied by a smithy yard, small factory and group of houses loosely arranged with waste space, all under one ownership. The remaining 100 or so properties on the route of the approach line were occupied cellars and houses, bakehouses, coachmaker's works and stables, wheelwright's shop and houses under construction, costing the railway company £40,000 altogether. Again, the number of properties affected by a two-mile extension of the London and South Western Railway from Nine Elms to Waterloo in 1845 was 2,367.[41] These cases exemplify what happened in many towns and were a foretaste of bigger things yet to come.

BUILDING FORM

Densities

Many of the building types which appeared in the first half of the nineteenth century were without architectural precedent and a large proportion of the remainder were novel developments of what had gone before. In the remainder of this chapter we look at some general characteristics of typical building form and construction of the period.

Movement from rural to urban living meant that the number of buildings erected in tightly packed groups increased and that those conceived as freestanding pavilions surrounded by open space diminished in proportion. Higher building densities applied to established places as well as new ones due to the practice of infilling new buildings among existing ones. New houses and workshops were inserted in gardens and yards and old premises were subdivided and extended in a restless search for more accommodation. In these ways remarkably large total floor areas were squeezed into the pre-existing framework of many towns, pre-eminent (or notorious) among which were Nottingham and Liverpool. Building by-laws did not much inhibit such development, either because they were ineffective (no new Metropolitan Acts were passed between 1774 and 1844) or because in many places they did not exist at all. While the resulting densely packed warrens utilized building materials exceedingly sparingly, the intolerable price of economy was paid in lethal and well-known consequences for public health. In more detail, the amount of party wall was relatively great and that of external wall was small; public open space, or indeed any open space, was minimal while the numbers and size of revenue-earning rooms were as large as possible; construction was likely to be piecemeal and scanty, with a profusion of interlocking plans, varied storey heights, short floor spans and tangled roof planes; as improvisations succeeded one another, standards of structural adequacy and weather exclusion are likely to have declined. Conditions perhaps were approaching their worst and densities their greatest by mid-century in the oldest quarters of the largest towns. Here, arguably at its most tangible, was the kind of world which followed the unbridled pursuit by each individual of his own interest. As Mumford[42] wrote '. . . the devil, if he did not take the hindmost, at least reserved for himself the privilege of building the cities', with the result that when a reaction to dense development eventually came it affected all subsequent urban form and remains evident even today.

While slums became more dense, newer and better-off development began to change in quite the opposite way so that some housing layouts became more ordered and open. In earlier times, when buildings had been added mostly in only ones and twos, the resulting pattern had been irregular and jumbled but, to borrow Engels' words again, 'More recently another different method of building was adopted . . . Working men's cottages are almost never built singly, but always by the dozen or score; a single contractor building up one or two streets at a time.' The horrific example of the poorest areas must have served as a warning against excessive density and unplanned irregularity, even where by-laws had little influence.

Yet the quality of individual houses was not necessarily rising everywhere, rather the meandering and informal character of old streets was beginning to give way to greater spatial formality and regimentation.

Building scale and complexity

That an ever-growing building stock was serving an increasingly complicated society was evident in several ways, one of which was the increasing number of large buildings. As industrialization advanced, they were used more and more for purposes of conspicuous expenditure, to house large institutions and manufacturing processes, and to store great quantities of goods. In examining the design of large buildings, distinctions are difficult to draw between architectural expression of display (arising from desire to impress) and necessity arising from physical function (unavoidable or unselfconscious largeness). Great size was accompanied frequently by corresponding complexity where large spaces, or numbers of smaller spaces, gave rise to technical problems not soluble by simple traditional means. Wide floor and roof spans and heavy floor loadings required resort to, or celebration of, advanced technology; buildings which contained heavy flows of people or goods demanded well thought out patterns of circulation, perhaps on several levels; the large number of servants necessary to run a major country house required to be segregated from owners and guests and this meant duplicated staircases and corridors. Just as the prevailing economic preoccupation was with the division of labour, of splitting into component parts, so buildings frequently were planned to provide specialized accommodation for each separate activity or function. A society characterized by hierarchy and differentiation of the parts preferred its buildings to express this wherever possible.[43]

Diversity of form

Pevsner[44] has noted growing diversification of building function among major works of architecture, which took place at least from the Middle Ages. This process accelerated in the nineteenth century, when new institutions and activities demanded new functions of buildings, leading to close investigation of them which resulted in novel building forms. Unfamiliar shapes such as multi-storey framed buildings, wide spans, factory chimneys, massive public institutions like workhouses, and revived Gothic forms are evidence enough of diversification; where it was not the shape which was entirely new, it was often the scale. Diversification was most prominent among purpose-built and unique buildings yet it was visible also at the level of certain commonplace buildings as varied as workshops, railway goods sheds and plate glass fronted shops. However, the extent of diversification among many speculatively produced buildings is less clear with, for example, the upper part of the housing market a conservative one in which continuity in design was more evident than cumulative change and increasing variety.[45]

Lower down the housing market there may well have been increased repetition in design, rather than the diversification visible in other fields. Certainly strong regional differences persisted in respect of materials and form, with distinctive characteristics such as cellar dwellings in Liverpool and back-to-backs in Leeds. Yet the increasing increments of town growth favoured repetition, if not on a national scale, at least locally where it gave ease and rapidity of building. Bigger towns meant that more and more individual buildings looked similar, even if the total number of building types was on the increase. Awareness of the growing monotony of increased repetition, and a desire to escape from it, may have been one of the reasons for growing application of ornament to buildings.

Building technology

Details of the technology of building are outside the scope of this chapter except to the extent that they exerted an influence on the basic physical form of buildings. A prominent example of such influence was the growing adoption of skeletal structures and concomitant decline in use of loadbearing walls. Increased use of cast iron for structural purposes after about 1830, despite high costs, matched the stimulus given by the Gothic revival to use of skeletal forms of masonry. Structural use of iron offered advantages in resistance to fire and vibration, but equally, if not more important, it reflected growing admiration for bold engineering innovations in general. In building design there were circumstances in which it was considered appropriate not only to divide and compartmentalize (as we saw above), but also to break down barriers and call into question established practice. Among the barriers deemed suitable for reduction were walls which excluded daylight and otherwise inhibited exacting tasks at the work-place, both sedentary and active. New domestic windows and openings in walls in general, appear to have been made larger and more numerous by mid-century than in 1815. If so, this was not, as sometimes thought, a consequence of abatement of the window tax on residential buildings, since this lasted until 1851 and did not apply to small houses with fewer than six, later seven, windows. Rather, the reasons for larger openings may be surmised as a combination of changing technology (beam materials, cheaper glazing, etc.) and changing needs of occupants, now more literate, but living under ever more smokey coketown skies.

Although impressive constructional possibilities were suggested by innovations in wide span structures and the like, no great or ingenious engineers, or anyone else, came forward to revolutionize common building technology. There were, to be sure, developments in prefabrication[46] and factory gas lighting, but technical change nowhere amounted to comprehensive or dramatic transformation. This may be explained in part by a preoccupation with problems of architectural style in higher quality work, together with the unfavourable cost of innovations. Technical conservatism of architects of the time may be contrasted with daring progressiveness of engineers, but in middle and lower quality work what really counted was the cost. If technical innovations had been economically competitive with traditional practices, one may be sure that they would have been adopted widely in order to reduce costs.

In all, while there was far more building activity than hitherto, the technology employed was not very different from that which it had long been, an assortment of methods involving the fashioning and assembly of small parts in their finished positions. It is from completed buildings to the industry which created them, to which our attention turns in the following chapter.

2

Masterbuilders and Jerrybuilders: 1815-50

'Example VII. You have a piece of timber 60 inches (or 5 feet) thick, and 96 inches (or 8 feet) broad, and want to know . . .'
(*E. Hoppus,* Hoppus's Tables for Measuring Made Easy, 1837)

BUILDING INDUSTRY IN THE NATIONAL ECONOMY

Large dispersed industry

The building industry occupied a prominent position in the national economy, both as means of support for many families, and as source of products which underpinned economic growth and sustained the comfort and convenience of the people. Yet the great size of the industry was disguised by its dispersed and fragmented nature, in contrast to the concentrated textile and heavy mineral industries. Even at the site of major building work, activity was only transitory and the men engaged there soon scattered to new locations. Only in a few places such as large slate quarries was there a hint of the true size of the industry elsewhere, yet seldom was it possible to be far from the scene of some building activity, no matter how trifling in scale.

The size of the industry cannot be defined precisely because its boundaries were so indistinct. Workload and labour force fluctuated according to the building cycle so that unskilled labourers and, to a lesser extent, craftsmen were employed casually with frequent unemployment and under-employment. Building was carried out to an unknown extent by farmers during slack times, and by agricultural labourers like those at Stonesfield, Oxfordshire who occupied the lull after the harvest by quarrying stone slates.[1] The building of primitive do-it-yourself accommodation in depressed rural localities cannot be given a clear economic definition and there are similar problems in the case of men, such as a joiner and undertaker, who straddled the boundaries of the industry. Because of these difficulties only a general indication of the size of the industry may be gained from the numbers of people employed in it. In 1831 the census showed that there were 203,000 men of twenty years or more in Great Britain who were either masons, carpenters, bricklayers, plasterers, plumbers, house-painters, slaters or glaziers; Clapham considered that this number was very nearly doubled by the inclusion of boys, apprentices and labourers.[2] Twenty years later in 1851 there were 497,000 people (including 1,000 women) occupied in building and construction out of a total occupied workforce of 9.4m (of which 6.5m were male). By way of comparison the only larger categories were 2.0m in agriculture, horticulture and forestry, 1.3m each in domestic service and textiles, 0.9m in clothing, and 0.6m in metal manufacture, machines, implements, vehicles, etc.[3] In addition to the 497,000 building workers there was an unknown proportion of people connected with building, but listed in census categories associated with mining, quarrying, wood, furniture, fittings, bricks, cement, pottery and glass. Even by the strictest definition of occupations, one person out of every nineteen in the workforce was occupied in building and, if male workers alone are considered, the proportion was as many as one in thirteen.

National influences at local level

An industry of such importance to the national economy was bound to be related in many ways to the national and international fortunes of the country. When rates of interest changed not only were sponsors' decisions to build affected, but so was the ease, or lack of it, with which builders operated. An obvious example of national influences on local building decisions was the effect of taxes on some primary materials. Another example was that of local building labour shortage which, it may be conjectured, resulted from rival work opportunities opened up by the railway mania. Most major events in the economic and social life of the nation sooner or later were likely to have repercussions on the building industry. Not all of them were necessarily bad for it either, as any Chartist rioter might have reflected when incarcerated during the 1830s in a new and very expensive gaol.

Links with other industries

The flow of cause and effect which connected society and building industry was not entirely in one direction. The level of building activity at a particular time influenced to a lesser or greater degree all manner of other trades connected with raw materials and finished goods: workers in innumerable quarries, processors of lead and copper, glass makers and those who worked or traded in bricks, tiles, pipes, timber, paint, wallpaper, plaster and lime. The industry also created a demand for coal for firing clay, processing metals and making lime and glass, and was a great user (perhaps the greatest) of such transport as was available. Baltic softwood and West Indian hardwood arrived by ocean-going vessels, while joinery and ironmongery found its way from yard to site by horse-drawn wagon. Canals competed with railways for the carriage of all bulk materials, from timber and sand to bricks and tiles. Building also demanded a variety of skilled services provided by the middle classes, such as transactions and loans involving land, materials, and buildings and, it must be said, disputes and bankruptcies which together provided sustenance for lawyers, bankers, accountants, surveyors and clerks of all descriptions.

STRUCTURE OF THE BUILDING INDUSTRY

Roles and relationships

The figures who populated the world of building seem as shadowy and ill-defined as those who took decisions to build. This was due partly to the transition through which their relationships and activities were passing and partly to the practice of combining roles so that some individuals were at once builder and architect or surveyor, or builder and estate agent. Similarly, some firms were general ones capable of carrying out entire projects and others were specialized ones interested in only one or two trades. New pressures outside and inside the industry made for fluidity, roused contention and stimulated a search for effective organization and ways of working.

Contracts

Such circumstances focused the attention of large sponsors on ways in which to protect themselves from sharp practice and incompetence, and promote efficiency. One way was to arrange for tradesmen and builders to submit detailed estimates for proposed work in advance of carrying it out. An estimate could take the form of rates for specified building tasks or a lump sum for a project, either form enabling the sponsor to compare competing submissions and choose the cheapest. Hitherto much work, for example the construction of large barracks during the Napoleonic Wars, was carried out on the basis of measure and value. This involved advancing money, usually to separate tradesmen, as the work proceeded (or at its conclusion) so as to cover current labour and materials costs plus a customary allowance of fifteen per cent for profit. Measurement of completed building work prior to payment caused enormous difficulties and frequent disputes, with the '. . . distressful, often the ruinous, uncertainty of common estimates . . .' by measurers said to be '. . . seldom or ever right in their conjectures'.[4] The response of Commissioners reporting on the public Office of Works in 1812–1813 was to favour competitive tendering as a superior alternative to measure and value.

Competitive tendering became more attractive and by the 1830s opinion, particularly outside the industry and in respect of small and simple buildings, had moved considerably further in the same direction. By then competitive tendering for contracts in gross was becoming increasingly favoured, that is for one builder to agree to erect the whole project (rather than the work only of a single trade) at a predetermined price. By mid-century, despite reservations particularly among some architects, contracting in gross prevailed widely, although it was not universal. The advantages of the method for sponsors were that they secured economic benefits of competition, knowledge of financial commitment before work began, better control of subsequent expenditure, and that they entered into a single contractual relationship with one builder instead of with a host of less coordinated independent tradesmen.[5,6]

Specialization

These changes in contractual arrangements were matched by evolving relationships within the industry which began to set the pattern for the future. From the 1820s architects gradually divorced themselves from direct involvement in building, seeking instead to represent and protect sponsors' interests, in addition to maintaining design responsibility. More and more they were employed to provide detailed drawings, specifications and tender documents required for contractors to base their tenders upon. The foundation of the Institute of British Architects in 1834 enhanced professional standing and was associated with the drive to discourage older style builder-architects. Similar specialization and differentiation took place in the measurement of building work, where the old practice of measuring after completion was being supplanted by more precise measurement before work began. The method was for a group of contractors who had been invited to submit tenders to appoint a surveyor whose task was to take from the architect's drawings the quantities of materials required. Sometimes two surveyors were employed, one to serve the interests of contractors and the other those of the sponsor.[7] The resulting new profession of quantity surveyor began to emerge in the 1820s, about the same time that architects began to relinquish direct commercial interest in building. One of the earliest prominent quantity surveyors was Henry Hunt, a well established figure involved in work on the new Houses of Parliament.[8,9] Further evidence of a general ferment in the structure and procedures of the industry in the earlier part of the nineteenth century was the foundation in 1818 of the Institute of Civil Engineers and, later in the 1830s, the formation of the Builders' Society, followed by the London Master Builders' Association.

Range of firms

Developments of this sort applied mainly to the more respectable part of the industry contracting with large sponsors to construct higher cost buildings. A great mass of cheaper building was created by speculative firms, although this is not to suggest that all speculative work was necessarily cheap. The range of businesses engaged in building conformed roughly to a hierarchy in which the simplest units were individual master craftsmen whose trade might be bricklayer, carpenter and joiner, mason, plasterer, plumber, slater, glazier or painter. They confined themselves to work in their own trade and often employed a few journeymen, apprentices and labourers. Much of their work was small, but not all; for instance when the owner of Black Dyke Mills began a £4,700 building in Queensbury in 1835, using his own direct labour for excavations, he let separate contracts to various small craftsmen in trades such as masonry (spending £585 on stone and £627 on labour), glazing, 'plaistering', etc.[10]

A development of these small master craftsmens' businesses were those of masters who contracted for, or speculated in, the erection of whole buildings. They employed only workmen in their own trade, usually bricklayers or carpenters and joiners, and they subcontracted with other masters for the remainder of the work in the other trades. An evolutionary step from these single trade contractors (first found in the later eighteenth century) were builders who worked in the same way but who had no trade skill of their own. They operated by making subcontracts with the master craftsmen of each trade and contributing financial and managerial skills of their own.

The most advanced businesses in the hierarchy were those of master builders who erected whole buildings and employed more or less permanently most of the necessary labour. They confined subcontracting to minor specialized trades for which continuity of work between projects was not possible and to times when activity was sufficiently brisk to justify the work of a few extra men for a short time. One of the very earliest of such firms, just outside our period, was the exceptional case of Alexander Copeland, who was paid over £1.3m for barrack building between 1796 and 1806, and at one time employed 700 men. Such larger firms with comprehensive establishments and substantial capital eventually showed themselves better able than small craftsmen to meet the greater risks inseparable from large projects. The result was that they undertook a growing proportion of work, particularly it seems in London, to some detriment of the most simple businesses.

Fluidity and size of firms

The range in size and complexity of businesses remained wide, with some retreat among the smallest being compensated by advance among the largest and, no doubt, adaptation from one form in times of boom to another in slump. Those who were energetic and fortunate enough, proceeded from small beginnings to accumulate enough capital to become firms of some size, yet small firms continued to predominate. An increase in total output, largely by proliferation of quite small firms, was in contrast to certain other key industries which secured growth by means of technical innovations and new forms of business unit. Many building firms ceased to exist when their proprietors withdrew, since company formation was almost unknown in the industry, thereby hindering accumulation of experience and capital.

The outlook of most tradesmen and builders was conservative, perhaps being preoccupied with mere survival in a field in which trade fluctuations were violent and competition fierce. London housebuilders seldom ventured more than a mile or two from their yards or, elsewhere, put up more than ten houses in a year. On the Mercers' Company estate in Stepney between 1811 and 1850, one builder managed to erect as many as 570 houses, but only two others reached 100 houses each during the period. In 1845 in North Kensington, where it took as many as 31 firms to build 137 houses, two firms built 26 and 28 houses each, but none of the others produced more than eleven. The sizeable London firm of Thomas Burton employed an average of 170 men between 1825 and 1832, but most of the work was repairs and alterations. There were nine London firms reported in the 1851 census as employing more than 200 men, and 57 firms which employed 50 men or more. Over 700 individuals called themselves builders, many of whom employed fewer than ten men each, a figure regarded outside London as large. Such builders (who, presumably, were able to cope with whole projects) were easily outnumbered by older one-trade master craftsmen, most of whom employed about six men each.[11]

Bad repute and good

The observer outside the industry saw a bewildering array of firms from a majority which were very small to a few which were large and prestigious. Of the lowest end of the industry Olsen[12] has written that no one of the time had anything very good to say about the speculative builders, who were themselves generally too busy building (as well as too poorly educated) to speak for themselves. Some subcontractors were so unreliable that general contractors found it necessary to pay men direct to ensure that wages reached the right pockets. The relative ease with which builders were able to enter and leave the industry was in contrast to many other industries which required much greater initial capital. The way in which firms could be established in an ill-considered manner was an attraction to men of straw, particularly when business was booming, but the inevitable harvest of failure made for unreliability.

A strong contrast to this not always edifying scene was provided by the case of Thomas Cubitt who pioneered one of the first recognizably modern firms.[13] Starting as a journeyman in London he set up on his own as a master carpenter about 1809 and in 1815 contracted to build the London Institution in Finsbury Circus. He soon determined not to remain at the mercy of subcontractors and invested heavily in workshops and yard and engaged tradesmen on a semi-permanent basis. In order to support this costly establishment, Cubitt was dependent on continuity of work which he achieved by deep involvement in high quality housing speculations in Bloomsbury, Belgravia and elsewhere. His exceptional organization consisted of three parts, the first concerned with law business and the second being a general office staffed by builders' clerks. These talented jacks-of-all-trades were 'expected to be fully competent to fulfil the several duties of architects, builders, and artizans, to be thorough draughtsmen and accountants and yet be practically acquainted with work.' Operations were large enough for each trade to be under the control of a principal foreman who was responsible for other foremen below him. The third section of the organization dealt with financial affairs under the direction of a confidential clerk. Cubitt's success, such that he employed a thousand men by 1828 and later possessed a works covering eleven acres, culminated in the building of Osborne House for Queen Victoria. He died in 1855, his achievement having attracted many emulators.

LABOUR

Range of trades and skills

The men who worked on site and in the builder's shop or yard possessed a great range of skills which conferred a matching variety of status and wages. At the top were skilled craftsmen, specialists in particular trades, who were journeymen having served apprenticeships and from whose ranks small masters from time to time arose. Below came the apprentices who learned craft skills while assisting the journeymen, and at the foot of the pyramid, overlapping in income, was the great mass of unskilled and semi-skilled labour which provided the brute force essential to building. A good proportion of the 367,000 unspecified labourers recorded in the 1851 census were probably connected with building. Here was the rough, tough, casual labour which cut foundations and basements, shifted muck and performed the hundred and one heavy tasks associated with unmechanized construction.[14] The field was a favourite entry point into employment for migrants and particularly for fugitives from the Irish famine.

The skill and reward of masons reflected their eminence among craft tradesmen, particularly where high quality building work prevailed, although in other places 'stone cutters' were identified with the less prestigious bricklayers. Carpenters and joiners also enjoyed a high place among the trades and were relatively numerous. Bricklayers were required on most sites, too, but appear to have had a slightly lower standing, perhaps reflecting heavy involvement with cheap building. The plastering trade appears to have endured a poor popular reputation because of a high proportion of men with moderate or low skill. Other trades were the plumbers, slaters, painters, and, in smaller numbers, glaziers and paviours. Trades connected with materials supply rather than site work included quarrymen, limeburners, sawyers, who suffered technological obsolescence due to introduction of steam power, and brickmakers, an unruly group about to face similar problems.

The quality of workmanship achieved by craftsmen was a cause of anxiety in some quarters. One origin of this was the erosion of autonomy of craftsmen by the growing practice of drawing up full details of buildings in advance of construction, in order to aid estimating. The effect was to move decisions from site and workshop to the relatively remote designer's office. Hitherto craftsmen had decided for themselves details of ornament and window, staircase and dormer, but now they were forced to yield responsibility to professional designers, often with different priorities. Another origin of concern for quality probably lay with the greatly increased volume of work carried out, much of it of low quality, as always. At all events, scamping of supposedly high quality work had occurred earlier in the eighteenth century, and the lowest standards could hardly have reached new depths, even if the intention existed. It seems likely that the level of skill exercised on the best work remained as high as ever; what happened to lesser work took place in circumstances so different from previous times as to call into question the validity of comparisons.

Wages

An understanding of wages is hindered by variations from place to place and time to time, depending on local labour market and work load. Broad generalizations may be based on the index of real wages compiled by Professor Phelps Brown[15] which shows a small rise in wages from 1813 to 1820 during a time when prices generally were rising. Between 1820 and 1840 wages were fairly stable, with small gains for those fortunate enough to remain in full employment, and from 1840 to 1849 wages improved somewhat while prices fell slowly. The average London price in 1826 for 'day work,' which included nearly 20% allowance for profit, ranged from 8/- for well-paid stone carvers (few masons got as much as this), to 6/6d for carpenters and joiners, slightly less for bricklayers and plasterers, down to 5/6d for slaters, plumbers, painters and glaziers.[16] Several shillings below were bricklayers' and plasterers' labourers, and below them at the foot were unskilled labourers. According to Postgate[17] the rate of wages computed on the basis of a ten-hour day between 1826 and 1847 for major trades was 5/-, and the same authority gives average wages of operative builders in 1834 as between 27/- and 30/- for a sixty-hour week. The working week was reduced by an hour-and-a-half in 1847, at which time the hourly rate stood at about 5½d to 6d.

Unemployment due to bad weather, slack trade or whatever, was liable at any time to reduce the earnings of an individual below average wage levels. Allowance for loss of earnings due to unemployment among Leeds bricklayers in the late 1830s was said to reduce average wages of 23/- per week to average earnings of 17/3d.[18] Another potentially misleading aspect of average figures is the differences which they conceal between one place and another, as when unskilled London labourers received 3/- per day while similar men in depressed rural areas earned only 1/9d or less. In general, wages (if not always earnings) in building compared reasonably well with those in other industries and men, if not among the labour 'aristocrats', at least were among the 'respectable' skilled workers. In the 1840s near the upper end of the income scale, skilled Manchester engineering ironmoulders earned 34/- to 36/- per week, only about 5/- more than the major building trades,[19] and less than the best paid masons and bricklayers working on intricate oven-work and the like; near the lower end of the scale, in conditions where agricultural labourers could expect about 10/4d per week, semi-skilled building labourers earned about 16/-, incentive enough to forsake the land for a new life in the towns.

Working conditions

The working life of many highly-skilled craftsmen was relatively good by the standards of the day and as yet sheltered from the effects of industrialization. Helped in part by combination, they were fairly secure and quite well rewarded, unlike the unskilled labourers and young apprentices whose lot was rather more bleak. Their lives and those of the elderly were dominated by the ever-present threat of loss of livelihood. A slackening in building activity, flood of migrant labour, introduction of new machinery, faltering health, a capricious master or merely a spell of bad weather could bring trouble. During the severely depressed years of 1841 and 1842 two thirds of the masons in Bolton were said to be without work, together with well over four fifths of the carpenters and bricklayers. When work was available it was strenuous or at least prolonged, though not necessarily any more so than employment in other industries. When work was not to be found there was the prospect of tramping in the hope of picking up a job somewhere else. The leading trades had a system of providing cheap temporary accommodation in major towns for use by tramping journeymen,[20] but by mid-century the masons' system, which had allowed men 6d per day, was in decay and those of other trades soon began to follow.

Another possible escape from the unemployment which even skilled men could expect in winter was to venture into speculative building on their own account.[21] The inexperience and unsuitability of some men, driven by desperation, may well explain the common occurrence of business failures in the field. The authentic voice of those on site emerges perhaps in this *cri de coeur* found written on a roof timber during repairs to a Chatham Dockyard workshop.[22] Original spelling and punctuation are retained.

'This floor was layed August 1835 by Shipwrights under the Disgraceful System of Classification And at a time when that valuable Body of Men laboured Under so many Grevences, ere this is found may that Dibolical treatment be Confounded, and all promoters of it, the day pay at this time 4s 6d, 4s, 3s 6d only every gang was 15 men, 3 of whom had 4s 6d, the other 4s and 3s 6d. Reader, pause and think seriously of the suffering of your forefather. Fare thee well.'

Organization

The collective organization of labour appears to have been patchy, all the more so because surviving evidence is fragmentary. Early in the period some local groups of skilled men formed builders' operatives' clubs which seem to have led relatively quiet existences free from much conflict with masters. Such organizations suffered the disrupting effects of violent fluctuations in building activity which alternately flooded trades with new semi-skilled recruits and plunged many into unemployment. The repeal of the Combination Acts in 1824 was followed by increased trade union activity, typically at local rather than national level, which included some strikes staged by the journeymen carpenters' society.[23] In 1832, the ambitious but shortlived Operative Builders' Union was formed and developed a connection with Robert Owen, but collapsed within two years. It took with it some craft organizations and weakened others, but the masons' union survived to remain one of the most stable in a harsh and turbulent climate. In 1841 and 1842, the Operative Stonemasons' Society was embroiled in a stoppage on the site of the new Houses of Parliament, serving to exemplify the bitter relations between employers and men which often characterized the period. The dispute was resolved eventually and the Stonemasons' Society later went on under Richard Harnott painstakingly to construct a centralized and forward-looking union.[24,25]

MATERIALS

Applications of stone

The atmosphere of change and experiment which existed in building professions and businesses scarcely extended as far as work on site, where most operatives exercised similar skills to those of their forefathers. We look now at the range of goods of which new buildings were composed and consider some influences on their levels of usage. The example of stone as a walling and paving material well illustrates relative changelessness in the nature of much building work. The walls of many better quality buildings were of well-cut ashlar, many cheaper examples were of rubble (which entailed less labour in shaping) and stone flags were widely used nearly everywhere. The sources of stone included a small number of very large quarries trading nationally in high quality material, such as the Portland group, where 800 men and boys worked in 1812 and from which 25,000 tons were produced annually. Elsewhere there were very many small quarries used only intermittently, for example, in the Cotswolds where almost every village had its own. Nationally, stones ranged from prestige-conferring granites to lowly sandstone rubble and chalk. In the mid-1820s, Portland and Painswick limestones cost about 5/- per cub. ft including transport to London, but excluding carriage to site. When economy was unimportant, Aberdeen granite was available for 5/9d per cub. ft and where economy was paramount, in poor country districts, rough local rubble walling cost as little as 6d per cub. ft. This great difference reflected in part the high cost of transport of all bulk materials. For example, Ketton stone at the quarry near Stamford in 1839 cost 1/9d per cub. ft but delivered to London it was 3/4d. Increased use of inland waterways, which could bring down transport rates to about one third of overland charges,[26] had the important effect of reducing local price differences of materials, and railways accentuated the same trend.

Limestone and, to a lesser extent, sandstone, were also used as roof finishes, particularly during the first decade or two after 1815. After that their use declined in the face of intensified competition from other materials, some of which benefited from lifting of taxes in the early 1830s. A leading rival was North Wales slate which cost in the mid-1820s between £2 and £3-7s (depending on quality) for 100 sq. ft of roof complete with boarding and nails, rather more than clay tiles. The decline of stone and rise of slate exemplified a more general trend in the use of materials. Early in the period typical roofs (where they were not thatched) were finished with variably sized units of considerable weight and thickness. At mid-century typical roofs had regular sized units of some precision and weighing perhaps only one-fifth of earlier types. Similar, or better, performance (though more monotonous appearance) was being achieved with less material and site labour, using goods carried far longer distances from their places of origin.

Brick and tile

Another instance of a similar trend was the growing use of brick for walling, which offered the advantage over many types of stone of regularity in shape and size. This aided the progress of assembly on site and minimized the amount of redundant material in the finished building. Applications of brick included thick, often decorated work in large multi-storey buildings; arches, jambs and other work in predominantly stone walls; domestic walling and infill in stud partitions. Provided there were local supplies of clay and fuel, bricks possessed the attractive properties of cheapness, durability and incombustibility. A result of these practical advantages was that production increased greatly, so that quinquennial average production beginning in 1845 (1749m) was double that beginning in 1815 (841m). More building (and civil engineering) appears to have been carried out in brick by 1850 than ever before, but it is not easy to be sure whether brick was maintaining or increasing its share of the market relative to other walling materials. Observation, at least, would suggest that brick increased its share for cheaper work, although may not have made equal progress in all higher quality building.

Brickwork amounted to a considerable proportion of total costs of typical buildings, estimated,[27] together with carpentry and joinery, at not less than two-thirds in the case of new houses in the first decade of the century, making other trades small in comparison. In a large house built at Deal, the bricklaying and plastering amounted to 42% (£362) of the total cost, carpentry 50%, and painting and glazing about 4%. In another example of two houses built at Brighton, bricklaying and plastering cost about 38% of the total and carpentry about 55%. The cost of completed brickwork was mainly in the materials, with labour charges considerably less. An estimate for new houses for Boulton and Watt near Birmingham in 1810 showed the proportion spent on brickwork materials was 27%, and timber materials 23%, while main labour charges were only 23% altogether. Until 1850 there was a tax on bricks which must have prolonged the competitiveness of various alternatives such as stone, timber cladding and mathematical tile hanging. The rate of duty payable from 1803 was 5/- per thousand bricks, rising to 5/10d from 1833. This was a sizeable proportion of the prime cost which in the mid-1820s ranged from about £1-12s per thousand for cheap London place bricks for foundations and party walls, up to £6-10s for best stocks. High quality brick walling, including lime, sand, labour, use of scaffolding and 15% profit, was estimated to cost 2/9d per cub. ft, cheap compared with good stonework.

The number of brickworks was large and their average size small, activity being local, technically simple and often transitory, with clay dug direct from the building site, if possible. Where site material was inadequate, large contractors for brickwork sometimes leased a brickfield nearby to supply a specific contract; elsewhere independent brickmakers acted as suppliers to builders on a more permanent basis for a whole series of projects. In London, the largest single market, demand for bricks exceeded strictly local capacity and it was worthwhile to bring in supplies from outlying Essex, Kent and Middlesex to supplement what was made in Islington, Fulham and Hammersmith. Brickmakers, generally working in an expanding market in which competition was limited by transport costs, increased output by multiplying the numbers of suppliers rather than by sweeping technical innovations. Early and not always very popular attempts at mechanization in the 1830s included pug-mills for grinding clay, brick pressing machine, extruder and wire cutter, and driers.[28]

Clay roof tiles shared with bricks their type of raw material, production processes and, frequently, manufacturers and work-force. The two main types of tile were plain, which could be used on walls as well as roofs, and the larger pantiles. The estimated cost in London in the mid-1820s of 100 sq. ft of roof, including laths, nails and labour was £2-18-10d for plain tiles and £1-16-4d for pantiles, although the favourable price of pantiles compared with that of slates was not sustained every-where throughout the period. Among other associated clay products which were available were floor tiles and chimney pots.

Cob, pisé, thatch

In inaccessible places with high transport costs, old building practices[29] survived with cheaper materials not only taken directly from the site itself, or nearly so, but avoiding as far as possible the use of heat in processing. There is little record of the quantities in which such materials were used or of their costs, but by their nature they were bound to be labour intensive and often demanded skill if early failure was to be avoided. Among the main walling materials were mud, cob, pisé and clay lump using various combinations of earth, lime, chalk, chopped straw, gravel and sand. The economic circumstances favouring use of these indigenous materials for walling applied equally to roofing where the choice was likely to be reed, straw or heather thatch. It is probable that the use of all these materials diminished relatively and absolutely, quickest in areas of population growth, slowest in remote areas such as west Wales, although they did not yet fall out of use entirely.

Timber

The applications of timber were very numerous and in many cases not susceptible to substitution with alternative materials. Nearly all roof structures used timber, and so did suspended floors, doors, cupboards and fittings; other uses included stud walls, lintels, claddings, window frames and stairs; there were also temporary uses such as scaffolding, arch centring and shoring. Adding to this list all non-building uses, it is not surprising that Britain was, and had long been, heavily de-pendent on imported timber. Although widely used for pur-poses other than building and although the amount of home grown supplies are unknown, the value of imported timber shows an upward trend which must have had significance in building. The average annual value of imports for the five years from 1846 was over one-and-a-half times that for the five years from 1826.[30] Following great increases during the Napoleonic Wars, the price of timber was relatively steady with softwood in the opening decade of the period at around £6 or £7 for a fifty cub. ft load, including duty. The best quality fir was European, but trans-Atlantic imports grew during and after the wartime shortages, and by 1850 Canadian imports exceeded in quantity and value all other sources put together.[31] The cost of cheapest pine at £4-10s per load contrasted sharply with that of West Indian mahogany at more than ten times that figure. English oak, where it could be obtained near the site, was competitive with best imported softwood, but elsewhere the additional cost of transport often took up the price to a third or so above that of softwood. Where no navigable waterways existed, and before the railways were built, overland transport of timber in general often added a sixth or quarter to its cost, encouraging reuse of old timbers (and other materials) wherever possible. When the prime cost of softwood stood at £6-13-4d per load, the price on site in London used in lintels and bonding timbers was estimated at 4/7d per cub. ft, in roofs, and floors 4/10d per cub. ft, and planed on all faces 5/1d per cub. ft. Powered machines, for planing and sawing were pioneered in the eighteenth century, but much timber continued to be worked laboriously by hand. One or two small innovations appeared, such as cheap machine-made nails in the 1830s, but most carpentry and joinery methods and products remained broadly unchanged.

Cement, plaster

A field in which some product development took place was that of more reliable and better-performing masonry bonding agents and surface finishes. Traditional lime mortar[32] began to be replaced on a small scale where conditions were onerous (especially in civil engineering structures) by the stronger Parker's hydraulic Roman cement and, later, Portland cement, the manufacture of early forms of which expanded in the 1840s.[33] Renderings for external walls, encouraged by the first London Building Act (concerned with incombustibility) and by a fashion for stucco on superior houses before about 1850, increasingly incorporated patent products such as Dehl's mastic, patented in 1815. Internal walls were finished generally with plaster, sometimes decorated with paper costing in 1825 from 4d to 1/- or more for a yard 20 in. in width, with extra for labour. For a given area this could cost more than four coats of paint on woodwork, to be had at a rate of about 1/2d per sq. yd.

Glass

By the standards of building and materials producers, glass making was exceptional in demanding very considerable capital and in producing goods which, despite fragility, lent themselves to economical long distance transport. In the 1820s and 1830s glass making was dominated by price agreements between makers, but when these dissolved there was intense competition. Costly improvements in methods of production for cylinder and unpolished plate glass were made by leading firms which proceeded to force out of business the smaller crown glass makers. In 1845, when concentration into fewer and larger firms was accelerating, the excise duty on glass was repealed, reducing costs.

A miscellany of materials remains to be mentioned, most of which were quite highly processed and used in relatively small quantities. Among them were lead, which was fairly widely used for roofing, flashings, pipework and cisterns, despite high and fluctuating costs; copper, which shared some of these applications; and zinc, which was used as a cost-saving substitute for lead from about 1830.[34] In the still somewhat rudimentary field of services, glazed ware and cast iron increasingly replaced wooden pipes; w.c.s were a considerable rarity, costing up to £6-6s complete with valve apparatus in the 1820s; and various patterns of kitchen range proliferated at prices of about £1 for every foot in width, in the 1840s. Cast iron was used for balconies, verandahs, balustrades, and window frames,[35] gradually supplanting the more costly wrought product less suited to repetitive production. Among heavy items of iron in the 1820s were structural columns and beams, costing from 15/- to £1 per cwt, and helical stairs. Remaining products, which conclude this chapter at the basement floor, included waterproof mastic asphalt, introduced in 1837, and bitumen pavings.

3

Buildings Upward and Outward: 1851-1914

'... *houses, churches, hospitals, gaols ... exhibition buildings, and hotels springing up with wonderful speed, and in dimensions beyond precedent.*'
(*Leone Levi,* Wages and Earnings of the Working Classes ..., *1867*)

DECISION TO BUILD

Growth of stock

The growing national economy generated apace new buildings, suburbs and whole towns, on a scale never before seen in Britain. Expansion of manufacture, trade and social control meant investment in buildings; the two were mutually dependent and inextricably mixed. Sometimes expansion took place in large increments giving rise to large and costly building projects, but more often it was composed of numerous smaller increments giving rise to appropriately small projects. The great majority of such minor buildings individually lacked both architectural distinction and financial significance except, no doubt, to those directly concerned. Today, the only reminder of many of the men and methods underlying the provision of terraces, industrial sheds, small shops and cottages is a diminishing stock of obsolescent buildings; a wasting memorial to largely forgotten aspirations and labours, upon which subsequent generations have built both figuratively and, sometimes, literally.

Speculative building

Building projects continued to be initiated in a variety of ways among landowners, developers, builders and others with capital or access to credit. One illustration of the making of decisions to build in later Victorian towns comes from Cardiff during a phase of spectacularly rapid growth after 1870.[1] Most building land was owned by three large estates whose development policy was to lease building sites for ninety-nine years rather than sell outright, a practice which resembled that in London prior to the exhaustion of major estate land supplies by about 1870.[2] Strict control of the quality of Cardiff development was exercised by estate officials whose activity in this respect approximated to that of modern town planners. Most building was by small firms which built houses as speculation, hoping to sell quickly to pay off debts and move on to fresh ventures. Their sources of short term credit are uncertain, but included mortgages given by solicitors (at least before the 1890s), insurance companies and building societies. Buyers of new houses, who thereby provided the necessary long-term investment, were local people seeking a safe outlet for small amounts of capital and wishing to keep an eye on their assets rather than invest in other places where, at times, returns were higher. Such investors appear hardly ever to have been in short supply and when building flagged it was likely to be due to problems with short-term credit or finding tenants able to pay economic rents. About nine out of ten houses were let rather than owner-occupied, and ownership was widely spread with only about a quarter to a third of houses owned by investors holding more than ten houses each, and only six men holding more than fifty houses each.

Custom building

An illustration of a quite different approach to the decision to build comes from Bromborough, near Birkenhead,[3] the place chosen by the Wilson brothers in 1853 when they decided to move part of the Price's Patent Candle Company. They had several motives for moving, since their Battersea site was unhealthy, fully developed and they wished to reduce transport costs. The principal market for their goods lay in Lancashire and raw materials were imported through Liverpool docks, so the Bromborough site was a logical choice. The Wilsons built a new works, houses, school and other facilities, making one example among very many of 'footloose' capital searching for a suitable site after the decision to build had been taken. In this particular case site choice was based mainly on economics of industrial location, but there were innumerable other cases in which sponsors also decided what to build in advance of where to build it. For example, schools and tenement blocks often had their location determined by combinations of social need and chance factors, such as the availability of sites. This sequence of building decision before site decision was the reverse of that represented by the Cardiff example in which estate owners took the first step in development without knowing what sort of buildings eventually would appear. Another distinction was that Bromborough represented cases in which buildings were likely (though not necessarily) to be custom built under contract. Cardiff, on the other hand, represented cases in which buildings were likely (again not necessarily) to be speculatively built. Almost certainly it was the speculative, piecemeal approach which continued to be dominant throughout the country during this period.

Institutional investment

A changing aspect of the decision to build was the scale of activity of some developers and investors in the later decades, as it were from the level of drawing room to that of board room. This reflected growth elsewhere, for towns were bigger and so were many individual buildings and the institutions which occupied them. Capital continued to flow into building from private individuals, much in the form of advances to speculative builders from landlords, but there were also institutional sources. For better quality London housing, particularly before the 1880s, insurance companies made capital available,[4] and building societies were active widely. Older terminating societies gave way to permanent ones although the primitive pattern persisted for some time alongside the more modern. The evolution of societies was gradual, hampered by financially doubtful forms such as the Starr-Bowkett societies, falling property values in the 1880s, occasional dishonesty and, worst of all, the notorious Liberator Society collapse of 1892. Acts of Parliament intended to regulate the societies were passed in 1874 and in 1894, at which time total assets of incorporated societies were £42m.[5]

Another aspect of institutional sources of capital was provided by early property companies such as the City of London Real Property Company founded in 1864. This joint stock concern had property which grew from an original £330,000 to £2.5m by 1914.[6] Activities of such firms appear to have formed a relatively small proportion of all building activity, like one other category of sponsors, the local authorities. These augmented the efforts of other non-profit making sponsors, namely central authority, churches, occasional philanthropists and charitable trusts. Their activities increased in total, but did not challenge the established dominance of sponsors motivated by profit, private satisfaction and considerations of conspicuous expenditure.

ASPECTS OF DEMAND

Geographical distribution

Each of the countless sponsor's fortune or failure, endeavour or exploit was acted out against a vast backcloth of national change. A leading feature was the geographical location of building activity to give continued vigorous growth of towns, already so dramatically under way. At mid-century, an approximate numerical balance had been reached between the urban population of 9.0m and the rural one of 8.9m, but by 1911 the figures had changed to 28.2m people in the towns compared with only 7.9m in the country. The approximate proportions of urban and rural dwellers had been completely reversed during the course of the nineteenth century. The largest single concentration of population, and hence buildings, in 1911 was London where there were 4,541,000 living within the county boundary and 7,256,000 in the conurbation as a whole. Birmingham was the next largest city (840,000), followed by Liverpool (746,000), Manchester (714,000) and Sheffield (455,000).[7] Although the order had changed since 1851, the only newcomer among the largest five was Sheffield, just displacing Leeds. The growing dominance of the largest towns emerged from an index of population growth[8] having 1851 as the base year with an index of 100. The index for eighty-four great towns in 1901 was 254, compared with only 169 for the rest of England and Wales, and a fall to 95.5 for typical rural counties. While the largest towns generated proportionately more building activity than most other places, their percentage growth rates fell somewhat from the peaks attained before mid-century. There was, to be sure, a new generation of very rapidly growing places which sprang up in the later nineteenth century. One example, the Rhondda Valleys, grew from 8,000 in 1861 to 56,000 in 1881, but later developing centres such as this did not go on to challenge the sheer size of the great towns which arose before mid-century.

Continued growth among neighbouring centres in some cases led to their coming together to create huge physically continuous settlements. London was such a conurbation by the early nineteenth century, and other places followed later as groups of mill communities or scatters of overgrown colliery villages gradually coalesced. Old boundaries were blurred and then rendered meaningless as the scale of apparently limitless growth surpassed all precedent. That was one side of the picture, but another was decay in the countryside in which falling rural population, as distinct from relatively slower growth, first appeared in remote parts from mid-century. It gradually spread thereafter under increasing urban job attraction and rural unemployment repulsion.

Population

The pattern of advancing urbanization provided tangible evidence of demand for buildings, but what of the sources of that demand? One crucial one was the growth of population, for it was self-evident that within broad limits the more people there were, the more buildings were required. An effect of the uninterrupted expansion seen in the following table was that of a sustained stimulus to building activity.

Population growth in England and Wales 1811–1911 (in thousands)[9]

1811 . . . 10,164	1871 . . . 22,712
1821 . . . 12,000	1881 . . . 25,974
1831 . . . 13,897	1891 . . . 29,003
1841 . . . 15,914	1901 . . . 32,528
1851 . . . 17,928	1911 . . . 36,070
1861 . . . 20,066	

Business activity

Demand for buildings also continued to be associated with the level of prosperity derived from business activity and confidence which, until about 1873, was generally very high and, as yet, unchallenged by overseas competition. Apparently irresistible material progress created heavy current demand for buildings which promised to continue far into a future in which society would be changing ceaselessly. After 1873 there were more than two decades of rather less ebullient prosperity when the rate of economic expansion was retarded. Frustrated expectations led to the overstating sobriquet 'great depression', although optimism eventually revived somewhat to make the years from 1896 to 1914 a sort of Indian summer. Some measure of general expansion in the United Kingdom is seen in the near-tripling of gross national income in the half-century after 1851 (the figures were £523m advancing to £1643m). While the long-term trend in building demand (and size of stock) was upward, an important shorter term influence was the attractiveness or otherwise of investment in building. Potential sponsors weighed returns possible from investment in building and in the growing number of rival outlets for capital, such as joint-stock companies and overseas investments. What had once been purely local building investment decisions became more and more bound up with national and, later, international events. Seen in this light, the choice facing a potential sponsor might lie between new houses in Hoxton and a railway in Argentina.

Health and welfare

The increase in national wealth was unmistakable, with gross domestic product per person in the United Kingdom not far from doubling between 1855 and 1900–1913 (£26 and over £45 respectively, at constant 1913 prices).[10] Some of the increase filtered down to reach the pockets of more skilled wage earners and their families. Rising real incomes, at least until the early twentieth century, meant that some were able to afford better accommodation than their parents and, although the increment of enhanced spending power was not all that large, sooner or later it was bound to affect building demand. A small additional increase in demand stemmed from growing middle class awareness of the plight of the poor, matched by some willingness to help. Here lay the roots of sponsorship by local authorities, not intended merely to maintain social control as in the past, but to lend physical help to the needy. By 1914 it was apparent that local authority sponsorship of various types of building was established alongside that of central government as another source of public sector building, representing a small but significant start to the task of narrowing the abyss between effective demand and social need for buildings.

Volume of building

The total volume of new building was vast; in the twenty years from 1865 alone the capital tied up in buildings in the United Kingdom was estimated to have almost doubled from £1000m to £1900m.[11] Similarly, the estimated value of buildings as a percentage of the national capital of Great Britain went up from 22 in 1885 to 26 in 1912, a proportion not far short of double that of the early 1830s. Building activity continued to proceed in an erratically fluctuating manner, at this stage more influenced by international events than during the first half of the century.[12,13] While non-residential activity corresponded with fluctuations in the business cycle, the greater part of all building activity, house building, developed a pattern of its own in which cycles were both longer and more extreme than the fluctuations in national investment in general.[14] The national pattern of house building activity, seen in Parry Lewis' index,[15] was one of growth to a peak around 1876, after which activity fell away rapidly at first, then more slowly to a trough in 1890. It then picked up to reach a great peak in 1898, falling to a very low level before 1914, although local departures from this pattern remained wide.[16,17]

HOUSING

Quantitative importance

The continuing quantitative importance of house building is underlined by comparing the value of its output with the value of commercial and public building output. In 1907, the figure for housing was estimated to be £28m compared with £16.5m for commercial and public building;[18] and at other times, too, housing nearly always dominated all other types of building together. The great importance of house building, in absolute as well as relative senses, may be seen from the steadily increasing size of the housing stock. In 1811 there were approximately 1,849,000 houses, compared with no less than 7,550,000 a century later, three-quarters or more of which must have appeared during the period so far covered by this study. In every decade from 1851 and, indeed, from 1811, an expanding stock of houses was recorded. At mid-century the figure was 3,432,000 and the percentage addition during each successive decade never fell below 11.6 (in 1881–1891), exceeding 15 in the sixties, seventies and nineties.[19]

Sponsorship

It has been emphasized that most of this considerable output was speculatively built, although there were exceptions like the custom-built houses of the wealthy. There was some non-speculative house building, too, by industrialists whose employees might otherwise have lacked shelter or proved recalcitrant. Pioneering enterprises obliged to build houses in remote upland locations such as Merthyr Tydfil early in the century,[20] were joined later by some employers in lowland parts such as Swindon and Wolverton. House building inspired by philanthropy mixed to lesser or greater extent with self-interest was to be found in industrial colonies, among which were Saltaire (1851), Bourneville (1879), Port Sunlight (1888) and New Earswick (1903). Related motives were at work in such bodies as the Peabody Trust (1862) and Waterlow's Improved Industrial Dwellings Co. (1863),[21] at their most active in London from the 1850s to the 1880s. By 1914 they had provided about 100,000 rooms for London artisans, although this did little more than absorb the population growth of two years.[22]

More important were the building societies which, we saw, grew up by degrees and through vicissitudes into sizeable permanent (or would-be permanent) institutions with interests over quite large districts. In the process they shifted emphasis from direct sponsorship of specific building projects towards helping individual investors and, in doing so, became a major means by which private savings were channelled into speculatively built houses.

The remaining source of houses was the local authorities, pioneered by Liverpool with the St Martin's Cottages tenement scheme of 1869.[23] Subsequent national progress remained slow and patchy, despite Housing Acts in 1890 and 1909, although by 1914 Liverpool had completed nearly 3,000 dwellings and there were 12,000 in London. Notwithstanding the opposition of private interests, many local authorities in Edwardian times found themselves called upon to supplement the flagging efforts of speculators. By 1914 about 5% of house building was said to be in public hands, with a prospect of heavier commitment ahead.

Low cost urban housing

The local authorities built small numbers of houses within the reach only of the 'respectable' part of the working class and above. The cheap end of the housing market was supplied mostly with private suburban terraces as successors to court, and back-to-back types which appeared only in fast diminishing numbers. Low cost urban houses of the third quarter of the century were likely to be built for rather less than £100 each. In Liverpool, three-room cottages with cellars, having 12 ft frontage and 13 ft 6 in depth, cost from £80 to £110 to build.[24] In the 1850s at Copley, near Halifax, one-bedroom houses were built for £90 and £100,[25] while for £120 there were stone back-to-backs with cellar, 196 sq ft living room with small adjoining scullery, one bedroom of 145 sq ft and another of 52 sq ft. Some terraced houses in nearby Saltaire also cost £120 to build while others for about £100 gave Titus Salt, or rather his employees, accommodation consisting of a cellar and basement pantry, 182 sq ft living room, 126 sq ft scullery and three bedrooms. Enlightened opinion of the mid-1860s held that this cost represented the lower limit for a 'decent cottage house' in a town, although there was no doubt that very inferior cottages could be – and often were – run up much more cheaply. Well-paid workers, like Salt's overlookers, could expect to occupy a terraced house costing about £200 and having a respectably ornate frontage, a basement wash-house, pantry and coal cellar, a ground floor with 248 sq ft parlour and 203 sq ft kitchen, a first floor with three or more bedrooms, and a back yard with separate w.c. and ashpit.

As the century progressed the quality of the cheapest new houses improved, largely as a result of legislation, so as to resemble increasingly (if not always to equal) the example above. Higher quality in respect of floor area, volume, room numbers, and provision of services gradually raised the average cost of new houses. By 1913 the cost of workmen's cottages was said to range from about £150 to £240, and from 4d to 6½d per cub. ft.[26] In 1890 some Birmingham municipal cottages consisting of 169 sq ft living room, 108 sq ft kitchen, pantry, flush w.c., two bedrooms and attic, cost £175 each.[27] Municipal cottages built in Exeter in 1906 and consisting of a living room, a scullery with a bath, a larder, coal store, w.c. in the garden, and two bedrooms, appear to have been a bargain at £149 each (5d per cub. ft).

Artisans' multi-storey tenement blocks were more expensive to build than houses, but were able to accommodate more people on valuable urban sites. A six-storey London scheme for the Improved Industrial Dwellings Co. in 1870 had 294 dwellings of three rooms and a scullery each, costing £162 per dwelling, and 359 dwellings of two rooms and a scullery, costing £108 each. The equivalent cost per room of £54 was low in comparison with others in London in the 1890s, which ranged from £83 to £138 per room. The large LCC Boundary Street scheme of 1893 to 1900 cost £107 per room (9d per cub. ft) and a smaller three-storey example at Hornby Street, Liverpool, of 1906, cost £85 per room. In 1913, the estimated cost of tenement building was from £65 to £100 per room (8d to 9½d per cub. ft) in London and £60 to £90 elsewhere.

Low cost rural housing

Much rural house building was cheaper than urban for not only were building wages likely to be less (as, indeed, were land costs), but building quality could be lower. The reasons were connected with lower expectations and purchasing power of rural householders, together with less rigorous by-law control in country and suburbs.[28] At mid-century the Duke of Bedford built four and five-room estate cottages for between £90 and £100 each, examples which were not the cheapest for they included a kitchen range, copper, upstairs fireplace and some exterior ornament. In the last quarter of the century Birch[29] thought that rural labourers' cottages of quite high quality, having a porch, living room, scullery, pantry, fuel store, privy, ashpit and three bedrooms, could be built for between £113 and £200 each, a wide range possibly reflecting the desire to avoid discouraging potential clients. Costs had not changed dramatically in 1913 when attractive examples of four-room cottages in short terraces cost £112 each. Others costing a further £78 each, about 4½d per cub. ft altogether, offered a 138 sq ft parlour, 150 sq ft kitchen, 100 sq ft scullery and three bedrooms ranging from 115 sq ft to 200 sq ft.[30] The efforts of landowners were supplemented by a handful of rural local authorities, of which one of the first was Yeovil, building twelve three-bedroom houses at Montacute in 1912 for £162 each.[31]

Higher cost housing

The sharpest possible contrast to this sort of residential building came from the large country houses of the very rich. The nineteenth-century peak in highest quality domestic building activity was reached in the early 1870s[32] when, in five years, seventy-four large houses were begun, more than double the figure for the five years from 1835. One particularly impressive example straddling good times and the less rosy ones of the 1880s was Eaton Hall, near Chester, on which the Duke of Westminster lavished no less than £600,000, ably assisted by his architect Alfred Waterhouse. A later example was the smaller but still considerable undertaking of Castle Drogo, Devon, begun in 1910, but not finished for twenty years, seemingly making it one of the very last of its kind. The owner, Julius Drewe, instructed his architect Lutyens that it should not exceed £50,000 (with another £10,000 for the garden), sufficient, incidentally, for three hundred or more labourers' cottages. This vast gulf in quality was bridged by the houses of the middle class.

New houses occupied by lower middle class families were indistinguishable from those of 'respectable' artisans. Above them came the more costly, but less plentiful houses of the comfortably off, and near the top were the expensive houses of the wealthy few. Writing of the lower end of this market in 1857, Walsh[33] took the view that four or six-room houses cost about £50 for each room of 14 x 12 x 9 ft high. From this it followed that a house with a basement kitchen and scullery, two ground-floor rooms, and two bedrooms would cost £300 or more. A ten-room house was likely to be more expensive per room, with a cost which was near the upper limit of speculative building, of the order of £800 to £1,000, although sometimes it was less. A larger example cited by Birch not long before 1890, was built at Studland, Dorset for £1,300 and offered dining, drawing and morning rooms, kitchen, w.c., two staircases, together with five main and two servants' bedrooms. Examples of middle class houses built around 1860, ranging from the smallest of 1900 sq ft costing about £500 up to the largest of over 7600 sq ft and most expensive costing up to £2,800, had a typical cost per sq ft of 7/-. A £3,000 'relatively modest country house' designed in 1899 by C. H. B. Quenell included a billiard hall, conservatory, verandah, drawing room, dining room, ten bedrooms, two nurseries and servants' quarters. Here was lavishness not available to many; for every house costing that much there were many similar to an example in Gidea Park, Essex, in 1912, termed cottage but costing £900 and having a porch, sitting room, hall, lobby, dining room, kitchen, scullery, larder, two w.c.s, four bedrooms and a bathroom. In the following year the estimated cost of 'villas' lay between 8d and 10d per cub. ft and that of flats and the most expensive houses from 1/-d to 1/3d. The main parts of 'mansions' occupied by their owners and families, were said to cost between 10d and 1/6d per cub. ft. In comparison with this, servants' quarters, at only 7d to 9d per cub. ft, were decidedly low in cost, albeit high in their attic locations.

INDUSTRIAL AND COMMERCIAL BUILDINGS

Sources of demand

Building for industry and commerce took place in a context of foundation, expansion and amalgamation of businesses. In manufacturing, the amount of fixed capital relative to labour became higher so that processes once possible outdoors with only a few simple tools and many men now demanded workshops, a boilerhouse, equipment and fewer men for the same or greater output. The heavy industries of coal, shipbuilding, engineering, iron and steel came to achieve the commanding position in the economy held by textiles at mid-century. While these industries increased impressively, underlying many of the advances from the last quarter of the century was a technological conservatism which began to prolong the life of obsolescent buildings and equipment. Yet in other fields more progressive attitudes prevailed: rising real incomes stimulated demand for consumer goods leading to factories engaged in flow-line production, for example, of foodstuffs and clothing; elsewhere scientific approaches were introduced in processing dyes, rubber, oil, and other products; engineering, from basic foundries to precision machine tool shops, expanded along with chemical works making acid, soda, bleach and fertilizers. Older industries such as papermaking, printing, brewing and milling also benefitted from growing markets and by the turn of the century important emerging industries included cycle, electrical and motor concerns.

The endless list of manufacturers was matched by commercial enterprises engaged in controlling, administering, accounting and marketing, activities stimulated by the sheer number and size of firms and their increasingly complicated trading relations. There were insurance companies, banks, company headquarters, branches and the offices of a growing number of professions and agencies which provided services to businesses, the public and each other.[34] Numerous commercial concerns carried on their business closer to the public eye than this, among them front-room shops and opulent department stores, plain public houses and vast luxury hotels, seedy music halls and extravagant theatres, and much else besides.

Factories

Economic and social change was reflected clearly in the types of buildings[35] for which tenders were published in contemporary periodicals.[36] Random examples from the 1860s included industrial projects such as an engine house and chimney in Hull, costing £1,200; an 'earthenware manufactury' in Gt Fenton, Stoke-on-Trent, costing £6,400; Brighton railway workshops costing about the same; and a six-storey water mill at Bamford, near Sheffield, costing £1,100. Rather later, the growth of consumers' purchasing power may be detected, for example, in a tiny aerated water factory in Devizes, Wiltshire, costing £300 in 1886. The rising importance of the same field may be surmised from a 1913 Battersea ice factory costing £7,000. Novelties of 1894 were electricity generating stations at Gt Yarmouth for £2,600 and Wolverhampton for twice as much. Nineteen years later one at Wallasey was as much as £65,000, by which time they were estimated at 6d to 8d per cub. ft, a little more than both 'plain factories' at 5d to 6d per cub. ft and low cost housing.

Building for goods storage, movement

Warehouses could be great, like a group in Cripplegate in 1876 for £19,000, or relatively small, like an ornate ten-storey granary at Welsh Back, Bristol, for £6,600 in 1871. The unit costs of buildings such as these were considerable, from 10d to 1/- per cub. ft in Edwardian times, although simpler structures could be had down to 5½d, and corrugated iron shedding was very cheap at 3½d to 4½d. Impressive structures for large markets and exchanges were created at appropriately impressive prices, as in the case of Broderick's Leeds Corn Exchange of 1861, the subject of tenders ranging upwards from £12,000. Stores and markets were associated with short-distance transport requiring stables and coach houses and here the national fondness for animals was reflected in what was paid for their shelter. In 1913, new fitted stables cost from 6d to 10d per cub. ft compared, it will be remembered, with only 4d to 6½d per cub. ft for workmens' cottages. Even so, not many stables can have rivalled in cost the London General Omnibus Co. Ltd premises at Bromley, Bow, costing £3,600 in 1876.

Commercial buildings

Accumulation of wealth predictably led to banks becoming key commercial buildings of which simple examples cost of the order of £2,000 in the 1860s. A larger example was the West of England and South Wales District Bank, Cardiff, which included a 45 x 25 x 19 ft high banking room, a basement, clerks' rooms, manager's accommodation with eight bedrooms, for £7,000. This was a small project compared with some high quality offices which accounted for £30,000 or £40,000 apiece, also in the 1860s. Half-a-century later banks with offices or flats over them cost much the same as luxury houses, from 1/1½d to 1/3½d per cub. ft, and a few years later offices were said to range widely between 9d and 2/- or more per cub. ft. New banks and offices were where many men earned and kept their money, and new shops where they spent much of it. Mid-1880s shop projects of

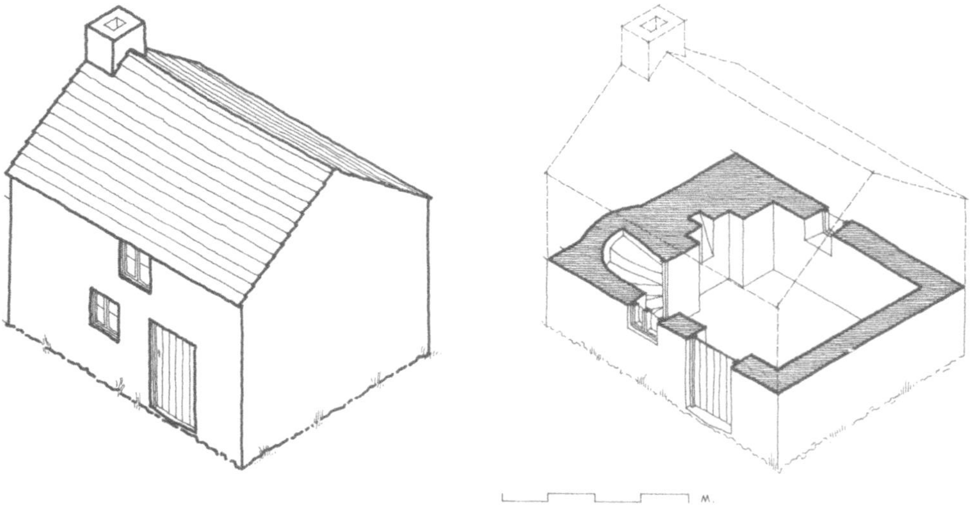

Rural cottage. This two-room example near Devauden, Gwent, appears to date from earlier decades of the nineteenth century. With a floor area of 265 sq. ft it probably cost less than £50. (*C. G. Powell*)

Urban back-to-backs. Repetitive *mass housing in Ancoats, Manchester, of similar date to the cottage above. Each two-room house had a floor area of about 405 sq. ft.* (*C. G. Powell; based on material in Central Library, Manchester*)

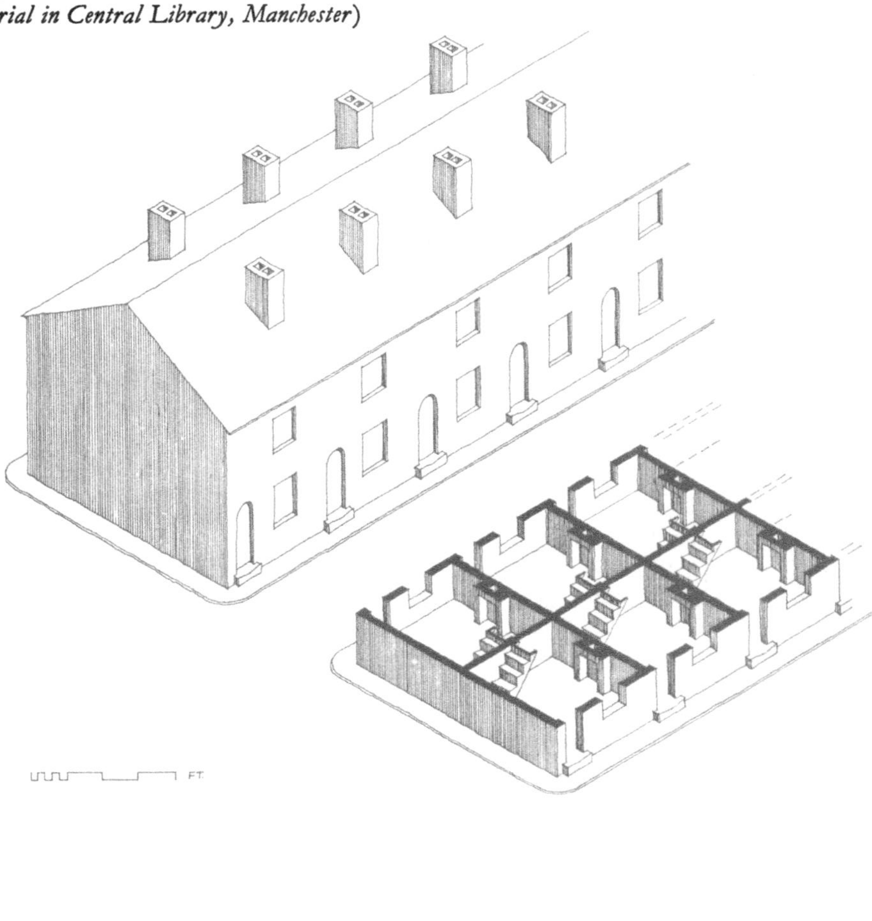

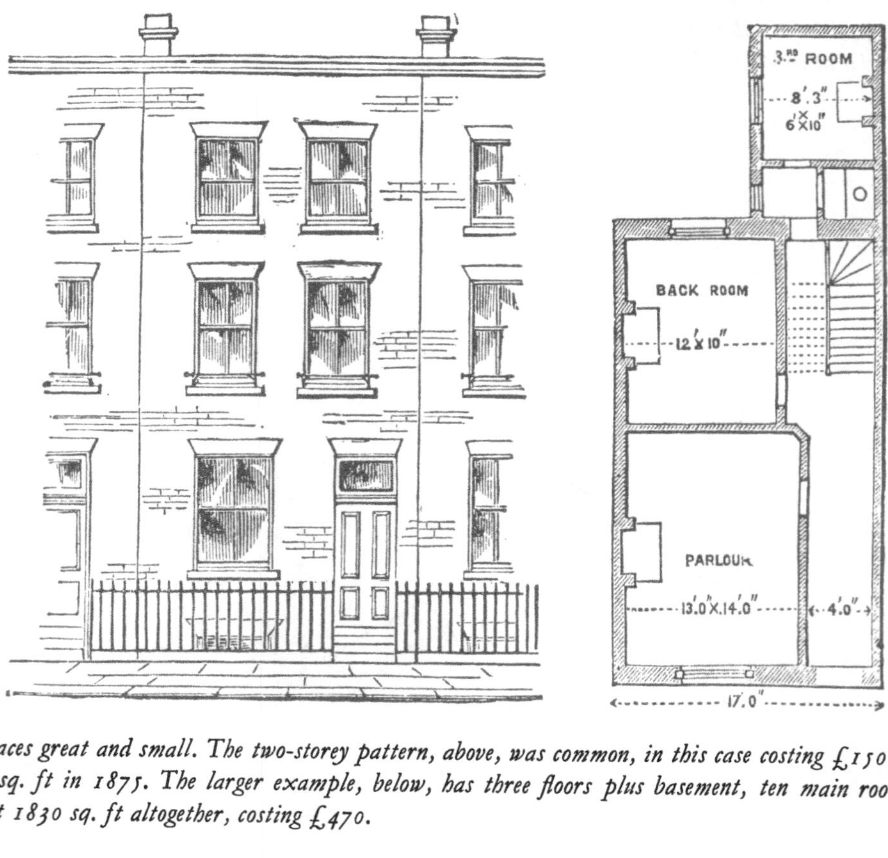

Terraces great and small. The two-storey pattern, above, was common, in this case costing £150 for 780 sq. ft in 1875. The larger example, below, has three floors plus basement, ten main rooms, about 1830 sq. ft altogether, costing £470.

Above: Early commercial prestige building. Sun Assurance Office, Threadneedle Street, designed by C. R. *Cockerell and costing £18,500 in 1842.* (RIBA)

Below: Large-scale public spending. Winson Green Workhouse, Birmingham. Designed by J. J. Bateman and built by Glenn of Liverpool Road, *London, for £29,000, it accommodated 1600 people.* (Builder, *1852*)

Above: Upper range of quality. This classical court house and prison was designed by R. *Elsam and estimated at £70,000. It appeared in Nicholson's* New Practical Builder and Workman's Companion *in 1823. (A. E. Powell)*

Above: Building material in the making. Limeburning depicted by W. H. Pyne in Microcosm, *1806, also the source of the next three illustrations. The sight was said to be 'An object by now [sic] means unterrific, particularly at night.' (Benjamin Blom, New York)*

Opposite page, top: Primitive building services. Smiths making copper chimney caps, a now-forgotten use of the material.

Opposite page, middle: Brickmaking. Taking bricks by barrow from a temporary kiln and, right, pumping water from a claypit.

Opposite page, bottom: Heavy transport. Moving large timbers with a suitably massive wagon emphasizes the difficulties of overland transport.

COPPER SMITHS,

Above: Victorian building site. Strangeways Courts, Manchester, under construction, 1853. Costume has changed but apparent chaos of planks and rubble remains familiar today. (*Manchester Public Libraries: Local History Library*)

Below: Victorian labour was plentiful. Men employed at Strangeways pose in 1853 for what must be one of the earliest records of its type. (*Manchester Public Libraries: Local History Library*)

Above: Rural labourer's cottage c.1890. This three-bedroom example was a great material advance on that shown in the first illustration but, at £150, so was its cost. It was designed by J. Birch and appeared in his Examples of Labourers' Cottages &c.

Below: Middle class house c.1890. Another design of Birch, having five main and two servants' bedrooms, costing £1300.

nary. An 1871 design in Bristol by Ponton and Gough
, no doubt a sum inflated by very rich ornament. (RIBA)

Comment on building quality. This was publish
The British Working Man *in 1878 but* Pu
same theme in the seventies. The subject itself was

four or five units cost £3,000 or more, but much small shop building must have been cheaper than this. Multiple retailers such as W. H. Smith emerged, particularly from the 1870s, followed in the 1890s by large and costly departmental stores sometimes incorporating residential space on upper floors.[37]

Hotels, theatres

Other built evidence of the advance of consumers, both humble and conspicuous, were hotels, public houses and theatres. Hotels, like other building types, varied greatly in size and cost; a small example in Malvern, designed in 1861 by E. W. Elmslie, cost £5,800 plus £800 for landscaping, while the much larger Victoria Hotel, Bradford, designed by Lockwood and Mawson several years later, cost £18,600. Even this was thoroughly overshadowed by the mighty Brighton Palace Hotel proposed in 1886 with 250 bedrooms on nine floors plus a basement for an estimated cost of £120,000. Succeeding schemes vied with each other in size and luxury and by 1913 hotel costs per cub. ft were reckoned to lie in about the same range as offices. 'Taverns' ranged from near-domestic scale up to examples of £4,000 and more in the 1870s, reaching as much as £30,000 by the turn of the century. Still commercial, but providing more mental than bodily sustenance, were theatre and music hall buildings, some of which were among the most sumptuous of buildings. The 1856 Surrey Gardens Music Hall costing £18,000[38] palled into insignificance when compared with D'Oyly Carte's Opera House which accommodated a 2,000 seated and 300 standing audience in 1891 for a cost of £150,000. Ten theatres built between 1876 and 1897[39] cost from £65 per place for the lavish example above, down to less than £6 per place at the Grand, Islington, but only three examples exceeded £20 per place. By 1913 increasing numbers of a rival attraction were appearing, with 500 'electric theatres' already in London and suburbs, and new provincial examples costing up to £3,000 each.

SOCIAL CONTROL AND WELFARE BUILDINGS

Growth of public sector

Buildings instrumental in social control and welfare, such as barracks, workhouses, churches, schools and hospitals, continued to appear and were supplemented by new, related provision. Enhanced mid-Victorian civic pride and identity were often expressed by architectural means, as in the case of the rivalry recorded by Asa Briggs[40] between Leeds and Bradford manifesting itself in two outstanding civic buildings, Leeds Town Hall and St George's Hall, Bradford. Improvement and modernization on a lesser scale were sought in many towns such as Middlesbrough where there were '... fine public buildings of the kind that grow up with the development of a municipality: a Town Hall, a Free Library, the various offices of the corporation, churches, schools, ... a big public square ...'[41] The purposes served by public buildings became progressively more diverse so that monumental examples were supplemented by mundane ones such as fire stations and tramway depots. The overall growth of activity by public authorities is seen by comparing their average annual expenditure with that of consumers; in the 1860s they spent about one-sixteenth that of consumers, rising to one-tenth in the decade after 1900.[42]

Provision for civil order, destitution, health

An appropriate place to begin examination of public building costs is in connection with the ultimate means of social control, the barracks. At Chatham in 1861 there was a large project for 500 officers and men estimated at £60,000 and at Albany, Parkhurst, there were building plans for 100 soldiers estimated at £18,000. Many police stations and courts also were costly, as represented by Norman Shaw's design for Kentish Town, estimated at £13,000 in 1894, and by Gt Marlborough Street police court and station costing £29,000 in 1913, but no doubt numerous country stations cost much less.

Sizeable public spending was forthcoming for accommodation for the sick and destitute in workhouses. Projects current in 1869 included one in Preston for 956 inmates for £30,000, a more costly one in Edmonton and a cheaper one in Monmouth. By 1913 the cost of workhouses was reckoned to be from £160 to £200 per inmate in London, slightly less elsewhere. At that time lunatics emerge as a more worthy cause than the destitute, with asylums costing from £200 to £400 per inmate (at 7d to 10d per cub. ft, much the same as villas) including wards, administrative buildings, chapel, mortuary and roads. Long Grove Asylum, Epsom, housed no less than 2,013 patients at a cost of £243 each in 1907. Yet provision for human derangement on such a superhuman scale was not to be found everywhere; 100 female patients of Worcester had a paltry £2,500 spent on them in the 1860s. Examples of hospitals of the same decade, when care of the sick poor outside workhouses became compulsory, were St Thomas's, Westminster Bridge, which housed 588 patients for £360,000 and Winchester County Hospital for only £23,000. After the 1860s cottage hospitals multiplied, with a twelve-bed example proposed in 1876 in Evesham estimated at £1,200, including the site. By 1911 there were nearly 2,200 institutions for the physically ill[43] and a first class urban hospital cost from £300 to £500 per bed (9d to 1/- per cub. ft). Below this were cottage hospitals at £200 to £300 (8d to 10d per cub. ft) and, not very reassuringly, 'corrugated iron hospitals' at £100 to £150 (5d to 6d per cub. ft).

Provision for education

A picture of mid-century provision for education comes from Seaborne[44] who gave data on eleven schools designed by J. Clarke. The largest, at Leigh, Essex, had three rooms for 260 children and the smallest, Monk's Horton, Kent, had one room for fifty children. Costs ranged upwards from £2-8s per place at Monk's Horton and £3-16s per place at Lydd, Romney Marsh, to £8-4s per place at Coopersale, Essex. During the 1850s and 1860s school building accelerated and costs of £3 to £4 per place seem to have been accepted as reasonable. The same source tabulated elementary day schools illustrated in the *Builder* between 1850 and 1870, giving an average cost for twenty-four schools of £1,859, with a maximum of £5,000 at St Saviour's, Paddington, and a minimum of £600 at Mansel Lacy, Herefordshire. The average cost per place among the fifteen schools for which data was published was £5-2s with a maximum of £16-14s at St Saviour's and a minimum of £2-12s at Hythe National School. The 1870 Education Act stimulated a large programme of elementary school building[45] among which were the London Board Schools which cost around £8 per place in the early 1870s, rising to over £20 per place in 1899, by which time more than 400 existed. In 1913, elementary schools were said to range from £7 to £12 per child (6d to 7½d per cub. ft) in the country and up to £15 or £20 (6d to 9d per cub. ft) in large towns. Overall sizes were often large as, for example, at Portlane Road, Croydon, with 1,300 places in 1901. Rather different provision for education was made for upper and middle class children, accommodated in public schools such as Lancing, Sussex. Such building was likely to be costly and frequently shared a neo-Gothic character with university work.

Among other higher education buildings were the technical colleges, of which more than thirty appeared after about 1890.

Finsbury Technical School cost £21,000 for three storeys plus a basement, with another £15,000 for furnishings, appliances and fittings. It measured about 130 x 70 ft and accommodated 150 day and 750 evening students. This was cheap compared with the 300 student Central Technical Institute, South Kensington, which amounted to £80,000 plus £20,000 for furnishings (1/3d per cub. ft). Educational building appears to have been less expensive in the north, where many of the colleges were situated, for example, Huddersfield Technical School cost about 5½d per cub. ft, and Oldham School of Science and Art about 8d per cub. ft.[46]

Provision for worship

Church and chapel building retained the prominence which it gained in the first half of the century. For instance, in the Diocese of Manchester, between 1869 and 1885, £730,000 was spent building over 100 new churches.[47] In Middlesbrough in 1907, where 100,000 people lived, of the sixty places of worship twenty were nonconformist (compared, incidentally, with twenty-five elementary schools). Micklethwaite[48] writing of costs in 1874 believed that the great majority of churches cost from £5 to £10 per sitting, although he knew of rare cases of £50 or more. He continued, 'We do indeed hear of churches at £4 and even at £3, but . . . they are nearly always . . . unfit to be called churches at all, every consideration of decency and convenience in performing the service being sacrificed . . .' From £10 to £12 per sitting was a '. . . fair estimating price for an ordinary well-appointed, but unpretentious parish church, exclusive of the tower' allowing 9 or 10 sq ft per sitting. An example of 1865 at Yardley Gobion, Northamptonshire, was comfortably within this limit, being 60 x 28 ft, with 150 places and estimated at £1,750. It may be imagined that Micklethwaite would have been unimpressed by the likes of St Paul's, Ryhope, Co. Durham at only £4-4s per place in 1869. Likewise he would certainly have recoiled from a chapel at West Green, Tottenham, built in 1861 for about £2-10s per place, surely to standards less sacred than profane.

Miscellaneous municipal provision

Returning to the less spiritual subject of municipal building, we find the peak of quality in that field represented by a few monumental town halls, followed by a host of lesser buildings of similar purpose. In 1861 Skipton Town Hall was expected to cost £4,500 and fifteen years later the citizens of Reading faced an estimated bill of £10,000 for their municipal buildings. Alfred Waterhouse's three-storey Gothic design included a 36 x 25 x 24 ft high council chamber, a clock tower, strong rooms, coal lift and accommodation for committees, town clerk and keeper. If this was too lavish, at least it was only half the 1886 estimate for the Queen Anne style St George's Vestry and Union Offices, Hanover Square, sited in Mount Street. At about 11½d per cub. ft, St George's Vestry Hall was reckoned by 1913 to be not at all unreasonable, lying comfortably within the range of 10d to 1/6d per cub. ft typical for such buildings.

As well as administration there were various new municipal enterprises such as public libraries,[49] pioneered in Manchester following an act of 1850. There were twenty-five library projects by 1860 and by 1913 typical costs were a moderate 7½d to 10½d per cub. ft. Swimming baths were built occasionally and were expected to cost from 1/-d to 1/2d per cub. ft in 1913, the year in which one at Sevenoaks cost £3,000. Amenity buildings of this sort depended in part on the mobility of their users, so it is no surprise to find heavy Edwardian public authority investment in tramways, both serving leisure-seekers and stimulating suburban growth in general. Examples of 1912 included costly tramway depot sheds by Bradford Corporation for £46,000 and by the LCC at Camberwell for £29,000. There appeared also an increasing number of buildings more useful than agreeable, among which were mortuaries, refuse destructors, abattoirs, fire stations and not least, public conveniences.

Non-municipal provision

There remains a category of buildings such as public halls and private clubs which were non-profit making yet not initiated by public authorities. Examples from 1861 included a public hall for 1,000 at Guildford for £2,500, built when poor nearby Godalming had to rest content with one of 'unpretending appearance' which accommodated only half that number and cost £600. Among innumerable other examples were the likes of Bishop Auckland Temperance Hall, a Gothic edifice of 1876 which included a Band of Hope room, committee room, tea preparation room and assembly room of 2,600 sq ft, costing about £3,000. Other examples included Salvation Army barracks, drill halls, bowling club pavilions, working men's clubs and golf club houses.

AGRICULTURAL BUILDINGS

Farms

A crucial turning point in the prosperity of Victorian high farming came soon after the onset of the great depression, after which agriculture suffered heavily from overseas competition. Investment in buildings fell away, no longer inspired by industrial precedents, and little occurred except steady deterioration and, at most, small improvisations. An example of the scale of investment before prosperity waned was a new group of buildings at Tranwell, near Morpeth for the Earl of Carlisle, costing £1,040. The architects, J. & J. Girdwood, were from London, maybe an indication of the importance attached to such ventures. Similarly, when a farm, which included house and cottages, was proposed for a site in Wilsthorpe, Lincolnshire, it attracted tenders from as far away as London, although the lowest at £1,250 came from neighbouring Baston. This was mere financial chickenfeed, as it were, compared with Lord Bateman's Uphampton Farm, Shobdon, Herefordshire planned in 1861, like the previous examples. This was estimated to be nearly four times as costly and included elaborate equipment and even a light railway.[50] The small amount of agricultural building which was undertaken later, around 1913, was likely to be among the cheapest of all building, from 3½d to 4d per cub. ft for barns and from 4d to 6d per cub. ft for cow houses.

LOSSES FROM STOCK

Motives for demolition

The buildings most susceptible to loss were the dwellings of the poor, most likely pre-industrial in origin and almost certainly worn out. In 1889, the Royal Commissioners for Inquiring into the Housing of the Working Classes[51] believed that demolition was undertaken for five purposes. The first was property improvement by building owners, mainly in big city centres where prosperity and the pace of change were greatest. Old town houses fell from decrepitude to oblivion when they were replaced by spanking new commercial buildings, a fate which by 1905 had probably overtaken four-fifths of the buildings which had stood in the City of London in 1855.[52] The second purpose of demolition noted by the Commissioners was railway construction which, in London at least, reached its most hectic in the 1860s. In that decade there appeared five new termini and the Metropolitan line connection between Paddington and Moorgate. The effect was nothing less than traumatic for the unfortunate occupants of the housing which was wiped out, but contemporary public concern was not generally echoed in the railway boardrooms. As many as 120,000 people and 800 acres of urban land may well have been affected by railway development in London alone.[53]

Railways were not the only agency to pursue the poor from one slum to the next, for local authority town-making was preceded by a long apprenticeship in town-breaking, or at least slum-breaking. They were connected with all three remaining purposes of demolition identified by the Commissioners: creation of sites for new artisan dwellings; street improvements; and new public buildings such as Board Schools. Slum clearance for public health reasons took over, tentatively at first, after the main onslaught by the railways had passed. Legislation proliferated to give local authorities powers of clearance, although initially there was reluctance to use Torrens's Act of 1868, Cross's Act of 1875 and a further Act of 1890. The Metropolitan Board of Works displaced about 29,000 slum dwellers before it was succeeded by the LCC in 1889, and by 1914 the area of cleared land in London was said to be over 100 acres.[54] Further losses to stock were caused by street widening schemes intended both to clear unhealthy buildings and ease road congestion, among them Victoria Street, High Holborn and Charing Cross Road. A different sort of loss took place on an increasing scale in the declining countryside. Countless old cottages, barns, sties and byres, some of great antiquity, many of the poorest construction, quietly mouldered back into the land from which they had been, often quite literally, created.

BUILDING FORM

Opportunities for novelty

New needs, products and approaches opened up further opportunities for new building form and detail. Unfamiliar plans, circulation patterns, architectural styles, materials, structures and services, all were tried in addition to, and in competition with, orthodox solutions. Many of the more bold innovations were embodied in high quality buildings where money restrictions lay lightest and talented individuals clustered thickest. In many lower quality buildings there was novelty of a less dramatic sort, where bulk-produced goods competed increasingly with materials made locally by hand. Here the novelty was less the appearance and performance of the new goods than their near-universal availability.

Building by-laws

As well as new freedoms there were new constraints to be taken into account, predominant among which was public health legislation. The influence of by-laws joined that of the emerging national market in materials to edge designers towards a common style for cheap buildings. Prior to the closing decades of the century, the legislative framework of building was rather confused and, where legislation applied at all, it differed from place to place so as to defy generalization. The London Building Act of 1844 was a key piece of legislation,[55] but other major cities such as Liverpool and Bristol also were governed by early local Acts dealing with fire, party walls and structural stability. Urged from the front by Chadwick and pushed from the back by fear of cholera, public opinion gradually swung away from a tolerance of this minimum and often ineffective control. The provisions of the Public Health Act of 1848 in respect of drainage and space about buildings, as well as the older concerns, were extended ten years later by the Local Government Act. Localized and permissive laws gained favour and eventually a system of national control in towns emerged, aided by the Public Health Act of 1875, although even then some towns appear not to have adopted by-laws at least until 1890.

In the earlier years some seemingly crucial points had been left to the discretion of the local boards, thereby creating a number of loopholes in the application of controls. For example, where new cesspools apparently were prohibited, they might still be permitted where unavoidable; similarly, party walls might not need to be incombustible if the proposed alternative material was approved by the local board. The first important section of typical early by-laws[56] was concerned with the level, width, construction and drainage of new streets and the second section dealt with walls with respect to stability and fire prevention. The third section regulated the space about buildings for purposes of ventilation and the fourth section made provisions regarding drainage, w.c.s, privies, ashpits and cesspools. The required standards were not always very onerous: in 1865 party walls of only 4½ in. thickness were permitted in Manchester and only 70 sq ft of open space was required at the side or rear of new buildings. The 1875 Public Health Act appears to have been instrumental in securing a semblance of comprehensive national control over new urban building, rather than profoundly altering the nature of control in places already covered.

Many big towns were probably less immediately affected by the Act than were smaller and less progressive towns which had not troubled themselves hitherto with permissive legislation. Rural authorities were granted by the Public Health Amendment Act 1890 some of the powers already exercised by their urban counterparts.[57] By-laws retained similar subject headings to the four already described but their scope and requirements were extended in succeeding versions of the Model form. One of the results of this steadily intensifying pressure for safer buildings was to be seen eventually in falling urban death rates.

Suburban forms

The mixture of opportunity and constraint had many effects on the physical form and grouping of buildings. Suburban development, spurred by revulsion against high-density slums and freed by mechanized transport, gave sites less enclosed by nearby buildings. Larger plots enabled many new buildings to be a storey or two lower than hitherto for a given quantity of accommodation, and have larger frontages. Enclosed courts and other spaces were fewer as ventilation was valued and its provision enforced more and more. The pattern was unmistakable: middle class households forsook town houses for villas, while artisan households abandoned back-to-backs for by-law terraces and, later, cottage estates; congested communal courts yielded first to private back yards and then to gardens front and rear.

Urban forms

But suburban growth was not all; we have already noted renewal in town centres, where numbers of old plots were combined to give wide frontages and where land values were so high that it became more desirable than ever to use sites to their fullest possible extent. The result was buildings of ever greater height, bulk and complexity, erected in forms which demonstrated rising concern with ventilation and daylight. The scale of whole streets in major cities increased appreciably after mid-century, as new succeeded old. Massive new hotels and offices, many with receding upper floors and pinnacled rooflines, began to dominate the shrinking townscape of Georgian London, a picture echoed elsewhere among hospitals, mills and warehouses. Growing diversity of buildings was such that where once children were taught in large single classrooms, now some had multiple specialised spaces like gymnasia and laboratories. Where once the subnormal and the tubercular had managed as best they could within their own homes, now some had special institutional buildings. Where textiles had once come from two-room cottage, now they emerged from vast weaving shed; time and again new buildings were called upon to meet larger, more complicated and more specialised needs than before.

Standardization

While variety blossomed in such ways, largely among good quality buildings, it withered among some of the lesser ones. Weakening of the considerable local and regional differences in mass housing before 1850 accelerated after that time and particularly after the 1875 Public Health Act. The lowest quality of building was raised, but stereotyped by-law streets spread ever more widely. To be sure, the idiosyncratic builders of Leeds somehow contrived to carry on building back-to-backs long after they were outlawed elsewhere (right up to 1937), but this defied all probability. In that majority of cases in which strongly individualistic design was not sought, the trend was towards universal building forms and away from local peculiarities and distinctive regional characteristics. At one time the character of cheap houses had been decided largely by their geographical location, but now the date, rather than place, of construction became more significant. Not that standardization (for that was what was taking place) was confined only to cheap housing, for it appeared also in other places such as multi-storey office blocks and mills where there was increasing repetition from one floor to the next. Other buildings such as warehouses and workshops increasingly were laid out in series of identical bays and, similarly, some railway companies were sufficiently large to perceive benefits in standardizing certain whole buildings. The Great Western Railway erected standard signal boxes, halts and stations in Edwardian years and also, to a lesser extent, before then.[58] Other standardization of an unsung sort came from makers of corrugated metal sheeting, patented in 1829, and increasingly evident from mid-century. By 1886 there were at least twenty-three builders of prefabricated sheet metal buildings in London alone,[59] making churches, mission rooms, schools, cottages and farm buildings.

Construction of carcass

In the design of larger and costly buildings the offensive was continued against obstructive effects of walls, partitions and columns. For example, workshop floors and shopfronts were freed where possible by spacing supports more widely than hitherto, and minimum permissable sizes for domestic windows were now stipulated in the by-laws. Ease of movement for people and goods, greater visibility, daylighting and ventilation were all in the ascendant, being developments which were both the cause and effect of new methods and materials. Prominent examples of the latter included continued growth in the use of cast iron frames and the introduction of wrought iron beams and trusses in the 1850s and 1860s. Mild steel joists were available by the mid-1880s, although subsequent growth in the use of steel for frames was slow. Floors of large buildings of concrete infill between wrought iron joists dated from the 1860s, being superseded by reinforced concrete early in the twentieth century.[60]

Deeper scientific understanding of the behaviour of some structures and materials made it possible to predict their performance and to eliminate that which was functionally redundant. Materials in their naturally occurring condition, whether clay, stone or timber were ousted increasingly where conditions were onerous and where preference could be exercised: where a heavy rubble wall once sufficed now there were slim metal columns; where once were uneven hand-made bricks, now were regular machine-pressed ones or terra-cotta products; where once were wooden window frames, now was patent glazing. Yet the advance of engineering and processed products at the expense of tradition and natural materials was not the whole story. There was also a quite distinct stream of development in building design which was rooted in aesthetic rather than functional criteria, one in which traditional building methods were employed by revivalists of historical architectural styles. In the case of architect-designed churches, country houses and some other monumental buildings bold innovations in construction usually were thought inappropriate and to be avoided or disguised. Whether a design in this field was inspired by Roman example or derived from the teaching of William Morris it generally used traditional construction. When it came to creating beauty, symbolizing function or evoking a sense of magnificence, nearly all architects continued to turn first to the well-tried vocabulary of masonry wall, column and arch, relieved by applied ornament. Often the best of both worlds was sought so that elaborate façades co-existed uneasily with backs and concealed interiors of unadorned plainness.

These considerations applied to expensive buildings where there was sufficient money to offer a choice of form from a range of alternatives. The position was different in lower-quality buildings where choice was restricted by cost and where the most striking feature of form probably was continuity with the past. A simple coach house or store was not likely to be profoundly different whether built in 1860 or 1910: maybe storey heights or window areas increased a little, or construction of the ground floor or roof varied slightly, but essentially the form was unaltered. Indeed, continuity was stronger than this, for the craftsmen who made such buildings would not have been unfamiliar with the work of their counterparts a century or more earlier.

Services

Circumstances were rather different when it came to building services where all manner of pipes, cisterns, fittings and wires for the first time began to amount to more than a trivial afterthought to building work. The rising proportion of services in the total cost of building was a response to several stimuli, among which was heightened concern with public health resulting in waste-disposal systems improved beyond recognition. There were growing expectations of convenience and comfort and an enhanced capacity to pay for them, together with new problems of circulation and communication in large buildings, soluble by means of new services. Finally, there were new inventions such as telephones, sprinkler fire-fighting systems and improved devices, such as domestic cookers, which must have stimulated hitherto unvoiced demand as well as meeting established wants. Among services and appliances which increasingly replaced builders' work of earlier and technically more simple times were iron ranges, lifts and details like ready-finished ceramic sinks instead of made-up hardwood ones. Services increasingly penetrated throughout buildings rather than being confined to all-too-insalubrious extremities, so that where once a combination of bucket and unwashed humanity was enough, now there were basins, tanks and pipes. Householders who once cheerfully endured a garden-long walk to the sole privy now expected a w.c. on every floor, and at least a few office workers basked in the warmth of central heating instead of taking their own coke supplies to work. Where the corridors of business once echoed with the footsteps of messenger boys, now they resounded to gadgets such as speaking tube and electric or pneumatic bell.

If such services were not always all that far-reaching in their effect on building form, at least they gave people cause to wonder and, usually, be thankful.

Leading developments in space heating were a more generous provision of open fireplaces in cheaper buildings, and new systems which arose from efforts in the 1860s to separate the point of combustion of fuel from occupied rooms. Some costly buildings employed steam or hot water circulation systems connected to boilers carefully placed out of sight and smell.[61] By the early years of the new century advanced systems incorporated underfloor air cleaners, ducts and concealed radiators[62], although well-tried enclosed stoves remained plentiful. The first gas lighting systems appeared in early nineteenth-century mills, but it was not much before mid-century that a growing network of mains made possible widespread domestic installations to replace candles and oil lamps. Nearly 1,000 gasworks existed by 1859[63] and consumption increased thereafter until lower installation costs of electric lighting helped it to compete with gas in the towns from the 1890s. Despite higher running costs electricity supply began to spread to the suburbs from about 1900 and by 1910 about 2% of homes were connected to mains.[64]

Variety was the keynote of the remarkable range of appliances supplying water for kitchen, washing and sanitary purposes.[65] As with space heating, invention was followed by adoption on the part of the wealthy few, then acceptance by the middle class, and finally use in the mass market. This process could take a very long time; decades for purpose-built bathrooms and a century or more for flush w.c.s. Around mid-century baths began to cease being regarded as portable and gas began to be used for water heating, bringing formidable geysers in the late 1860s and piped water to bedrooms sometime after 1870. Earth closets may be said to have lost ground to water closets as the latter became more reliable and hence acceptable inside the house, and as new public systems of water supply and waste disposal replaced old private arrangements, often inadequate and sometimes lethally mixed. Innovations in the provision of the various services proceeded as far as, perhaps farther than, those in other aspects of building; in this field, if anywhere, a builder of mid-century would have had cause for surprise by what was visible by 1914.

4

Ragged Trousered Philanthropy: The Industry 1851-1914

'"*The house . . . should be built entirely of stone, but, as I thought you wouldn't stand that, I've compromised for a facing. It ought to have a copper roof, but I've made it green slate. As it is . . . it'll cost you eight thousand five hundred.*"

"*Eight thousand five hundred?*" *said Soames.* "*Why, I gave you an outside limit of eight!*"

"*Can't be done for a penny less,*" *replied Bosinney coolly.* "*You must take it or leave it!*"'

(*John Galsworthy,* The Man of Property, *1906*)

SIGNIFICANCE OF BUILDING INDUSTRY

Growth of industry

The building stock was transformed in size by an industry which itself showed many signs of change. Some were of methods and organization, but the most evident was that of magnitude; the great untidy, far-flung and much-ramified building industry expanded to massive proportions. Despite continuing cycles of boom and slump, of frenetic activity alternating with slackness, the industry moved ahead of certain aspects of national growth. One aspect was workforce: males occupied in building and construction, as a proportion of all occupied males in Great Britain, increased from 1:13.2 in 1851 to 1:11.3 in 1911, although the peak in relative importance of building employment was recorded in the 1901 census with a proportion of 1:9.5. The building workforce expanded from 497,000 at mid-century to 1,219,000 (including 3,000 women) in 1901, although depression dragged down the 1911 total to 1,145,000.[1] Building was a key part of the economy and could hardly have been otherwise, with its proportion of investment at around one-third of total fixed investment (ranging between 31% and 38% in each decade after 1870).[2] Building activity was on a sufficiently large scale to be more likely to exert influence on the national economy than to be subject itself to influence from that quarter.[3]

DESIGNERS AND ADVISERS

Contract procedure

The open and changeable roles and relationships which existed among the providers of new buildings in the first half of the century became less fluid in the second half. Procedures were refined and consolidated and widely accepted practice emerged for the non-speculative, generally higher quality, minority of work. In such cases a sponsor would commission and accept a design from a professional architect, whereupon general building contractors were invited to submit competitive tenders on the basis of detailed drawings, specification and bills of quantities. The successful contractor, usually the one with lowest tender, was chosen to carry out the work under contract to the sponsor and under the supervision of the architect. Standard guidance documents for contracts began to appear in 1870, subsequently developing into standard forms.[4]

Architects

Apart from the person who paid for the building, the central figure in this procedure was the architect, whose profession developed significantly in nature and size in consequence of heavy building activity, changes in the industry, and increasing numbers of commercial clients, many of whom worked by committee rather than as individuals. The concerns of the rising profession were public approval, movement towards legalized closure to non-professional outsiders, and a plea for a code of ethics.[5] With evident emotion Micklethwaite stigmatized professional circumstances in which

> *'Any man worth a brass plate and a door to put it on may dub himself an architect, and a very large number of surveyors, auctioneers, house-agents, upholsterers, &c., with a sprinkling of bankrupt builders and retired clerks of works, find it in their interest to do so.'*[6]

Leading practitioners began to remedy this state of affairs

and by the 1860s the professional institute was elevated to a position of some distinction with the broad mass of the profession, who did not yet belong, gradually following it in the same direction. Old direct links with trades became tenuous and, for members of the Royal Institute of British Architects at least, were severed entirely in 1887. Numbers grew from 3,000 'architects' recorded in the 1851 census (many of whom also must have been builders and so on) to over 10,000 by 1901 and the proportion who were members of the RIBA increased from 8% to 15% in the same interval.[7] A more businesslike approach began to supplant earlier artistic leanings and somewhat menial and repetitive work assumed a fair proportion of the total carried out in architects' offices. Sir John Summerson has observed that the profession of the 1860s was a gentleman's profession – but only just.[8] The rise of general contractors and large projects emphasized a host of legal and financial matters such as contract procedure, insurance, costs and arbitration. There was increasing need to draw and specify every last detail of ever more technically complicated buildings, to facilitate estimating and replace the ebbing autonomy of individual craftsmen. These new responsibilities which accumulated round central creative and aesthetic skills perhaps made more hard-earned the customary fee of 5% of building cost.

Quantity surveyors, engineers

Quantity surveying practice in compiling bills of quantities varied according to locality, but slowly evolved in directions first set in London. There the issue of the 1860s and 1870s was whether two quantity surveyors, one for the architect and one for the contractor, or only one were needed for each project. The Surveyors' Institution (which included quantity surveyors among land surveyors) was founded in 1868, and the professional standing of quantity surveyors slowly grew. By 1909, when the first RIBA Form of Contract was issued and quantities became part of the contract, the quantity surveyors were fully fledged professionals standing above the more commercial builders' estimators.[9] Occupying a position between architects as leading professionals and quantity surveyors were civil engineers who contributed to certain larger and technically advanced projects. Retaining some direct links with contractors, engineers were concerned mainly with heavy structural elements such as wide floor and roof spans and deep foundations.

BUILDING FIRMS

Range of firms

The bewildering variety of firms with interests in building gradually changed and the recognizable order in one field lent by the rise of the professions was counterbalanced elsewhere by other forces. The average size of building firms became larger, although very many remained small, and new specialists emerged in response to greater technical complexity in products and processes. An index of 1886[10] listed over 400 trades from alabaster warehouses to zinc workers, including well-sinkers and weathervane manufacturers. In London alone there were eighty-three firms listed as shop front builders, fourteen asbestos manufacturers, ten laundry fitters, nineteen plasterers' hair merchants and over one hundred paint manufacturers.

Contractors

Upper position in the teeming mass of firms was held by the general contractors, the sort of firms which had risen to ascendancy in London during the second quarter of the century. They engaged in work under contract to sponsors and directed by professional architects and engineers. Unlike the masterbuilders whom they supplanted, their work forces included all main trades, although they were prepared to call in sub-contractors when fully occupied, for occasional specialized tasks and when required by architects. Most high quality buildings were produced by general contractors so it followed that they were regarded as the most respectable firms in the industry. However in some parts, particularly the north, they appear not to have occupied so dominant a position and the practice persisted of tendering separately for each trade. Leading firms associated from time to time, usually to present a united front in dealing with organized labour. Various organizations, some purely local, of different strength and longevity appeared, one of the more important being the National Association of Master Builders of Great Britain. This dated from 1878 and led in 1899 to the foundation of the National Federation of Building Trade Employers.

Speculative builders and sub-contractors

The superior status of general contractors did not necessarily prevent them from engaging also in speculative building to varying degrees, depending on market condition and the inclination of their proprietors. Below the general contractors in public esteem were the wholly speculative builders,[11] greatly outnumbering contractors and for the most part engaged in commonplace buildings not much influenced by professional designers. Speculative builders also were prepared to sub-contract work as circumstances required, although their straightforward buildings usually demanded few specialized skills. The sub-contractors were a loosely defined group which included firms of highly skilled traditional craftsmen such as ornamental masons, up-to-date technicians such as electricians, down to more-or-less disreputable tradesmen such as low-skilled painters. Between these extremes was a growing range of specialist sub-contractors who contributed only small parts to any one project. Their degree of specialization limited scope and adaptability and obliged them to seek continuity of work on numerous widely spread projects. It is probable that specialization advanced furthest where the total volume of building was largest, in the conurbations, and that the more specialized the firm, the further it had to travel to get work. Examples were specialists in design and fabrication of metal frames, and makers and installers of patent glazing and gas fittings. Architects frequently nominated such sub-contractors in order to assure the quality of intricate work, while arranging in the normal way for the main contract to be let by competitive tender.

Merchants and suppliers

Contractors and sub-contractors alike obtained most of their materials from suppliers and builders' merchants who, in addition to their function as wholesale stockists, acted as a major source of short-term credit for firms on site. The importance of merchants can only have been enhanced by the increasing range of goods resulting from growing use of ready-finished components to replace builders' work, for example in the case of heating appliances and prefabricated joinery. Suppliers and merchants in turn were kept stocked by manufacturers and processors who, in some cases, also supplied builders direct.

The number of manufacturers and range of products proliferated as advancing technology created new opportunities. Some new products were intended to be substituted for laborious or difficult traditional methods, and others were intended to improve the appearance or performance of finished buildings. For example, many timber roof members ceased to be connected by painstakingly cut joints and instead were joined by metal bolts from Birmingham, handled wholesale by merchants. Similarly, some time-consuming brick flue building was avoided by use of iron pipes, brought from afar but quick to fix in position. Likewise, makers of fencing wire and so on found a large market open to them, and one which was easy to enter. Even if the effect was insufficient to change building methods fundamentally, at least it brought into existence a whole network of makers, dealers and stockists complete with an apparatus of publicity, sales, deliveries and accounts. One result of the increase of branded goods was to intensify the demands made of builders and specifiers so that an understanding of building crafts alone was ceasing to be enough; skills in administration and management were rising to the forefront.

Size of building firms

The pattern of more and often bigger firms extended less strongly to work on site. Firms in south-east London with 150 skilled men were regarded as large and ones with twenty or thirty were more typical.[12] Approximately one half of all London house builders around 1845 are thought to have built only one or two houses each per year, and about four-fifths of them built six or fewer houses per year. There appears to have been little change in the size of firms for another thirty years or so, but in the booming late 1870s and early 1880s the number of small firms increased less than the number of larger firms. Small firms suffered more when the boom ended and when the next one came in the late 1890s some really large firms benefited. In 1899 seventeen firms, less than 3% of the total, put up over 40% of new houses.[13]

Examples of firms

The life of many small building firms continued to be precarious, with bankruptcy a common end to unrealistic hopes nurtured in boom times, abetted by easy access to credit and often doomed by under-pricing of work. A single example from North Kensington serves to represent a tragically large number of failures. One George Ingersent undertook to build ninety houses around Westbourne Grove in the heady atmosphere of the early 1850s, but had run into financial difficulties by 1854. Soon he came down heavily in the world and was to be found building a mere four houses in Palace Gardens Terrace. One of them was the Mall Tavern of which he was licensee by 1856,[14] no doubt a sadder but wiser man.

Larger firms appear to have been rather less accident-prone than smaller,[15] although Bowley[16] has questioned whether they possessed any obvious competitive advantage in relation to small projects. Some larger firms were active well outside their home towns, as in the case of George Myers who employed 2,000 men in 1851 from premises in Belvedere Road on the South Bank. His 1861 tender for the Glamorganshire Lunatic Asylum illustrates the national scope of large contracting, with competition between two local firms, two from Birmingham (one the winner) and one from Bristol. In 1865, Myers is known to have submitted tenders for at least sixty-five projects and to have been successful on five occasions. A smaller firm, one of the more successful at work in North Kensington in the third quarter of the century, was William and Francis Radford. They built over 200 houses between 1848 and 1880, and Francis Radford left £256,000 when he died. A similar firm was owned by Jeremiah Little, a Yorkshireman like Myers, who built about 150 houses in the Campden Hill area between 1848 and 1873. He employed sixty men in 1861 and died leaving £120,000.[17] A more dramatic tale of rags to riches was that of Edward Yates who arrived in London, also from the north, early in the 1850s to build houses in south London, at first in small numbers, but after 1870 on a steadily expanding scale. Professor Dyos has shown that between 1867 and 1895 Yates borrowed over £280,000, to finance his ventures, mostly at the normal rates of 4½ to 5%, reaching a peak around 1890 when he built about 150 houses a year. He died in 1907 a millionaire, having built over 2,500 houses,[18] showing that some builders, at least, managed to rise above the tough proving-ground of small speculation and went on to achieve positions of some social standing.

LABOUR

Variety and numbers

Building workers suggested to Robert Tressell[19] the description of ragged-trousered philanthropists, blind and exploited men who willingly handed over the results of their labour to their employers. His bleak narrative well illustrates the arduous nature of life on site, although probably no worse, or better, than in other industries. The worst off were the unskilled labourers, of whom there were perhaps a quarter of a million in the 1870s and 1880s,[20] a large proportion of all labourers. Especially at their level, but also among skilled men, employment at best remained intermittent and vulnerable, with seldom a time when nobody was waiting to step into a job vacated because of sickness or unsuitability. Casual employment and surplus labour meant that movement in and out of jobs was very frequent, as was movement between trades and between building and other industries. Instances of mobility were carpenter-greengrocers, small-holders who occasionally tried their hands at brickmaking, and labourers employed in a brickfield one day and a quarry the next. Some adaptable individuals took on stonemasonry, bricklaying, roof mending and even the erection of entire small buildings, on a fairly casual basis interspersed with gardening.[21] The contribution of these versatile and unclassifiable figures, and that of the great anonymous mass of unskilled labourers, was crucial but remains largely unquantified.

The circumstances of skilled tradesmen are better recorded and few groups more so than those of the carpenters and joiners. Theirs was the largest trade, being 177,000 strong at the time of the 1861 census, rising to 270,000 by 1901. A typical mid-century figure was said to be the young carpenter and joiner working for a London speculative builder, after having left the country in search of improvement. No doubt some found it, for Clapham noted that foremen were recruited generally from the ranks of their trade. Bricklayers displaced the masons as the second largest trade by 1871, growing from 79,000 in 1861 to 213,000 by 1901 although, like the carpenters and joiners, the total fell back during the ensuing slump.[22] The 86,000 masons recorded in 1861 did not change in number dramatically during the remainder of the century, expansion being arrested by changing materials usage. The painting trade was large but, with low levels of skill and casual employment, it had indistinct boundaries. Combined with the glaziers, over 100,000 painters were recorded in 1881, along with 37,000 plumbers, 29,000 plasterers and 7,000 slaters and tilers. Not least were those who described themselves as builders, a term which might be used to cover both the great such as Edward Yates, and the very much lesser jobbing builders and repair men. Nearly 16,000 of this heterogeneous kind were recorded in 1861 and twenty years later the number had almost doubled.

Wages

The trend of building wages was upward and broadly in sympathy with levels of activity, with a slow rise from the 1850s accelerating towards the beginning of the last quarter of the century. Thereafter increases levelled off until the boom of the 1890s took wages to a peak, followed by stagnation until shortly before the outbreak of war.[23] In the 1850s wages in southern England were of the order of 54d per ten-hour day for craftsmen and 34d for labourers.[24] In 1867 Levi[25] thought that London wages were about 8d per hour for first class men, and one halfpenny less for second class. He also noted wide regional differences such as the range between 6½d and 8d per hour in Yorkshire and 4½d and 5d in Norfolk. The national average rates were estimated to be about 7d per hour, 30/- to 32/- per week for skilled adults, 12/- to 25/- per week for labourers, and 5/- per week for boys and lads. As well as losses from such figures due to bad weather and slack trade, allowance had to be made for payments for tools. For bricklayers this amounted to only about £1 initially and 5/- annually, but for some joiners it was as much as £20 or more initially and £1-15s annually. Between 1873 and 1892 typical craftsmen's wages were 72d per ten-hour day and labourers' 46d or more. In the mid-1880s the highest London day rates were for decorators, followed by grainers, plaster modellers and smiths' and founders' engineers. Next came slate masons followed by plumbers and smiths, then stonemasons, bellhangers, plasterers, gasfitters and glaziers. Slightly lower was the large category of excavator gangers, slaters, carpenters and joiners, painters and paper-hangers, slightly ahead of bricklayers and tilers. Below these skilled men were their respective labourers, headed by slate masons' labourers and completed by bricklayers' and excavators' labourers.[26]

At the outbreak of war craftsmen's wages had advanced to something of the order of 85d per ten-hour day, and those of labourers about 60d. On the basis of annual earnings in 1906, building craftsmen were paid slightly more than the average for all skilled manual workers although labourers, of course, did less well. Carpenters were said to earn about £98 and bricklayers a few pounds less, while the almost revered railway engine drivers earned £119, pottery turners and engineering fitters £90 and bakers £75.[27]

Organization

Wages were related in part to the organization of building trade unions which was hampered by fragmentation of the industry into numerous, mostly small, firms offering mainly short-term employment on dispersed sites. Identity of interest between men of different trades and districts was hard for them to perceive and even harder to use advantageously. Disputes between employers and labour usually remained narrowly confined by the relative insularity and lack of organization of the men. Nevertheless some skilled workers successfully combined to form effective unions, prominent among which was the Operative Stonemasons Society, in its heyday in the late 1870s. As other leading trades also organized themselves, loose collections of local branches began to become more centralized, but the process was slow and the number of unions long remained very large.

Building unions of the 1860s were for skilled men who could afford high contributions in exchange for correspondingly large benefits. Policies were moderate and based on the belief that the best way to obtain a share of growing prosperity was to adopt a conciliatory posture towards employers,[28] an attitude epitomized by Robert Applegarth, influential leader of the Amalgamated Society of Carpenters and Joiners. The two main aims of this union, and others, were to reduce working hours and resist employers who sought to replace payment by the day with payment by the hour. These issues were central to a lock-out by large London builders in 1859–60, during which the men pressed for shorter hours while employers tried to enforce the terms of 'The Document' intended to ban union members from work. Inflamed feelings and rousing talk of a 'tyranny of fustian' by 'dastards of the hod and trowel' subsided eventually when the threat of 'The Document' was withdrawn. However, payment by the hour, and with it one hour's notice of dismissal, was accepted gradually, and significantly shorter hours did not come until the early 1870s. By that time London masons, with a fifty-one-hour week, seem to have enjoyed one of the happiest positions, but very wide variations long persisted up and down the country.

Union militancy was discouraged by slack building activity during the 1880s and early 1890s, although there were said to be more than 100,000 union members in 1885,[29] perhaps an eighth of the building labour force. Returning prosperity in the 1890s brought a near-doubling in the proportion of craftsmen, approaching one in five, who belonged to unions, but neither this growth or more radical leadership much changed the structure of the unions. Local claims continued to be contested without control from union head offices which, for their part, ignored significant developments in other industries. In addition to the perennials of pay and hours, a key issue was piece-work, which was opposed on the grounds that it depressed pay and standards of craftsmanship. Another issue was apprenticeship, threatened by employers who sought to ease labour shortages in times of boom, and defended by unions fearing the effects of future labour surplus when the boom passed. National conciliation boards, on which employers and unions met, began to appear towards the end of the century by which time the main basis of working rules was becoming established.

A quarter of a century or more of very gradual improvement in living and working conditions was halted by economic adversity which came with the new century. Employment was scarce (12% unemployment among carpenters in 1909) while wages were stationary and prices rising. Worse, technological obsolescence began to threaten parts of certain trades, calling for adaptation: less stone was used; joinery work was mechanized; brick and timber began to yield to steel and concrete; lead roofing sometimes was replaced by asphalt; and gas began to give way to electricity. Here, if anywhere, were fertile grounds for demarcation disputes and competition among unions to hinder relations and amalgamation.[30] In the last few years of peace, union membership declined and active members' views shifted from thoughts of reform to ideas of more profound change.

MATERIALS AND COMPONENTS

Costs

While labour costs followed an upward trend, the same was not true of the cost of materials and components, which generally fell gradually in sympathy with wholesale prices. The most notable exceptions to the downward trend were peaks around 1873 and 1900, and a rise after 1909. The effect of rising labour and falling materials costs was to keep total building costs fairly stable; at the same time labour began to assume greater significance within total costs than materials. Around mid-century the proportion of total cost represented by materials on a typical project probably was about two-thirds or more but this appears to have fallen to about one half by early Edwardian times.[31] The fall was due largely to increased productivity and efficiency resulting from mechanization in workshop and yard and from improved transport. The circumstances of each trade varied so that some experienced technical development or increased usage while others did not, and some were more costly in materials and others in labour. In the 1890s the trades with high materials costs were plumbing, bricklaying and carpentry, and those with high labour costs were plastering, painting, masonry and joinery.

Range and transport of goods

The combination of increasing labour costs and fairly stable total building costs was associated loosely with the already noted broadening range of goods for building. Contemporary advertisers leave us in no doubt of the real or supposed advantages of new products such as partitioning systems, and metal and wire lathing which offered 'expedition in erecting' as well as being hygienic, fireproof and soundproof. Countless other products were alleged to save time and labour and to contribute to better finished buildings: window control gear which 'cannot run down or become deranged'; patent roof ridge slates which we were assured, were 'handsome, neat, artistic and durable'; and assorted patent preparations such as Browning's colourless preservative of which it was boasted 'Cleopatra's needle preserved by this solution.'

The market for such products was extended greatly by cheapening and accelerating transport, particularly by rail. Freight tonnage conveyed annually by that means in Great Britain increased more than eight-fold between mid-century and 1914, by which time virtually all communities of any size had been served by rail for some years. Typical late Victorian rates were 4/3d per ton-mile up to twenty miles and less for greater distances. Coastal and inland water transport was slower and less flexible, but still important for bulky goods like lime and bricks. The new century brought another competitor to the field, with the number of goods road vehicles swelling from 4,000 to 64,000 between 1904 and 1913,[32] to further sharpen competition among hitherto sheltered materials producers. When brickmakers and others added lorries to their ownership of horses and traction engines, vulnerable local producers like quarries, unable to adapt to new trading conditions, perished.

Brick

Foremost among materials was brick: formerly only one of several alternative walling materials, it now advanced to near-domination and became synonymous with building itself. It accounted for a large proportion of the total cost of materials, often not far short of one half. In part the usefulness of brick was due to the availability of brick earth near most of the largest towns, but even where suitable stone was plentiful, brick was preferred for most uses. A result was that output by

1907 (4800m) was more than two-and-a-half times that of 1845. Aesthetic preference was mostly for uniform machine-made bricks rather than uneven hand-made ones, and fondness for ornament favoured many different colours and shapes intended to lend interest and contrast. Terra-cotta decorations also gained popularity, sand-lime bricks were patented in 1866, and hollow clay blocks for use in composite suspended floors appeared later in the century. Cavity walls were built occasionally (they were proposed in 1821), but the great majority of walls put up before 1914 were solid. The Fletton brick industry arose in the 1880s, expanding strongly in the London market around the turn of the century[33] and eroding cost advantages previously held by small yards. The price of bricks was relatively stable and not so very different from the levels of the 1820s. In London, in the mid-1890s, it ranged from about £6 per 1000 for very high quality products for arches, down to £1-3s for place bricks for use in concealed positions.[34] The average price at Fletton works was rather less than the latter, although subsequent cut-throat competition sometimes brought prices so low as to force unlucky makers out of business.

Stone

The fortunes of stone as a building material were different from brick, with a general decline except in monumental architectural and decorative uses. Many quarries which survived were ones which managed to find outlets either for superior products or which avoided costly transport and kept to a minimum laborious cutting, for example around window openings. The problem with stone, apart from a possible aesthetic preference for processed rather than natural materials, was that of bringing closely together irregular shapes and sizes to make walls as quickly and cheaply as was possible with bricks. Where cutting was unavoidable it was mechanized increasingly and carried out at the quarry rather than on site. Although the cost of stone remained steady from mid-century, having fallen somewhat since the 1820s, the impact of rising labour costs counted against the material. Rough rubble walling cost in the region of 15/6d per cub. yd in the two final decades of the century, when the cost of rubble delivered to site was 5/- per cub. yd. For higher quality work, typical prices at the quarry were about 1/- per cub. ft for Corsham and Doulting stones and triple that amount for Hopton Wood carboniferous limestone.

Timber

Timber was perhaps the next most important material after brick, with the cost of carpentry and joinery work on typical small buildings of the 1860s often amounting to something between a quarter and a third of total building costs. The timber import trade was one of the few overseas contacts for the building industry and one carried out on a greatly increasing scale. The annual value of imports to the United Kingdom expanded, fluctuating between £8m and £13m in the decade from 1854, and between £23m and £34m in the decade from 1903.[35] The cost trend was downward until the 1890s with a slight rise thereafter, but there were marked short-term fluctuations. In the 1850s a typical prime cost of softwood was about £4-15s per load, on site in bonding plates and lintels it was 3/6d per cub. ft, and more when wrought and framed. By that time English oak was much more expensive than this, over 7/-d per cub. ft when used in bonding plates. By the 1880s typical prime costs of softwood had declined by about £1 per load, reducing the cost of plates and lintels on site to only about 2/6d per cub. ft. Joinery items such as doors and windows, as well as hewn timber, were imported at that time and within another decade Swedish and American goods were undercutting home-produced ones, despite increasing workshop mechanization.[36]

Slate and tile

If brick was ever one half of our stereotype of Victorian buildings, then slate must have been the other half; its use for roofing reached a peak in the final years of the nineteenth century, by which time North Wales output had nearly devastated rival roofing producers. In the third quarter of the century, slaters' work probably accounted for between 5 and 10% of total building cost, and slate prices in London appear to have been lower than they were earlier in the century, no doubt helped by cheaper transport. In the 1850s a square (100 sq ft) of small slates including labour and metal nails cost £1-6s, or more for larger slates with superior copper nails. Welsh prices increased as output went up and the selling price of best quality slates had more than doubled by 1877, although it fell somewhat in the ensuing depression. By the mid-1880s a square of small slates cost £2, but within ten years the cost had fallen to £1-5s-6d. Having vanquished so many producers of traditional roofing materials, slate itself faced stiffening competition from early Edwardian years when coloured asbestos-cement tiles appeared alongside the concrete tiles already in limited use. Just as the use of brick represented in several respects the obverse of the use of stone, so slate usage represented the obverse of that of clay tiles. Pantiles, in particular, were rejected in favour of slates, although prices remained fairly stable: a square of pantiles complete with laths, nails and labour in the 1850s cost between £1-4s and £1-15s,[37] and thirty years later was a few shillings cheaper. Plain tiles belied their name by costing more than pantiles, at £2-5s per square in the 1850s, falling by several shillings late in the century. Tile making followed the example of brick with the gradual introduction of machinery and some concentration into larger businesses alongside the survival of older methods.

Plaster and cement

Plastering costs were typical of others in following a generally downward trend, with lathing plastered with one coat and set costing about 1/5d per sq yd in the 1850s and about 1½d less in the 1880s. Laxton's price for cement did not vary much more than a few pence from 30d per bushel (1.28 cub. ft, or about 135 lb) between 1854 and the late 1880s, after which it fell by about 6d by 1893–95 but recovered thereafter.[38] Portland cement gradually became more reliable, largely superseding the older Roman cement, but applications remained cautious and directed towards foundations and fire-proof suspended floors. By 1912 reinforced concrete beams and columns were said to be cheaper than steel, brick arches and timber[39] but, like cement mortar for brickwork, were not yet adopted widely.

Services

Nowhere was the increasing variety of goods more evident than in the field of building services where the rate of obsolescence probably was faster than in other fields of building. The wide price range for many goods is notable, with 1880s examples which included £1-8s-6d for a cheap dry earth closet of deal, compared with £5 for a similar article in mahogany or slightly less for a w.c. with valve; from £1-5s to £11 for hand basins of various sizes and materials; and wide differences between cheap japanned cast iron baths and costly zinc and copper ones. Similarly the range was wide among the large array of gas appliances of the 1890s, with stoves costing from £1 each up to £12 or more, and fires from 14/6d up to £4. The cost of electric lighting installations also varied very widely, with a reasonable sum for a fifty-lamp system in an office or larger house said to be about £100. Where the affluent householder had no access to public electricity supply, a private generator with dynamo, cables, fittings, accumulators and steam, gas or oil engine, could add a further £300 or so, more than double the cost of a private gasworks. Lifts of the 1890s ranged from about £32, for supplying and fitting a small dinner lift, to ten times that sum or more, for an 8 cwt hydraulic passenger lift of 50 ft travel.

Miscellaneous goods

Painting and decorating was a minor trade in terms of total building costs, but one which was ubiquitous for new work and which increased somewhat in importance with growing standards of living. Prices fell until around the turn of the century when there was a peak, then a fall, followed by a rise towards 1914.[40] Glass usage and prices moved in a similar way, with prices falling as the size of glassworks increased over time. In the 1850s small panes of crown glass were available for between 9d and 1/3d per sq ft and polished plate could be had for about 4/9d per sq ft. Forty years later polished plate was down to a half or two-thirds of its earlier price and crown glass had been superseded by qualitatively superior sheet glass costing between 4½d and 1/8d per sq ft. By then glassmaking had become very centralized and among new products which had appeared, or were soon to do so, were patent glazing, wired glass and glass blocks.

Like glass, iron and steel demanded very large capital investment for production and was supplied to other markets as well as building. Iron prices stood relatively high at mid-century and climbed haltingly to a sharp peak in the early 1870s. They fell to their lowest level around 1890, but climbed temporarily at the turn of the century, and again as the war approached. The cost of rolled iron girders in the 1880s was from 10/- to 15/- per cwt (wrought iron weighed 480 lb per cub. ft; 6 x 6 in girders weighed 56 lb per ft) Ten years later cast iron members cost between 9/- and 11/6d per cwt delivered in London, far cheaper than in the 1820s. Competition from newer rolled mild steel joists appears not to have been intense, with some reluctance to use the material. Lighter applications of iron included galvanized sheeting, cast window frames and cast kitchen ranges. Among the wide range of other materials, space permits only passing mention of new low cost sheets available in the decade or so before the war, such as asbestos-cement roofing, fibreboard and millboard for use in commercial and industrial interiors.

Plant

Although builders' plant is neither a material or component, some brief mention of its nature and cost is called for. Small builders and larger ones engaged on small buildings, operated quite happily with a minimum of craftsmen's hand tools, ladders and odd scraps of timber for scaffolding and shoring. On the other hand larger firms which worked at great heights or depths, with large buildings, or with civil engineering interests, were prepared increasingly to buy or hire plant to speed their progress. In larger joinery shops of the 1880s there might be a moulding and planing machine, lathes and morticing machines and a steam engine to provide power. In order to move goods to site the builder could hire a horse, cart and a man at a rate of 1/6d per hour or, if the load demanded, a traction engine at £4 per hour, including fuel and attendance. Heavy handling might require a portable crane (£34 for one ton capacity, £120 for five tons) and on the largest sites it could be economical to hire a steam excavator at £12 per month. A two-foot gauge light railway (£300 per mile) was a far cry from a wheelbarrow (price about 15/-) but both had a part to play in shifting spoil. Other plant included mortar mills (£35 to £90 in the 1890s), donkey pumps and power sources in the shape of steam or 'Otto' gas engines.[41] Such elaborate plant, like the more advanced materials, still had little influence on typical small-scale building. As one progressive gloomily observed in 1891:[42]

'Unfortunately the practices . . . are greatly of an empirical character, and have been handed down from one generation to another with little or no thought as to how far they are judicious, or in what respects they may be improved upon.'

5

Buildings in Ribbons and Suburbs: 1915-39

'Nina looked down and saw . . . a horizon of straggling red suburb; arterial roads dotted with little cars; factories, some of them working, others empty and decaying; a disused canal; some distant hills sown with bungalows; wireless masts and overhead power cables . . . "I think I'm going to be sick," said Nina.'

(*Evelyn Waugh,* Vile Bodies, *1930*)

DECISION TO BUILD

Sponsorship

National transformation from a rural agricultural economy to an urban industrial one was substantially complete by 1914. Each economy in turn had given rise to its own characteristic legacy of buildings; in the interwar years the visible contrast between the two legacies lost much of its former clarity. Large new suburbs encircled the more prosperous towns and spilled out into open countryside, to wreak a striking change in the national stock of buildings, qualitatively in respect of density and form, and quantitatively in sheer numbers and geographical extent. Like most major changes to the stock it was consequent on the decisions of building sponsors interpreting the signs of demand for new buildings and acting to meet them. Here two prominent features were evident: vigour, to be seen in the exceptional quantity of new building; and growth of attempts to satisfy social need as a motive for building. Although the profit motive retained its primacy in sponsorship, the public sector quickly rose to a new importance with the annual average level of public building expenditure increasing five-fold between 1920–23 and 1935–38.[1] Each new responsibility taken on by the State for the well-being of the people brought expansion in the sponsorship of public buildings. Efforts to replace slums, improve education, create employment and resist the Nazi threat all led directly or indirectly to public sector building. Hitherto the total volume of building activity in the country at one time had been regarded, if at all, rather as an incidental consequence of innumerable private decisions. With the stress and shortages of the First World War this attitude began to change and the government started to regard the total volume of building as a national priority. After recovery from the war, itself protracted, the volume of building still remained as a fit subject for government policies although frequently of a short-term and changeable nature.

Public authority sponsors

The rise of public sector sponsorship affected many departments of central and local government: during the First World War the Ministry of Munitions and Office of Works, for example, were heavily engaged; after the war came the turn of the local authorities. In the housing field, particularly, national policies and public debate moved back and forth between local authorities and private builders and from additions to stock towards replacement and relief of overcrowding. Despite policy changes imposed from above, the 1,500 or so local authorities accumulated considerable experience as sponsors. Their building programmes, having large numbers of small units of building rather than occasional large units, gave continuity of work to those responsible for administration and execution. While local authority organizations grew and the provision of houses became almost a matter of routine, levels of competence were variable.[2] Repetitive procedures applied less in the case of other local authority buildings: for example the number of new schools was considerable, but never rivalled house building in either total expenditure or continuity of programme. Important buildings such as town halls and central libraries were sufficiently rare for most to be treated as unique ventures. Various departments of central authority also continued after the war to sponsor their share of buildings, among them post offices, telephone exchanges, labour exchanges, training centres and installations for the armed forces. There was another smaller category of sponsors which came to occupy a position mid-way between public sponsors and private, the newly founded public corporations such as the Central Electricity Board and London Passenger Transport Board.

Private sponsors

Private sponsors were motivated mainly by considerations of profit, although some minor exceptions should not be overlooked. Among them were private trusts, those whose interest was more in long-term security than immediate gain, and those in receipt of State subsidies. Private sponsorship was undertaken with one of several intentions in mind: occupation by the sponsor himself, as in the case of many industrial and commercial ventures and larger houses; rental to others or sale for capital gain, as in the case of many cheaper houses. The customary initial act of developers of suburban houses, often specialist land or estate agents, was to buy land either for themselves or on behalf of others. Much was bought from land speculators who had themselves originally acquired it in order to 'hold for a rise', that is to await the reversionary value which would accrue from advancing demand or development of nearby amenities. Having bought the land the developer laid out roads, arranged the installation of mains services and offered plots to buyers. In the case of expensive prime sites the plots might be sold singly for detached houses, otherwise multiples of plots were sold for groups of semi-detached and terraced houses. Occasionally the land speculator or original landowner himself arranged development, employing agents to lay out the site and sell the plots. To attract early buyers the developers often erected a few prominently placed houses by means of a contract with a builder. The speculative builders who bought or leased the plots often paid only a deposit to the developers; the remainder followed after they had sold the houses which they intended to build. In this they perpetuated the rather shaky precedent of many of their Victorian forerunners who had survived, if lucky, on the barest minimum of working capital. At some stage of the development process, often later rather than sooner, sites were taken by other private interests for shops, and by public interests for church, school and other non-residential buildings. Developers generally hoped to dispose of entire sites within five years and to recover costs plus interest and make a profit of not less than 10%. Speculative builders sometimes kept houses as investments or sold them to other investors but most were sold to owner-occupiers, at which point building societies played a crucial part in lending money to those wishing to buy.

The growth of building societies was spectacular, with a nine-fold increase in both shares and deposits over the period, and a five or six-fold increase in the annual amount advanced on mortgage. The size of some societies, such as the Halifax, increased greatly, transforming the movement from a fragmented pattern of mainly local societies, each with its own traditions and methods, into one of large national societies with competing networks of branch offices up and down the country.

A variation on the method of development, more typical of the south-east during the 1930s than the 1920s, was for large building firms themselves to handle all the various stages from site purchase to finished building. A series of interlocked development, sales and building companies, with related financial support, carried out much of the work formerly done by a number of independent firms.[3,4] Increases in the size and scope of larger concerns was akin to that visible among local authorities and other sponsors, for example, high street retailers and railway companies, where there were amalgamations and emergence of large organizations. Both private and public building sponsors, or at least the largest of them, increasingly undertook continuous building programmes instead of intermittent or occasional commitments characteristic of smaller concerns. In the process they accumulated first-hand knowledge about the nature, cost, timescale and procedures of building.

ASPECTS OF DEMAND

Location

The largest additions to the stock of buildings appeared in hitherto agricultural landscapes near the towns. Early in the century the percentage of land area occupied by urban development was just short of 5.5, rising slightly to 6.2 in 1925 and then rapidly to 8.6 in 1939. Towards the end of the period the spread of building and other constructional development took place at a rate of over 60,000 acres per year.[5] This was fast enough to provoke cries of anxiety and protest which did little to redeem the doubtful reputation of speculative builders. Yet little effective action emerged to stem or direct the flood of development which followed the rising popularity and accessibility of suburban living.

Among the stimuli of suburban growth were the established centrifugal repulsion from often unattractive towns, and the magnetism of the countryside. A newer influence enabling old ambitions to be realized was the increasing mobility brought by mechanized transport and rising incomes. Other influences included the ideals and examples of the garden city movement, possibly abetted by growing anxiety about the effects of bombing on town centres. Yet by no means was there unbridled growth right across the country, for sharp contrasts existed between one region and another. In the south and midlands, where economic prospects were good, new houses and light industry expanded the building stock. In the depressed or 'special' areas occupied by declining old industries in the north and west were to be found neglect and decay. J. B. Priestley's[6] comparison was between the '. . . England of arterial and by-pass roads, of filling stations and factories . . . of giant cinemas and dance halls and cafes, bungalows with tiny garages . . .' and sad places of '. . . cindery waste ground, mill chimneys, slums, fried-fish shops . . . sooty dismal little towns.' In some depressed places the only new buildings before the mid-1930s were small outlying council estates sometimes joined, when the worst of the slump eventually passed, by a few new shops and private houses.

Fluctuations

The turning point in the fortunes of older industrial towns, and heavy industrial expansion generally, was the First World War. During the four years of conflict the cycle of boom and slump in building activity was halted and non-essential building tapered away. New work required an official licence and output was drastically curtailed, although not before completion of buildings in some cases as large as part of Heal's store, Tottenham Court Road, in 1916. Uncertainty over the outcome of the war, stagnant incomes and conversion of means of production to meet war needs all hindered change to the building stock. The obvious exception was accommodation for war purposes, in which industrial buildings for armaments and related fields appeared at a faster than average peacetime rate, along with hutted camps and hospitals for the armed services.

The armistice was followed by intractable national problems of readjustment, both in building and heavy industries. A brief postwar economic boom brought sizeable but short-lived demand for industrial buildings at about the same time that local authorities struggled to meet the housing shortage, but soon came collapse and the fall of prices from high levels. Recovery in building (but not now-crippled heavy industries) came in 1924 and activity increased so that gross capital formation in United Kingdom building expanded from about £109m in 1923 to £201m in 1927. Activity then slipped back a little, but remained fairly high, largely due to house building, until a vigorous burst of growth took place from 1932 leading to the interwar peak of £272m in 1937. By then not only was the volume of building greater than hitherto, but old violent fluctuations between boom and slump had been much reduced. The great interwar overall addition to stock is exemplified by the case of Birmingham in 1938, when over one-third of all dwellings in the city were younger than nineteen years old.

Influences on demand

Details of the impressive national performance in meeting demand for buildings have been set down elsewhere by Richardson and Aldcroft,[7] so it is necessary here only to note some of the more important influences at work. High among them were demographic changes, of which the most significant was an increase in the number of families. While population growth was very moderate compared with nineteenth-century levels, the number of families in the United Kingdom increased considerably, by 3.5m between 1921 and 1938. This meant that although the average family size was much smaller than it had been, the need for separate houses increased greatly. Housing need also was stimulated by movement between regions, mostly by unemployed manual workers from depressed areas in search of jobs in the south-east and midlands, which gained over a million people by immigration between 1921 and 1936. Most of those who found jobs benefited from increases in real income, enabling them to translate housing need into effective demand. Better paid households were tempted to move to better houses, often changing from rented to owner-occupied dwellings in the process. Another stimulus for building came from the fashion for suburban living[8] which must have persuaded many households to move to new localities. In doing so they increased demand for more than houses alone, for even the most soulless ribbon development eventually generated shops and other amenity buildings. A further source of building demand was connected with replacement of worn-out accommodation, although this was not as large as the condition of the stock appeared to warrant, being depressed by housing shortage. Where good accommodation was scarce, people made do with obsolete buildings and replacements were few, but in other places where emigration eased the shortage, local authorities could demolish and replace dwellings instead of confining their limited resources to adding to stock.

Most of the sources of demand noted so far concerned occupants (or would-be occupants), but there was demand also from investors who either sold or let buildings. Demand from this source was influenced by the level of rents which could be expected. From 1915 these were controlled by government and returns generally were smaller than hitherto, although rents slowly increased on average between the wars. Another influence on investment demand was the level of general interest rates: when high, investors put their money in fields outside building in order to get greatest returns; when low, their money flowed into building. Interest rates were particularly low after 1931 and many investors were attracted by the favourable returns possible from property and building societies. Being replete with funds, the societies found that they could offer mortgages to householders of smaller and smaller incomes, thereby broadening their market. New industrial and commercial building was determined mainly by business activity such that growth of manufacturing soon led to new building, particularly if interest rates on loans available for expansion happened to be low. The volumes of industrial and house building activity alike were influenced by the cost of building: the cheaper it was, the more activity was stimulated. Here, once postwar difficulties were overcome, the pattern was favourable with costs moving downwards for the most part until the late 1930s. One other influence on activity, and not the least, was government policy, in which efforts to stimulate local authority house building could indirectly affect the cost of all other kinds of building activity. Subsidies to private house-builders had more limited impact, but still were significant and, similarly, municipal non-residential building could exert an influence, particularly where it happened to be close to building for rearmament purposes.

HOUSING

Private provision

The number of dwellings built in England and Wales between the wars was 3,998,000, a large output which maintained the annual value of new housing at over half that of all building. The peak was reached in 1937 with 347,000 house completions, equivalent to over 1000 every working day. Nearly three-quarters of the interwar total, 2,886,000, were built by private agencies, most for sale rather than rent, and we begin our examination with this type. At the outset private house builders recovered slowly from wartime dislocation and there were fewer than 100,000 completions before March 1923, of which less than half were built with the aid of subsidy introduced by the Housing (Additional Powers) Act 1919. This was intended to stimulate private house building by means of a lump sum of about £150 for each new house not exceeding a specified size. The inducement was not long-lived however, and it was Chamberlain's Housing Act of 1923 which triggered more lasting expansion by offering a subsidy of £6 per house for a maximum of twenty years, again subject to restriction on house size. The rate of house building, subsidized and unsubsidized, increased until the late 1920s when subsidized completions fell away. Although they subsequently reached 430,000, subsidized houses were eclipsed by a strong upsurge in the number of unsubsidized houses. Great activity in the late 1920s was followed by a slight slackening during the slump and by another burst through the golden years of speculative building after 1932. Only the approaching threat of the Second World War and market saturation retarded intense activity which had brought home ownership within reach of lower middle and upper working class households. As Professor Burnett has written,[9] new houses have probably never been so cheap or so widely available as in the mid-thirties.

Many typical 1930s speculative houses were known as 'five fifties',[10] taking their name from the selling price of £550. For this sum the mortgaged householder could expect a semi-detached house of 'Tudorbethan' style on an estate of similar houses at a density of eight or ten per acre. Typical ground floor accommodation consisted of a hall and stairs; a 125 sq ft parlour; a 140 sq ft living room; and a 65 sq ft 'kitchenette'. Upstairs were a bathroom and a separate w.c.; two larger bedrooms roughly corresponding with main rooms below; and a small bedroom of 50 sq ft, sometimes tactfully named a box-room in view of its minimal size. The average cost per cub. ft was about 1/- with lower and upper limits of 10d and 1/4d. Not all houses cost as much as the 'five fifties'; in London a reasonable minimum was £400 and elsewhere it was £300 or even £250.[11] At this end of the market, houses and bungalows were decidedly tightly planned with cramped circulation spaces and floor areas cut down to 800 sq ft or less. In the late 1920s, somewhere very near the lower reaches, came corrugated iron, plaster and stud bungalows for 9d per cub. ft.[12] Before that, just after the First World War when prices generally were high, even the cheapest houses were far above such levels. For a while, around 1920, small London houses cost as much as £1,000 although when the fall came it was a steep one, dropping from over £1 per sq ft to less than 10/- by 1922. Thereafter costs continued to drift downwards slowly under the influence of low interest rates and building costs.

The upper part of the 1930s suburban speculative market contained houses at £1,000 to £1,250 or occasionally more. For example, semi-detached houses offered by A. W. Curton at Edgware for £1,200 consisted of a hall and stairs; a dining room 13 ft 6 in x 14 ft 9 in (into bay); drawing room 12 ft 3 in x 17 ft 3 in (into bay); kitchen 9 ft 3 in x 10 ft 6 in (into door); a garage; a separate bathroom and w.c.; two bedrooms of 175 sq ft each; and one bedroom of 70 sq ft.[13] The cost of individual architect-designed houses overlapped with the better speculatively built ones, but most were more expensive.[14] The size, and probably number, of new larger private houses was less than it had been before 1914 owing to the effects of higher taxes, economic depression and shortage of domestic servants. The proportion of new privately built houses large enough to have rateable values between £27 and £78 fell from 33% before 1931 to only 13% between that year and 1939.[15] Individuals wishing to build their own architect-designed houses faced a typical expenditure of over £1,400 for a detached house with four or more bedrooms, about 1/2d per cub. ft, more or less, depending on means and taste. Total costs of £2,500 and upwards were reached, along with unit costs of 1/8d per cub. ft, and near the top the wealthiest few could pay 2/6d per cub. ft for a mansion or compact town service flat.

Public provision

Public sector housing sponsorship[16] was sustained during the First World War by the Ministry of Munitions which erected both temporary and permanent accommodation for war workers.[17] After the armistice local authorities were quickly plunged into action, urged and guided by central government to produce as many 'Homes Fit for Heroes' as required to meet a severe shortage. They attempted to do so, through vicissitudes,[18] to the extent of a total of 1,112,000 new dwellings by

1939. Provision was initiated by Addison's Housing and Town Planning Act 1919 which required (no longer merely permitted) local authorities to ascertain housing need and take steps, with Ministry approval, to meet it. Financial losses to local authorities in excess of a penny in the pound rate were met by the Treasury. Soon, estates of houses, showing the influence of the forward-looking Tudor Walters Report, [19,20] began to appear, but so, too, did alarming price increases reflecting overstretched resources. With the passing of the postwar boom went the incomplete housing drive, yielding only 170,000 local authority houses to make small impact on the shortage. The Chamberlain Housing Act which followed in 1923 stimulated some local authority activity despite demanding greater financial responsibility from them and being aimed mainly at private builders. Local authorities were restored fully to their new-found place of importance in the provision of houses in 1924 by the Wheatley Act. This made available a subsidy of £9 per year for forty years for each new house, with the result that local authority activity soon picked up to reach the interwar peak of 104,000 new houses in 1928. From the early 1930s official attention turned from additions to stock towards replacement of slums by means of subsidies created by the Greenwood Housing Act, 1930. Progress was slow at first, but eventually this, and later measures intended to abate overcrowding, led to a switch away from houses towards flat building. In the last few years of the decade, under the shadow of the war with Hitler, local authority activity expanded almost to its 1928 peak level.

Houses built under the Addison Act of 1919 were of relatively high quality, generous size (most had three bedrooms) and commensurate cost. Floor areas ranged between about 950 sq ft and as much as 1,400 sq ft, containing living room, scullery and, in two-fifths of cases, a parlour. A typical plan produced by the Ministry of Health for local authority guidance had hall and stairs, a 174 sq ft living room, 132 sq ft parlour, 80 sq ft scullery, larder and coal store. There were three bedrooms corresponding with the main rooms downstairs and a separate bathroom and w.c.[21] In 1920 the cost was about £955, equivalent to nearly £1 per sq ft, although smaller houses without parlours cost £870. By 1923 non-parlour three-bedroom houses on average had fallen to £365, or 9/9d per sq ft. Chamberlain and Wheatley Act houses which soon followed were smaller and cheaper, but similar in fundamentals, being two-storey terraced houses on estates. Most were between 750 and 850 sq ft in floor area, with later examples (and succeeding ones built under the Greenwood Act) being smaller than earlier ones.[22] When quality was near its lowest in 1936 the average cost of non-parlour three-bedroom houses was £310 and that of parlour houses £487, approaching double the figures of 1913. The number of flats was not great in comparison with that of suburban estate houses, amounting to about one in twenty of local authority dwellings.[23] They were to be found in the largest cities and most of them took the form of four or five-storey blocks at densities of forty-five to sixty-five dwellings per acre. With special structures, circulation and services they consistently cost more than non-parlour houses, of the order of one-third to two-thirds more for equivalent accommodation. In the mid-1930s their cost was about 1/6d per cub. ft and by the late 1930s, when slum replacement and hence flat building was most active and building prices were beginning to rise, the average cost was about £600 each.

INDUSTRIAL BUILDINGS

Factories etc.

Opposite many a new estate of semi-detached houses, across an improved arterial road, were the long, usually low shapes of new factories. In 1935 about 5% of building investment was in industrial or warehouse buildings,[24] and although this proportion was not large, most individual units were imposing ones. They were built extensively during the boom of the early 1920s, but activity then fell away for a decade, whereupon there was fresh growth lasting for about five years. Like new private houses, most factories were located in the south and midlands where they benefited from effective distribution networks and the proximity of the largest consumer markets. Freed from earlier dependence on congested city-centre sites by improved communications and electric power, factories now could occupy more spacious suburban surroundings. In the sceptical words of the *Architects' Journal*:[25]

'Places like Slough are growing into towns . . . [with] . . . all the terrible signs of pig-headed industrialism . . . at Hayes, Southall and fanwise round the northern suburbs are springing up miles of new factories. Even the Great West Road . . . has, in places, the look of a motor track leading to an

absolute fun-fare of comic factories. It is as though London were now the absolutely irresistable magnet for all the money in the country.'

While the old staples remained depressed, expansion was to be found among motor, electrical, rubber, manufactured foodstuff, furniture, hosiery and other light finished consumer goods industries. Around London, in the late 1920s, were new factories making goods such as patent medicines, silk robes, chewing gum and soap.

Typical new factories were larger than earlier examples and many were owned rather than rented by their occupiers, although in the 1930s private trading estate companies commonly built standard factories for letting. Earlier in the period, in particular, they might well be multi-storey,[26,27] like the Maidstone works of Tilling-Stevens, the Acton motor works of Napier, and other designs by Wallis, Gilbert and Partners. The pattern of the 1930s was often a single-storey block with saw-tooth bays of north-light roofing concealed at the front by offices. In heavy chemical and electrical plants, purely engineering aspects might dominate or replace traditional building enclosures, so that tanks, pipes, valves and so on were exposed fully to view. Simple industrial buildings such as engine sheds cost 9d or 10d per cub. ft, factories were to be had for 1/-d to 1/4d per cub. ft (not much different from housing), while typical warehouses cost from 1/3d to 1/8d per cub. ft. Some examples were very large, like two cargo sheds planned by the Southern Railway Company in Southampton docks in 1934, 1,470 ft in length and estimated at £145,000. The scale of this expenditure is clarified by comparison with the cost to the same company of providing suburban passenger stations for about £8,000 each.

Not all industrial installations were quite as mundane as cargo sheds: for example there were airport terminals at such places as Heston and Croydon and novel multi-storey garages to house part of the six-fold increase in motor vehicles during the period. Some fast-growing enterprises serving new consumer markets were prepared to pay for showpiece designs which attracted the attention of the public. Sir Bannister Fletcher's Gillette factory, built in 1926 alongside the Great West Road, was one such building and another was the Boots factory at Beeston, Nottingham, designed by Sir Owen Williams in 1932.[28] The publicity and prestige which these examples were intended to confer on their owners was not at all akin to the aims of government in planning buildings for rearmament purposes. This occurred at an accelerating pace in the later 1930s as the fearful implications of Hitler's regime began to be seen and accepted. In 1934 major new RAF works amounted to a modest £900,000, but two years later the figure had jumped to £8m, and in 1938 it was £20m.[29] Nor was this all, for there was work for the other armed services and new ordnance factories, such as one at Glascoed expected to cost £3.7m in 1938.

From the pressing needs of the services to the more moderate ones of rural life is a long step; agricultural building activity remained light and of piecemeal adaptive nature, being confined largely to the needs of livestock. Desire for extreme economy encouraged many farmers to reuse 1914–18 wartime huts and discarded railway rolling stock bodies, while those who could afford better paid about 8d per cub. ft for new barns and 1/- per cub. ft for cow houses.[30]

COMMERCIAL BUILDINGS

Offices, shops etc.

Commercial buildings such as offices, shops and hotels together made up a category which generally was smaller in value than industrial work. The pattern of commercial building activity was uncertain, with depression in early 1920s and 1930s offset by periods of growth around 1922 to 1924, 1927 to 1929 and from 1932 to 1934.[31] Top quality office building included ponderous central headquarters and prestige premises such as South Africa House, Trafalgar Square, by Sir Herbert Baker and A. T. Scott, and Imperial Chemical House, Millbank, by Sir Frank Baines. Costly offices of this type cost 2/- or more per cub. ft, but lesser premises for rent on the open market, for branch banks and building societies, down to plain blocks associated with factories and depots, cost of the order of 1/6d per cub. ft. Large department stores cost about the same as the best offices and, with stone facings and ornament, many also resembled them. The number of stores increased, from about 200 in 1914 to over 500 in 1938,[32] and so did the number of premises occupied by multiple chains of tailors and so on. Smaller shops and showrooms cost between 1/6d and 1/8d per cub. ft, perhaps £10,000 each in total, while minor examples in suburban parades cost from £1,000 to £2,000, often including a sma'l first floor flat.

Many new shopping centres soon acquired a cinema: there were said to be about 3,000 in 1926 and another 1,300 within eight years, having a combined seating capacity of 3.8m; by 1939 the total had reached 4,800 buildings.[33] A suburban example like the Regal, Altrincham, by Drury and Gomersall, cost £27,000 while the exceptional 4,000-seat Gaumont State, Kilburn, by G. Cole cost as much as £345,000 in 1937.[34] In a sense, cinemas carried on where hotels left off in 1914 in competing with each other in conspicuous expenditure. New hotels still appeared, such as the Cumberland near Marble Arch and smaller examples at the resorts, but earlier exuberance was usually lacking. Costs appear to have advanced from 2/3d per cub. ft in 1927 to an upper limit of 4/- in 1936, although few other building types increased by more than a few pence per cub. ft. More basic accommodation available to holiday makers was in seaside holiday camps, built on a sufficient scale by 1939 to shelter up to 500,000 people. For leisure-seekers preferring alcohol to sea water, a moderate number of public houses was built serving new estates and picking up passing motor trade. These were likely to fall near the range of £10,000 to £15,000 apiece.[35]

PUBLIC AND SOCIAL BUILDINGS

Welfare buildings, education

A large proportion of all buildings for public and social purposes were put up by public authorities and it is probable that only a diminishing minority came from philanthropic individuals and charitable trusts. Public authority building expenditure soon recovered from low levels of 1918 to attain a size comparable with both industrial and commercial categories. The upward trend was almost continuous except for a pause during the slump, in contrast to other sorts of non-residential building which experienced periodic falls. Expenditure on public and social buildings of the order of £5m per year (at 1930 prices) in the early years after 1918 went up to over £30m by 1938.[36] This expansion is all the more notable since it occurred during a period widely regarded as one of government inactivity and lack of resolve. As Dr Stevenson[37] has written, probably the most pervasive impression is that of the 'long weekend' and 'wasted years' summed up in spectres of mass unemployment and appeasement. Yet, as he also pointed out, there was another side characterized by fairly widespread relief projects and municipal building. A key part of the latter, in addition to the ever-dominant housing activity, was building for education.

This began inauspiciously with a light programme, including reused army huts for classrooms, but later in the 1920s there was steady development in provision of secondary schools, followed by further resurgence after the slump. In 1934, a junior mixed and infant school for 600 children could be built for about £13,000 and a few years later senior schools with higher standards of accommodation cost about £50 per pupil.[38] A reasonable cost for cheaper school building was thought to be about 1/4d per cub. ft, with more for private and further education building, although the quantity of work in the field was not particularly large. Only about 5% of children attended private fee-paying schools and the increase in students in full-time higher education from 1924–25 to 1938–39 was only 8,000, to a total of 69,000.[39]

Medical, municipal, and library provision

The cost both of technical institutions and large hospitals, where there was some expansion, was fairly heavy at about 2/- per cub. ft. The total number of beds in hospitals and related institutions increased from 200,000 shortly before the First World War to 260,000 in 1938, while the number of hospital institutions went up from 2,190 to 3,140.[40] There was a wide variety of medical buildings ranging from small cottage hospitals and clinics complete for around £10,000 up to large hospitals like Chadwell Heath, Essex, for 1,120 patients, expected in 1938 to exceed £500,000. This was a large sum by the standards of the time and such expenditure in the public sector was not confined to health buildings. Town halls usually were conspicuously large and expensive, so much so that George Orwell[41] questioned the mystery by which so many northern towns saw fit to build themselves immense and luxurious examples at the same time as they were in crying need of houses. He pointed out that Barnsley spent close on £150,000 on a new town hall (enough for well over 350 council houses), and Southampton Guildhall cost almost the same. A typical cost for this sort of building (and also law courts) in the mid-1930s was about 2/4d per cub. ft in provincial towns, but London rate-payers might find the cost of upholding civic dignity nearer 3/- per cub. ft. Small numbers of museums and art galleries and, more frequently, libraries[42] were also thought to be appropriate subjects for heavy expenditure. Less pretentious branch libraries cost anything between £7,000 (Belsize Branch, Hampstead, 1937) and over £40,000 (Leytonstone Branch, Church Lane,

1934), or between 1/8d and 1/10d per cub. ft. Central libraries were more costly, for instance the three-storey example in Huddersfield completed one month after the outbreak of the Second World War cost 2/- per cub. ft, £87,000 altogether. Even this was quite insignificant compared with Vincent Harris's vast rotunda design in Manchester costing nearly £400,000 in 1934. Small generally meant cheaper, not only in total sum but also on the basis of cost per sq ft of floor area, which varied from £2 up to £4.[43]

Miscellaneous provision

As was the case before 1914, public authorities were called upon to provide numerous other far less monumental building types for more utilitarian purposes. Among them were police stations for about 1/8d per cub. ft, fire stations for slightly less, crematoria, and laundries. Some of the latter were immense temples in honour of cleanliness, or at least in honour of centralization; Surrey County Council's Carshalton central laundry was estimated at £186,000 in 1938. Construction of public baths and wash houses also was significant, with over £2½m in loans sanctioned during the three years to 1937,[44] and cubic costs similar to those of police stations. Various institutions sponsored hostel building such as a home for 220 nurses in Crumpsall, Manchester, which amounted to £80,000 in 1930, incidentally about enough to buy each nurse a house of her own. Plenty of other buildings, most of them cheaper, were sponsored for predominantly non-commercial purposes either by public authorities, private interests or combinations of both. They included drill halls at only 1/- per cub. ft, village halls at a few pence more, sports pavilions and a few community centres. The great impetus behind provision of religious buildings, so strong in the nineteenth century, was now much weakened, although new buildings exceeded 2,000 in number between 1921 and 1941. In the 1930s the cost of places of worship per cub. ft lay between 10d for uncompromising corrugated iron chapels ('tin tabernacles') and 1/6d for brick, while good quality examples cost about £11 to £14 per seat.

LOSSES FROM STOCK

Slum clearance and other obsolescence

The times were not outstandingly good ones for the demolition men. Clearance was restricted by unfettered suburban expansion together with a shortage of accommodation which encouraged patching and mending instead of full replacement. Limited damage (and over 5,000 casualties) were inflicted by air raids and coastal bombardment during the First World War. Later, in the 1920s, about 179,000 houses were demolished and slum clearance accelerated in the 1930s. The peak was reached in 1938 when 61,000 houses were cleared, and the total for the decade came to about 258,000.[45] Most of these houses were in the towns which had grown so quickly in the earlier phase of urbanization before 1850. Cataclysmic town growth eventually had led to wholesale obsolescence, as the fabric of entire groups of streets wore out more or less simultaneously. While the more willing of the local authorities attempted to tackle what had become sub-standard (some of it always had been), other agencies destroyed similar buildings to make way for new industrial and commercial accommodation. Some old industrial buildings also were lost, as in the case of redundant textile mills (700 premises closed between 1933 and 1938), buildings of shipbuilding, coal mining and other industries, all suffering from severe over-capacity and consequent rationalization. In prosperous industries, building obsolescence could arise as a result of need for new equipment requiring equally new buildings to shelter it.

In the country quiet decay continued among the less competitive farms and workshops of blacksmiths, saddlers, clogmakers and the rest. As markets and products changed and economies of scale increasingly were felt, so numerous small bakeries, breweries, mills and shops disappeared. Many premises found new owners and uses, but some simply were abandoned to ruin. A few of their urban counterparts suffered a similar fate but higher site values made building reuse or replacement much more probable. Many a commercial building was found to be too small, inconvenient, wrongly located, or guilty of conveying to the world an undesired image of its occupants. Small beer houses were replaced by large road houses; cramped converted stables were swept away to make room for filling stations; corner shops and tenements came down and department stores went up; and traces of earlier settlements all along the advancing suburban frontier were obliterated under the march of the ubiquitous 'five fifty'.

BUILDING FORM

Growth upward and outward

The appearance of typical new buildings changed in numerous ways, many of which remain forcefully apparent. Here, consideration of physical form must be limited to some general aspects which arose from broad economic and social influences. Foremost was the continued growth of building size to reflect that of the institutions and organizations which were housed. Heights attained by the tallest buildings were greater, and large groups of related buildings became more numerous, as visible in imposing new power stations, aircraft hangars and multi-storey factories. New offices, shops and department stores, and composite versions of all three, dwarfed neighbouring buildings in town centres. Some new giants were in groups which occupied whole street blocks, with the result that the streets in leading commercial districts became ever more canyon-like.

Intensified demand for all kinds of accommodation, transport and recreational facilities combined to drive up urban land values, encouraging sponsors to redevelop sites to the limit of every available cubic foot of space. Physical forms were more and more determined by regulations governing daylight, ventilation and fire precautions, among other legally enforceable constraints. Prominent legislation included Factory and Workshop Acts in 1929 and 1937 (following those of 1901 and 1907) and the Public Health Act of 1936. Larger buildings were encouraged by technical advances in services and framed structures, and possibly by an element of rivalry between instigators of succeeding projects.

Outside the intensified concentration in town centres, among more dispersed suburban development, the dominant emphasis of built form was not upward but outward, in the shape of predominantly horizontal buildings. There, a carpet of one and two-storey development, punctuated only occasionally by the height of a new cinema or engulfed old village church, was a product of lower site values (probably averaging £5 per ft of frontage around London, less elsewhere) than prevailed in town centres. Other practical and economic advantages also favoured lower and more dispersed buildings, since lofty, gravity-defying structures and basements were difficult and expensive to design, construct, and maintain, for all their powers to impress onlookers and exploit restricted sites. Where they could be avoided, and in the suburbs they nearly always could, it paid to do so.

Provision of universal space

Another changing aspect of building form was that which arose from differentiation between one building type and another, and between separate parts of the same building.

Needless to say, built form had always been tailored in size and shape to the specific functions and activities which it contained. Proliferation of building forms with the emergence of new functions, noted above in the nineteenth-century context, continued to take place, but there were also signs of a contrary trend. While some forms became more specialized according to function, others became less so by the development of universal space. Increasingly, it appears, whole floors were designed as unobstructed open spaces, without sub-division by partitions, columns or varied ceiling heights. Similarly, whole large buildings appear increasingly to have taken the form of repetitive uniform bays, having each part indistinguishable from the others. As well as speeding up building operations, this enabled early decisions about activities and functions to be postponed and, in the subsequent life of the building, to be changed at will without demanding difficult alterations to the building. One instance of need for flexibility came from the Board of Education, increasingly conscious that school activities sometimes were hampered by inability to make economical adjustment to the fabric.[46] Another instance arose from expansion in the market for offices, leading to building provision increasingly made by sponsors without prior knowledge of occupiers' identity.

Some offices were planned to permit space to be let either in single or multiple increments, depending on demand; final choice could be left open and various different demands for space met without undue difficulty. Likewise, in many factories there was need for unobstructed floors capable of meeting a variety of functions. Among numerous influences which encouraged this were availability of electric power, use of light plant making consumer goods for changeable markets, need to accommodate expansion and adaptation of equipment, and perhaps a desire to maintain factory resale value. An instance of pioneering provision to accommodate change came from the LMSR research laboratories, Derby, in 1935 where partitions were demountable and services specially positioned.[47] The penalty paid in some fields for inflexibility was recognized and obsolescence within five years or so not unknown.[48] An ability to cope with unforseeable change by means of undifferentiated floor space and general flexibility in some buildings was beginning to surpass in importance an outward impression of permanence.

Range of quality

The quality of buildings in terms of their spaciousness, durability and overall performance continued to vary widely. Before 1914 the range of new buildings, between highest quality and lowest, may be likened to a pyramid at the base of which were numerous low-quality examples and near the apex a small number of high quality. The pyramid reflected crudely the nature of society, so it is reasonable to suppose that in the interwar years the pyramid became rather more squat. As social and economic differences between the classes became less visible, so differences between highest and lowest quality buildings diminished. The quality of the best buildings was held down by the economic constraints felt by their sponsors, and so was the number of such buildings. The quality of the poorest buildings was elevated, if anything, by more effective by-laws, public sponsorship and economic growth.

Nowhere was this process of compression between the two extremes more visible than in the field of housing. Major country house building, already flagging before 1914, became all but extinct, replaced by smaller but often still sizeable new houses. At the same time the quality of new rural cottages, which had traditionally embodied the worst standards, improved. Likewise, new housing for some urban working class families also improved; indeed, many hitherto had never even had the possibility of new accommodation.

Modern methods and appearances

While quality differences appear to have narrowed, the variety of new ideas about architecture and ways of constructing buildings was maintained. The proportion of new buildings which showed uncompromising commitment to the Modern Movement was only small, but rather more exhibited at least some of its influence. There were severe white rendered houses and some schools, for example in Middlesex[49] and West Sussex, appeared with steel frames and flat roofs instead of following the customary neo-classical style. Seaborne and Lowe[50] have suggested that such change was connected with a need for economy, and this may have been the case in part, although the ideology of the Modern Movement laid stress in different directions outside our scope. Designers who did not accept fully the principles of the Modern Movement could find themselves at least obliged to economize on functionally redundant volumes and ornament. As a consequence some buildings were more lean and reduced to fundamentals than many of their predecessors had been.

In the constructional field there was wider acceptance of earlier innovations such as mild steel and reinforced concrete frames, and in-situ concrete walls and floors. Similarly, more use was made of light sheet claddings, linings and partitions of asbestos-cement, plywood, fibreboard and plasterboard, which offered cheapness, lightness and speed. There were many exceptions, but in general new methods and ideas which involved a manifest break with orthodoxy appear to have been regarded with ambivalence. Sometimes, where a sense of progressiveness was the aim or basic utilitarian considerations applied, innovations were thought to be appropriate; at other times, in housing and where a sense of dignity was sought, there was strong attachment to that which was tried and proven, or which appeared to be so. International-style factories were juxtaposed with homely mock-traditional half-timbering and stained glass; bold cinemas, embellished with neon lighting and chrome-plated tubes, contrasted oddly with heavy neo-classical town halls.

Services

Attitudes to mechanical and electrical services were much less ambivalent and virtually everyone was happy to forego the rigours of old forms of heating, lighting, plumbing and sanitation in exchange for modern comfort, convenience and cost. It was as if the money saved by eliminating traditional exterior decorations like plinths, fretted barge boards and ornamental ridge tiles, found its way indoors in the form of improved services. The general direction of development was already clear by 1914 and most subsequent changes were ones of consolidation. By the 1930s services in housing had grown in complexity and cost to amount to one third of total costs.

The greatest technical advances were in electrical systems, the market for which expanded vigorously such that British consumers increased from 730,000 in 1920 to 2.8m in 1929, and nearly 9.0m by the late 1930s. Gas lighting declined accordingly, although it continued to be installed for this purpose in some houses in the 1920s. Central heating systems, some fired by oil, appeared more widely in offices and public buildings but seldom in houses, while large non-residential buildings, particularly tall ones, relied more and more on lifts, and other complicated services. In houses there were increasing quantities of more reliable plumbing and drainage services, electric and gas water heaters, and fitted fires instead of small open ones. As well as new benefits to building users, services brought new goods and methods to the building industry, to which we return in the chapter which follows.

6

Men of Sprawl: The Industry 1915-39

'I know many . . . builders who find less trouble in building a house than in making an estimate, and whose method in ordering material is to get some along and order some more when they see it running out.'
(*Edwin Gunn,* Economy in House Design, *1932*)

POSITION IN THE NATIONAL ECONOMY

Importance of building

The position of the building industry and associated professions between the wars for the most part was marked by prosperity and independence. Being active at one time or another nearly everywhere, and being very large in total, building nevertheless remained aside from the most intense political and economic storm centres, relatively untouched by the devastating impact of lost markets which struck some other major industries. Variations in building activity were not closely similar to variations in other industries, yet upward and downward movements in building from time to time led movements in the other sectors. Growth of building activity stimulated materials producers and other loosely associated industries and services; what was good for building was likely to be good for providers of transport, public utilities, consumer durables and certain legal and financial services. If the national economy was not entirely carried forward by the growth of building, at least building appears to have exerted an important stabilizing influence[1] in troubled times.

While the exact influence of building on the national economy may be open to debate, the magnitude of the industry is beyond dispute: the share of building investment in United Kingdom gross domestic capital formation generally exceeded 40%. Even at its lowest (38% in 1923), building investment compared well with levels before the First World War and at its highest (58% in 1933) it took on a dominating stature. Moreover the rate of growth of building production was greater than that of industry generally, estimated[2] at 4% and 2% per year respectively, between 1913 and 1938. Indeed, it may be argued that investment in building was so large as to have effectively starved of capital other industries deserving modernization. The significance of building for good or ill was most evident in the capital market, but it was important also as a source of employment. In 1921, the number of males occupied in building in England and Wales (974,000) was barely more than it had been in 1901 and represented a smaller proportion (8.0%) of the total occupied male population. By 1931 the number in building had grown to 1,277,000 and the proportion of the male workforce was 9.6%,[3] figures which subsequently grew still further. After recovery from the low levels of output per man which followed the First World War, more men on more sites than ever before each carried out a larger volume of work. By 1937 output was reckoned to exceed by a third or half the levels of 1924, at least in respect of local authority houses.[4]

DESIGNERS AND ADVISERS

Contracts

The means by which demand for buildings was formulated and put before the builders remained broadly unchanged. Where sponsor and builder were separate individuals or firms, a contract usually was agreed between the two parties and its execution administered by professional designers and their advisers. Experienced sponsors, particularly local authorities, frequently made use of the services of architects, engineers and surveyors whom they permanently employed, otherwise they commissioned independent consultants. In cases in which sponsor and builder were the same, no contract was necessary, although often the services of employee or consultant professionals were still required. The aim of contract procedure and documentation was to minimize scope for disagreement between the parties, but the delicate balance of opposing interests was difficult to strike. Contract procedures continued to evolve, with the standard form of 1909 being superseded by another in 1931.[5]

Architects

Architects were estimated[6] to design about one half of all building work by value in the late 1930s. Repetitive housing was the largest field in which the cost of their services might be avoided and there engineers, surveyors and unqualified draughtsmen frequently were able to try their hands, with results not always beyond criticism. At York, Rowntree[7] found some 'quite frankly ugly' examples and everywhere 'a lack of real genius'. Partly reflecting such shortcomings and partly growing professional strength, the proportion of architect-designed speculative houses was said in 1938 to have doubled from the 5 or 10% of the late 1920s.[8] The proportion of architect-designed non-residential work amounted to far more, according to the *Architects' Journal* in 1939, about 85%. Consolidation of the profession may be seen in near quadrupling of RIBA membership between 1910, when it was 2,300, and 1940 when it exceeded 8,800, although the census indicated only a small increase in total numbers of architects from 8,900 to 9,200. The RIBA absorbed the Society of Architects in 1925, the year in which the Incorporated Association of Architects and Surveyors and the Faculty of Architects and Surveyors were founded by those remaining outside the RIBA. The Architects (Registration) Act of 1931, strengthened seven years later by a further Act, established a register of architects and protected their title, thereby closing the profession.[9]

These efforts to win a higher standing in society were accompanied by corresponding increases in professional responsibility and liability. Established trends continued to bring larger demands: bigger projects, new materials, methods and specialisms required fresh technical knowledge and management ability; new legislation governing structural stability, fire precautions and so on, protracted design times and negotiations. In 1919 the profession could take some consolation for the passing of earlier and more simple times, from the increase of fees by 1% of the cost of the works, to a total of 6%.[10] The 1938 Registration Act perhaps represented the apotheosis of private practitioners, inhabiting a professional world akin to that portrayed in the celebrated *Honeywood File*,[11] which described how the architect Spinlove picked a pitfall-strewn but broadly agreeable path through the process of putting up a house for a wealthy client.

Yet a real life rival to the private architect was already in the ascendant, propelled by the rise of experienced sponsors with continuous building programmes. This was the salaried employee local authority architect, either seen as the embodiment of a welcome extension of architectural influence or alternatively as a bureaucratic threat to independent practitioners. To be sure, official architects had existed in the 1920s and earlier, but then their numbers had been too small and their prestige too low to threaten private practitioners. This position was beginning to change by the late 1930s when official architects were becoming more powerful both in their number and in the strength of their progressive views.[12]

Allied professions and other bodies

This is not to suggest that progressiveness was the dominant force driving either architects or other professionals, among whom a narrow conservatism often prevailed. Bowley[13] has suggested that the climate was one of lethargy and inertia, due in part to a lack of incentive for innovation together with insufficient contact between co-professions and the industry. In purely technological respects the charge appears to have been justified, but in mitigation there were other broader preoccupations which also demanded attention, among them human and aesthetic considerations implicit in design, new legislation, contractual relations and the politics of professional consolidation.

Architects were not alone in this last respect, for structural engineers emerged in 1922 as a specialization in their own right, distinct from civil engineers, to form the Institution of Structural Engineers out of a transformed Concrete Institute.[14] Consolidation elsewhere included the founding of the Town Planning Institute in 1914, absorption of the Quantity Surveyors' Association by the Surveyors' Institution in 1922, and foundation of the Institute of Quantity Surveyors in 1938. These bodies were joined by other new organizations with interests in related fields, such as the Building Research Station which originated under official guidance in the early 1920s for the purpose of investigating new materials. Another example was the British Standards Institution which began as an Engineering Standards Committee in 1901, incorporated by Royal Charter in 1929, and became the national organization for promulgation of standard terms, codes of practice and specifications of materials.[15] Another body was the National House Builders' Registration Council, founded in 1937 in an attempt to safeguard the quality of new private houses, hitherto not always all that proud owners had hoped. A growing number of associations such as the British Constructional Steelwork Association of 1929 and the Cement and Concrete Association of 1935 were set up to protect and further the interests of their members. Whether commercial, or disinterested like BRS, these bodies added to the sum total of information and its exchange within the industry.

BUILDING FIRMS

Range of firms

Building firms maintained their own central body, the National Federation of Building Trade Employers, to represent them in wage negotiations with the unions. Firms eligible for membership, or engaged in related fields, included several novelties in addition to the established wide variety of size, ability and interest. At the largest scale, and already familiar, were a few large general contractors prepared to work anywhere in the country on both building and civil engineering. Smaller firms of contractors, speculative builders and specialist subcontractors operated at regional and local levels, and jobbing builders and maintenance men worked close to home, much as before.

Newcomers to local authority work in the early 1920s were a number of direct labour organizations (there was one at West Ham as early as 1893), council employees competing with private contractors and usually directed by the local authority surveyor. As a form of public enterprise the performance, and very existence, of direct labour was surrounded by heated controversy and political debate. The central government Office of Works was another minor source of house building in the early 1920s, entirely overshadowed by the output of private builders.[16] An even shorter-lived and less auspicious appearance was made at about the same time by Building Guilds, non-profit making local associations of operatives who built an insignificant number of local authority houses before failing, largely due to inexperience and lack of capital.[17]

Size of firms

The size of building firms remained predominantly small, with 84% in 1930 employing not more than ten people. Slightly larger firms employing between eleven and twenty-four amounted to only 7% of all firms, while at the largest extreme less than 1% (only 317) of firms employed more than 200 people.[18] The total number of firms increased slowly at first and then more quickly as the industry expanded. In 1930 there were 52,000 firms in Great Britain and Northern Ireland (to which the above figures also relate), over 2,000 more than in 1924, but 20,000 fewer than in 1935. The continued importance of very small firms was the reverse of that which applied in many other parts of the economy and may be attributed to two causes. Firstly, building still offered few economies of scale, unlike many other industries, so that most projects could be carried out as effectively and cheaply by small firms as by large, although it is likely that small firms were most vulnerable to adversity. Secondly, the building industry continued to be exceptionally easy to enter since working capital was readily available and plant requirements small. The established pattern persisted of building as a field attractive to entrepreneurs who were liable to find ease of entry matched only by ease of exit.

Contractors

Opportunities for contractors were not lacking in the first few years of recovery from the First World War, but there were severe problems arising from shortages of labour, materials and working capital. When these obstacles eventually were overcome and some semblance of stability restored, small firms of contractors could still be seen to form, and break up rather too quickly to make for a favourable public image. The performance of many firms attracted informed criticism on grounds of poor business planning and general inefficiency,[19,20] and the popular reputation of many firms was not improved by the low quality of some of their products.

Jerry-building, however, was not the whole picture for there were some firms which, if scarcely displaying revolutionary change, at least tried out some beneficial innovations. Among firms engaged on that minority of larger and non-residential contracts were some which were increasingly efficient in productivity, management and investment in equipment. Robinson[21] in 1939 thought that there had been very great changes in these fields over the previous twenty years, with new firms of general contractors which owed much to factories in their organization, being mainly concerned to co-ordinate numbers of specialized sub-contractors.

Speculative builders

Among speculative building firms and jobbing builders the chief exceptions to the general rule of traditionalism were some larger house builders, such as Costain and Laing, mainly active in the 1930s in the London area. As we saw in the preceding chapter, many large concerns were involved in all aspects of development so that building was only a part of their business. They raised capital by issuing shares, whereas smaller speculative builders relied more on bank overdrafts for current expenses and on credit from builders' merchants, in turn indebted to materials producers. Small builders also borrowed from developers, building societies and private individuals, usually at an interest rate of about 4%. Frequently competition between speculative builders was intense and profit margins of the order of 10% were small compared with those earned at times outside the field of building. When demand lagged, profits could be hard won and sales sustained only by resort to publicity stunts such as firework displays, floodlighting and free transport for house buyers.[22] Less commendable ways by which to keep pace with rivals included skimped construction to cut building cost, apparently more common among small firms than large.

Sub-contractors

Much of the most technically advanced work on site was executed by sub-contractors, some commissioned by main contractors and others nominated by architects. Sub-contractors appear to have been employed most extensively on non-residential building work where the size and complexity of construction tasks were greatest. An increasing proportion of work was sub-contracted during the period,[23] and with it increased the number and degree of specialization of sub-contracting firms. As many as thirty could be engaged during the course of a single large project, many of them on site at the same time, including specialists in demolition, excavation, structural steelwork, concreting, stonework, woodwork, various branches of services engineering, asphalt, floor finishes, plastering and painting. Just as the later nineteenth century was a time of proliferation of the products used in building, so this was a time of increase in the variety of firms working on site. This multiplication of sub-contractors, with attendant management responsibilities for main contractors, was one of the more far-reaching changes to occur among interwar building firms. It was a development which enabled the industry to handle new and unfamiliar products and to retain a necessary capacity for rapid change in scope of operations and workload. The contrast between traditional firms and progressive, say between masons and electrical engineers was striking; in this the industry reflected that which was visible in the broader national economic and social scene.

LABOUR

Place of work

The working life of most men on the sites went on much as ever, with operations from foundations up to roofs continuing to require the services of numerous workmen relying on manual skills and simple hand tools. Admittedly, mechanization and fabrication of components off site advanced in some fields, but as a rule orthodoxy and minor adaptations were more evident than thoroughgoing change. The prevailing methods of construction entailed fashioning raw materials on site at or near the point at which the finished product was required. This meant that large numbers of men worked on site rather than in workshop or factory, thereby avoiding some of the oppressively monotonous aspects of factory employment, but giving poor general amenities and lack of weather protection. Permanent employment was less available than short-term employment, especially among small firms, and much of it was casual, being seasonal, by the week or even by the day in the case of unskilled men, with little security. Tough working conditions taken for granted in the coarser world of the nineteenth century began to look anachronistic alongside conditions in up-to-date factories where non-building employment was to be found. Yet perhaps this comparison was more likely to be made by middle-class onlookers than by people on the sites, for even if the prospect of a waterlogged and apparently chaotic site was uninviting, it was a great deal better than unemployment as an alternative. Heavy demand for building labour provided welcome job opportunities for men who otherwise faced the rigours of the dole. In the high general unemployment of the interwar years, building held out at least some hope of work, and growing numbers availed themselves of the opportunity.

The geographical distribution of employment on sites was heavily concentrated in the prosperous south-east and midlands. In 1931, no less than 41% of employment in building existed in London and the south-east, where only 23% of the total population of Great Britain lived. The much more slender chance of a site job in the depressed regions represented the reverse of this picture, although prospects there were helped a little by the increasing amount of unavoidable maintenance work and some local authority activity. Regional imbalance was also ameliorated by the effect of various materials-producing industries, such as paint works, ironfoundries and quarries, employment in which was conservatively estimated to increase from 1.6% of British insured population in 1924 to 2.1% in 1936. Some such industries, while located in depressed regions, were stimulated by demand from prosperous ones; for instance glass needed in the housing estates of Middlesex helped to create jobs far away in Lancashire where much was made.

Employment and unemployment

The ease, or lack of it, with which jobs could be found in building varied widely in time as well as place. Low levels of employment during the First World War were followed briefly by labour shortage changing quickly to prolonged surplus and reverting eventually to some shortage. In the unsettled aftermath of war in 1919, unskilled building labour was only two-thirds of its prewar numerical strength and skilled labour was even less. Those who had survived the war and been demobilised did not attain prewar levels of output owing to the deterioration of their skills through disuse and lack of adequate training and experience. However, shortages gradually eased and the number of men at work increased year by year, but so did unemployment among their fellows. In 1925, about 10.5% of building workers were without jobs, swelling to 16% in 1930 and 30% at the worst of the depression in 1932. Some improvement followed that outstandingly bad year and by 1937 the proportion had fallen to 15%. Despite unemployment of these magnitudes, some shortages of skilled men developed in the late 1930s, due to coincidence of heavy house building activity with growing building work for rearmament. Unemployment in building in the interwar years generally was higher than the national average, a peculiarity (in view of the prosperity of building) attributable to the attraction of building to men forced out of work in other industries.[24]

Size of trades

Roughly half of building labour was skilled or semi-skilled and the other half unskilled, although even nominally unskilled navvies certainly possessed a degree of expert ability. Among craftsmen the relative size of different trades provides evidence of continuity rather than rapid change. In 1924 the largest trade still was carpentry and joinery, with 19% of the employed persons in building. Painters formed the second largest trade, having risen to prominence since 1914 with 15% of employed persons. A sizeable gap then followed before the bricklayers with 9%, followed in descending order by plumbers, masons (now well and truly eclipsed), plasterers and slaters. The position in the later 1930s was not very different, with carpenters and joiners, and painters retaining their respective leading positions but by smaller margins, and bricklayers still third, but with increased strength.

Minor variations were to be found in the regions, suggesting that some distinctive local building practices lingered on, such that masons declined least in the south-west and Wales, and bricklayers were relatively numerous in the south-east and midlands. There must have been wide differences also in the proportions of trades engaged on different projects, with housing work probably requiring trades in roughly typical proportions. Large city centre projects with numerous sub-contractors, on the other hand, required the full diversity of newer skills and proportionately fewer traditional ones. Among the newer skills were steel erectors, reinforcement benders, crane drivers and installers of electrical systems, lifts, central heating and other engineering services.

Wages

The movement of building wages developed dramatically after the stagnation of Edwardian times. Increases which began just before the war in 1914 accelerated during it and reached an unprecedented peak in 1920. In that year average rates, like prices, were double or more than double their prewar levels, with unskilled rather than skilled men making the biggest gains. A typical rate in 1920 for the main craft trades was about 18/8d for a ten-hour day and that for labourers about 16/8d for an eight-hour day.[25] In 1924, when the postwar peak had passed, the hourly rate in London for highly skilled stone carvers was said to be 1/9d, followed by the main trades at 1/7½d. Slightly below this were the slaters and tilers, then glaziers and painters, followed by scaffolders and then labourers at 1/2¾d.[26]

From the early 1920s wages began to be fixed on a nationwide basis related to the cost of living and graded according to place of work, but variations persisted due to payment of productivity bonuses. The fall from high wages and prices after 1920 was steep though it soon moderated, whereupon wages drifted down to a trough in 1933, near the time of greatest unemployment, then recovered mildly to reach approximately the level prevailing in 1928.[27] In 1937, the London hourly rate for most skilled trades was 1/8d, and that in the lowest paid rural localities was 1/2½d. The hours worked per week, like the rates of pay, lacked national uniformity, although forty-six hours appears to have been a fair average.

Comparison between the average annual earnings in building and in all industries show building in a moderately favourable light. The estimated figure in building in 1924 was £156 compared with £146 in all industries, despite slightly longer hours worked outside building. In 1933, the differential was unchanged, although within another five years it had narrowed somewhat, to £158 in building and £153 in all industries.[28] Building workers fortunate enough to retain their jobs between 1918 and 1939, like those in most other industries, experienced an increase in real earnings of the order of a third or half.

Organization

Building trades unions encountered widely changing circumstances brought initially by the war when, in 1914, the largest union was the woodworkers' with 79,000 members. Compared with this all others were small, with the next largest, the bricklayers', having less than half that membership.[29] Little normal building work took place and, since the Munitions of War Act of 1915 made arbitration compulsory for any disputes, there were few strikes.

One point of activity in an otherwise apparently quiet wartime scene was provided by unions having members engaged in building for war purposes. The leading example was the labourers' union which experienced eightfold growth of membership to reach 65,000 by 1919. Elsewhere beneath the surface some influence, perhaps international events, was eroding earlier isolationism and narrowness of vision within the craft unions. This began to be evident early in 1918 when the National Federation of Building Trade Operatives was formed with powers to bring about uniformity of action among affiliated unions. Other divisions were healed when woodworking unions joined forces to form the Amalgamated Society of Woodworkers and several 'trowel unions' combined to form the Amalgamated Union of Building Trades Operatives.

Economic turbulence and heavy labour demand in 1919 and 1920 brought a new phase of union activity, membership growth and a reduction of the working week.[30] Labour scarcity, difficulties in employing ex-servicemen, and housing shortage encouraged the government to press dilution, the employment of men less than fully trained. This was resisted by the unions, more concerned with their members' prospects in the event of a future surplus of labour than with the broader problems of ex-servicemen. Labour relations were aggravated further in 1922 and 1923 by the threat of lower wages and longer hours which accompanied falling prices and general depression. In 1924, year of the first nationwide building strike, renewed labour shortages led the Minister of Health, Wheatley, to devise a 'gentleman's agreement' as part of his housing policy, in which the unions accepted a shorter training period than the customary five-year apprenticeship, in exchange for guarantees of more employment. Subsequently, although building was one of the 'front line' industries in the 1926 general strike, disputes became fewer and smaller and in the later 1920s strength ebbed away.

There was no recovery until the worst of the depression was over and prosperity began to return in the later 1930s, when membership reached, and in some cases passed, the totals of the early 1920s. New technology called for some adaptation: unskilled men increasingly undertook tasks formerly carried out by craftsmen; some on-site woodworkers were displaced by prefabricated joinery; various crafts were displaced by the use of structural steelwork, concrete and artificial stone; plasterboard displaced some 'wet' plaster work, despite union opposition; plumbers continued to lose lead roofing to cheaper substitutes; and labourers were ousted in part by mechanized plant. However, the impact of such developments should not be overestimated for no leading trade suffered decline on the scale experienced by masons prior to the First World War, and the changes took effect relatively slowly.

METHODS, MATERIALS AND COMPONENTS

Prices

The cost of building roughly doubled during the war and continued to increase steeply for the several difficult years which followed it. Maiwald's index[31] shows that after the early 1920s prospects improved and it became progressively cheaper to build until 1933, when the lowest level was reached, whereupon costs began to rise slowly with the volume of building. In this pattern building approximately followed movements in general retail prices. The proportion of total building cost made up by materials varied from one building to another depending on design, and estimates differ as to relative importance. A rough

"I 'll tell yer what, Jack: if it wasn't as the District Surveyor 'ad said it was all right, I 'd a'most say as them columns down there wasn't enough to support this 'ere 'ouse."

Left: Trouble with by-laws. Here Sullivan's caustic wit is directed at incompetent officials.

Above: Gothic revival in progress. Men at work on the well-advanced structure of Ettington Park, Warwickshire, built between 1858 and 1863 to designs of Pritchard and Seddon. (*V & A*)

Aristocrats of labour under the eye of authority. Examination of stonemasons' work on the granite of the Albert Memorial, 1864–1876. (*V & A*)

Right: Welsh masons. Costly-looking stone dressings are being incorporated in a predominantly brick building. The project probably was a library in Cardiff near the turn of the century. (G. A. C. Dart, County Librarian for Glamorgan)

Ragged trousered philanthropist. The central figure carries bricks on his head while his mate, left, holds a trowel. A carpenter with apron stands among non-manual figures, but we can only guess how the seated woman and dog came to be there. This enigmatic roof-top scene in Cheltenham appears to date from the early twentieth century. (City of Bristol Museum and Art Gallery)

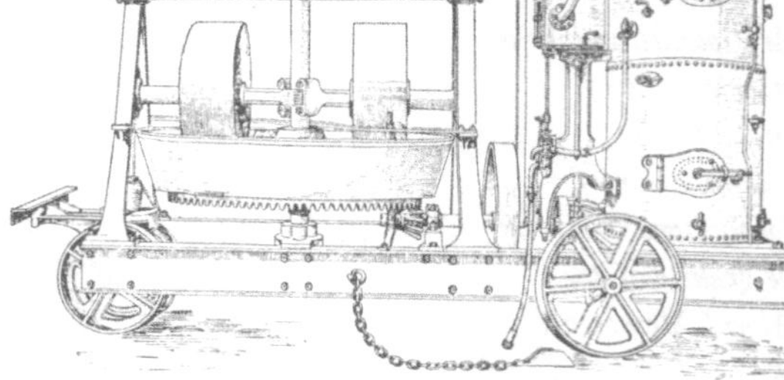

Steam supplants shovel. Portable mechanically powered mortar mill for use on large sites c.1905.

Above: County Hall progress I. Houses of Parliament visible, upper right. Steam rail cranes and narrow gauge trucks are in use while excavation proceeds, left, and arches emerge, right. (GLC)

Below: County Hall progress II. Basement view c.1910 showing bricks stacked ready on floor slab and walls begun, lower right. Steel columns are beginning to be erected, mid-right. The unpopulated scene is enlivened by advertisement for a 'stupendous production' of Ben Hur, *upper left.* (GLC)

Above: County Hall progress III. Brick walls are well advanced and so is a line of arches running diagonally lower left to upper right. Timber centring is propped near centre foreground and crane is just visible in background through South London murk. (GLC)

Below: County Hall progress IV. Public face of Knott's 1907 design for LCC begins to peep above hoarding. Stone is visible behind timber scaffolding and cranes tower overhead. Contractor's modest-size name board, Holland, Hannen and Cubitts, is upper left. Posters enjoin passers-by to 'Remember the Lusitania . . . Enlist Today.' War rages but work goes on. (GLC)

Top: Home Front. Houses for wartime shipbuilders in Chepstow, Gwent, c.1917, designed by Curtis Green. Concrete walling blocks (a novelty probably due to brick shortage) are made and stacked in foreground. Behind is temporary rail siding with government Office of Works trucks. Some houses already have planted gardens but scaffolding remains at right. (J. Pearson, Monmouth District Council Museums Service)

Middle: Suburban sprawl. Inter-war home counties speculative estate of houses priced at £595 each. (Fox Photos)

Right: Superior detached. This mid-1930s house cost double (£1250) the amount of those in the photograph above. Orthodox brick and tile alongside steel window frames with up-to-date horizontal-proportion panes. Designed by E. Garthside and built in Farnham Royal.

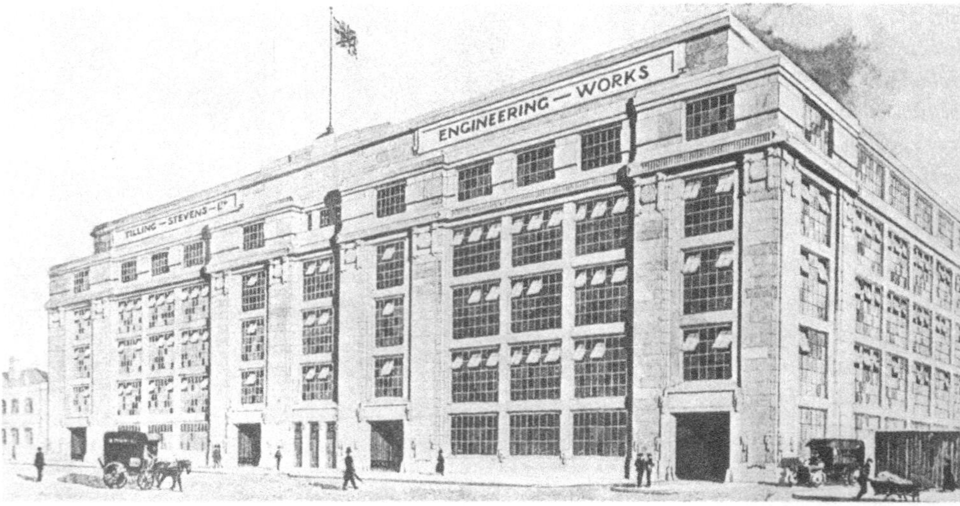

Above: Multi-storey industry. Tilling-Stevens works, Maidstone, designed by Wallis, Gilbert and Partners about 1917. A five-storey factory with ornamented frontage and plain sides.

Below: Factory floor. Plan of Tilling-Stevens works showing framed structure with two lifts at rear. The project was published in M. Kahn's Design and Construction of Industrial Buildings, *1917.*

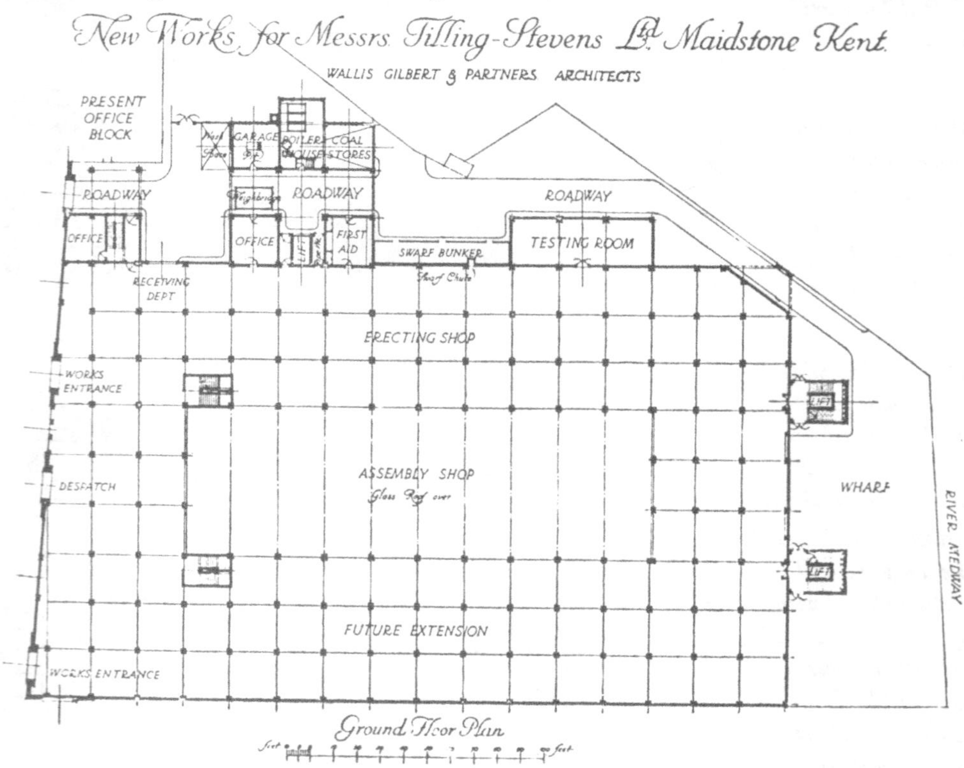

Above: Non-traditional house construction. Local authority Cornish Unit of pre-cast concrete and tile-hanging c.1950. Another unorthodox system also devised when the traditional industry was overstretched is visible on far left. (City of Bristol Housing Committee)

Right: High rise flats. An early local authority eleven-storey block, St. George, Bristol. Many later examples were higher and avoided use of brick, visible left. (City of Bristol Housing Committee)

Top: Repetitive bays for industry. Steel-framed factory, Avonmouth, 1969. Concrete floors are being laid and light wall cladding will quickly follow. Heavy plant will have been used to save time in lifting the many prefabricated components.

Middle: Big box completed. The factory above is now finished, showing the exterior of a building providing universal space, with flat roof and few windows. (R. G. *Hardcastle, Power Clark Hiscocks Partnership*)

Right: Modern traditional construction. Housing association project, Crosby, Lancashire, mid-1970s. Floor decking is being placed on concrete block walls, and brick and timber clad exteriors will follow. Light plant abounds on site, along with stored materials and discarded oddments. In background is a variety of earlier terraces overlooked by tower blocks. (J. Olley, Architects and Planning Consultants)

approximation was two-thirds of total cost for materials and the remaining third for labour, although a more equal balance probably applied in many cases. Changes in the prices of materials were similar to those of total building costs, but not all materials changed price by similar amounts; timber and cement fell particularly far, while some kinds of brick did not fall at all. Overall, materials prices fell somewhat less than those of all industrial materials and manufactures taken together.

Supply

The supply of materials at first was dominated by the war which caused disruption of timber imports, abandonment and flooding of claypits and widespread conversion of plant to make goods destined for destruction rather than construction. By the end of the war most materials were in short supply, and brick and tile production was down to only one third or less of the pre-1914 level. In 1919, the government released nearly all materials from wartime control and prices surged up in sympathy with those of other goods. Some materials prices doubled within months and tripled by 1920, and difficulties were worsened by transport problems on the congested and run-down railways. Soon however, this confused and gloomy picture brightened and by 1921 the production of bricks and cement exceeded that of 1914, even if timber and clay tiles took longer to regain 'normality'.[32] Output of materials climbed to a peak in 1927 and, after faltering during the slump, went on to new high levels in the late 1930s, by which time output was approximately double that of the troubled early 1920s.

Methods

The ways in which materials were fashioned into completed buildings deserves some elaboration although nowhere was it revolutionized. One development already evident before the First World War was the fabrication of a limited but widening range of component parts off the site, for incorporation in the ready-finished or near-finished state in a building. Provided costs were competitive (and this was by no means always so), the method offered several advantages: work was less dependent on the weather; specialized skills, plant and power could be used to full effect in the workshop where supervision was easier; building time could be cut; and shortages of skilled site labour eased. Some components lent themselves better than others to off-site fabrication and transport, although not all designers or builders were able or willing to grasp the advantage.

Suitable components included steel columns and beams (bearing the reassuring legend 'British Steel Only'); light sheet claddings, linings and panels which eliminated time-consuming 'wet' operations; joinery such as cupboards, standard doors and window frames; and a host of minor items replacing or altering traditional practice, such as surface finishes and plywood for fittings and duct covers.

The extreme development in off-site manufacture was that of the prefabricated houses of the 1920s, which came from various building and industrial concerns responding to official encouragement to overcome shortages and high prices afflicting traditional building. One of the most publicized examples was the 'Weir' house, made of steel plates and timber framing, which encountered stiff opposition from unions.[33] Other hopeful makers tried out a remarkable variety of different materials, including cast iron, pre-cast and in-situ concrete, and something called shredded wood and concrete. But novelty alone was not enough and most examples cost more than traditional ones, requiring subsidy and not always performing very well. Some types corroded so rapidly that they lasted less than forty years before requiring replacement. Only a relatively small number were built, not more than 50,000, before enthusiasm waned and traditional methods reasserted dominance by about 1928.

One of the lessons of prefabrication was that traditional methods were seldom susceptible to radical alteration, being more amenable to gradual evolution, if anything. The introduction of prefabricated joinery into traditional building was one example of evolution and another was the use of plant and power on sites in order to speed up operations without necessarily altering end products. This development probably was strongest in non-residential projects, although if we admit road motor haulage in our definition of building plant, then even the most doggedly traditional house building was affected. The flexibility and cheapness of road transport compared with rail was particularly important for the building industry with its characteristic restless movement from site to site. For example, the scene visible at the LCC St Hellier estate in 1929, where six locomotives puffed about an extensive light railway system in and out of the rising suburban terraces, seems not to have been perpetuated much after that time.

There was increasing mechanization also in the earlier stages of building operations to complement off-site fabrication in the later stages. Steam shovels were used more for large excavations, and other plant included hydraulic and pneumatic riveters for joining steelwork, spray guns for applying finishes, and artificial lighting and heating as aids for winter working. Departure from tried and tested nineteenth-century methods probably was most evident on large industrial and commercial projects where finished buildings often embodied most novelties, and where the scale of operations was largest and urgency greatest.

Yet to build faster and more efficiently, the aim of most new methods, was not necessarily to build better. The effect of changes of technology on quality appears to have been more or less neutral. The best work probably was as durable and well executed as before, if more rare; the shoddiest jerry-building probably was curtailed by the by-laws. Of the middle range some observers[34] were less sanguine, believing that small speculative houses were more lightly built than before 1914, and that the mediocre, if not the downright bad, generally outweighed the good.

Brick

The basis of much new building was brick, a material regarded as functionally effective, convenient to use, handsome and reasonably priced. These advantages together with a prosperous building industry led to the doubling of output in the United Kingdom between the depressed year of 1912 (3700m bricks) and 1937 (7800m).[35] The material lent itself to various treatments including concealment behind render and mock timber framing, but elaborate details exemplified by Edwardian string courses, cills and arches, were to be found less and less. The proportion of total materials cost represented by brick often approached one fifth in the case of houses, but obviously varied according to designs. In the early 1930s 9 in. thick brickwork with exterior distemper and interior plaster was estimated to cost 15/- per sq yd, compared with 18/4d for a cavity wall of rustic Fletton brickwork. The substitution of red facing bricks added about 5/- to the cost, but even this was cheaper than 16 in. thick rubble stone walling at about 25/-.[36]

The broad trend of brick prices did not depart greatly from that of other materials, but at a detailed level there were some differences. For example, between 1924 and 1937 Fletton prices fell from about 53/- per 1000 to 46/-, while the price of second hard-stocks moved in the opposite direction from about 78/6d to a far less competitive 88/-. Fletton producers made one third of all bricks produced in 1937 and their resounding commercial success in the south-eastern market, dominated by the London Brick Company which had emerged the previous year, was a striking feature of the time. Closure was forced upon many smaller makers unable to match the economies of scale of the newcomers, by 1939 reducing the number of brickyards to about a third of the 3,500 open at the beginning of the century.[37]

Blocks and stone

The main alternatives to brick were stone and blocks made from concrete, breeze, clinker and foamed slag. The variety of blocks and blockmakers, many of them small concerns, was wide and especially so early in the period when alternative materials were scarce. Although bricks were thought to look better than blocks, the latter could be handled more quickly, making them for the first time a widely used substitute where appearance was of secondary importance. Falling cement prices helped blocks to become ever cheaper, over 25% so, in the case of clinker blocks between 1924 and 1938, making them about the cheapest of all materials for partitions. In positions where their appearance mattered, concrete blocks could be faced with crushed and reconstructed stone or aggregate to make a cost-saving processed substitute for natural stone, although not always a visually pleasing one.

Stone itself was confined by price mainly to prestige uses, with Hopton Wood material priced at 14/- per cub. ft in 1924, rising slightly by the late 1930s.[38] Bath stone was considerably cheaper than this but, like other stones, suffered from an inability to compete widely with bricks and concrete blocks. Occasional country work in local stone was cheapest, sometimes a mere sixth of the price of prestige ashlar work, but still its use diminished.

Timber

Timber and timber products retained a position of importance in a typical house, amounting to about three-tenths of total materials costs. In low cost houses it is possible that more timber was used than formerly, in the provision of fittings and substitution of solid ground floors by suspended timber ones. In higher quality housing, however, it seems likely that structural members were rather smaller than formerly and that light timber-based sheets often replaced heavier frames and panels. Steel and concrete replaced some timber in larger buildings, but often there, too, were new timber-based sheet materials.

Timber imports suffered during the First World War and in 1918 were only one fifth of prewar level. By 1924 the value of imports into the United Kingdom (about 90% of supplies), not all destined for building purposes, exceeded £32m and in addition there was £9m worth of hardwood and £5m worth of manufactured joinery.[39] At that time sawn softwood cost about 4/6d per cub. ft in plates and lintels, compared with about 10/- per cub. ft for oak, a far cry from the days a century or more earlier when at times the two had been competitive. Plywood, which was much developed in the wartime aero-industry, was an inexpensive way of securing the appearance of far more expensive hardwood, and by 1937 cost between 3d and 1/- per sq ft depending on thickness and quality. A number of other sheet materials were tried and among the few which survived the passing of early postwar shortages were fibreboards.

Roof finishes

The advantages possessed by different roof finishes at different times, and hence the usage of one compared with another, continued to change more frequently than was the case with most major materials. The cost of roofing materials accounted for well over 10% of total materials costs of typical houses, so shifts of preference affected large volumes of goods. One such shift was the resurgence of clay tiles, the United Kingdom output of which approximately doubled between 1912 and 1924, and more than tripled from the original total by 1935. This success story was matched by that of the rival concrete tiles which increased in output from a low level after the First World War to about a third of combined clay and concrete tile output in 1935. On the other hand slate production declined by about a quarter between 1912 and 1924 and thereafter remained static in an expanding market. Underlying these successes and failures was a complicated pattern of price competition in which slate prices fell less than those of clay tiles. Concrete tile prices appear to have fallen most of all, by 1938 being of the order of three-quarters of clay prices.[40]

Different qualities and haulage rates make generalization hazardous, but typical prices of materials laid in 1937, per 100 sq ft, were around 35/- to 40/- for pantiles, rising to 50/- for Staffordshire machine-made plain tiles and Somerset double Roman tiles. Slate prices lay between 57/6d and 75/-, although the most expensive Westmorland products cost as much as 110/-, slightly more than fashionable glazed apple green clay tiles. Reed thatch at about 120/- now was priced decisively among luxury rather than humble utilitarian materials, although shorter lived straw was cheaper. Neither were Gloucestershire stone slates at 160/- any longer within the reach of simple cottagers, having moved against the predominantly downward price trend. Providing a sharp visual contrast to such rustic materials, there was strong growth in output of asbestos-cement tiles, costing between 45/- and 70/- per 100 sq ft depending on quality and colour. Larger corrugated sheets, at about 53/-, were slightly cheaper than corrugated steel sheets. Approximate comparative prices for the same area, but including fir timber, boarding and felt, were of the order of £10 for tiling and slating, £12 for zinc and asphalt, £18 for lead and a near-prohibitive £21-10s for copper.

Cement, concrete and plaster

Like concrete and asbestos roof materials, production of cement increasingly passed by amalgamation into the hands of a small number of large capital-intensive manufacturers. Production underwent technical development and output almost tripled between 1912 and 1938. Prices fell more than those of any other domestically produced building material, about 30% between 1924 and 1938, due in part to fierce price competition eventually curtailed by trading agreements between producers.

Apart from the technical advantages of cement, steep falls in price made new and extended uses of the material to be expected. Among them were cement mortar instead of lime for bonding masonry, in-situ and pre-cast concrete for walls, floors, roofs and structural frames, concrete lintels and cills, steps, fire-resisting cladding to steelwork, exterior rendering, paving, and, of course, concrete blocks. About 8% of materials costs in typical houses were absorbed by cement and aggregates, no doubt more in some other building types, while very few new buildings indeed contained no cement products whatever. In the late 1930s reinforced concrete beam and column members (between 4/6d and 7/- per cub. ft) were rather too costly to be competitive with steel for most applications,[41] but reinforced concrete floors had few fireproof competitors.

The other major 'wet' material was plaster where, again, lime was largely superseded, in this case by gypsum. Home production of plasterboard as a substitute for 'wet' plaster began in 1917 and, although opposed by organized labour and not yet of the highest quality, it was gradually accepted. By 1939 there were four plasterboard producers having a combined annual output of over 31m sq yd.

Services

The quantity of goods associated with building services continued to grow. Some 1930s domestic examples of costs were a cold water supply installation serving two sinks, bath, three basins and two w.c.s at £22 for galvanized pipework, or several pounds more for copper or lead;[42] a hot water system consisting of a small boiler, cylinder, pipework with a connection to the sink, bath and lavatory basin at about £35, and another £5 for an auxiliary gas or electric water heater; gas installations at about £2 per point, and electric lighting points complete with fittings, having fallen significantly to about 30/-.

Other goods and plant

So far, numerous goods have received no mention although some, such as ironmongery, ceramic tiles, paint and varnish, were used extensively in most buildings. Others, such as lifts and central heating, were used in only a small minority of projects, but were important and significant in overall cost. Again, there were other goods, such as aluminium extrusions to take a novel example, and cast iron window frames to take an obsolescent one, which were used only occasionally and in relatively small quantities. Among the ubiquitous materials was glass, produced by a duopoly making use of extensive technical innovations which helped to reduce the price of sheet by over a quarter between 1924 and 1936.[43]

An associated novelty dating from the timber scarcity of the early 1920s was standard metal window frames, while far larger and heavier steel members were used widely as structural frames in high and long span buildings. Rolled steel members often replaced timber beam and masonry arch alternatives because of advantages of reliability and faster building operations. Steel prices reached their lowest in 1932 when demand was at rock-bottom and by 1938 had risen above the level of 1924. Erection of heavy steelwork, and the excavation which preceded it, encouraged the use of heavy plant such as cranes and compressors, but such capital investment remained largely the province of specialists. Most builders between the wars preferred to confine themselves to use of smaller and simpler goods. Among them were barrows, carts, lorries and sheds in which to shelter foremen and clerks of works. If that now-vanished species, the nightwatchman and lamp were required to safeguard the works, the cost was about 1/4d per hour. In case his best endeavours should be in vain, the cost in 1937 of insuring the works for three months prior to handover was of the order of 8d per £100 value of building.

7

Buildings in Austerity and Affluence: 1940-73

'. . . it is perfectly possible to get rid of the slums within the next 10 years and to see that every family has a decent home; . . . to find all the land needed for building without spoiling the countryside; to rebuild our cities so that they will be a source of pride . . .'

(*The Labour Party,* Signposts for the Sixties, *1961*)

DECISION TO BUILD

Sponsorship: intensification, concentration

The motives and behaviour of people who decided to build during and after the Second World War were associated with four related themes. The first may be termed intensification, an increase in the scale and a quickening in the pace of building. Activity moved forward on a rising tide of economic growth which proceeded, despite setbacks, at a rate which compared favourably with that of the nineteenth century. Gross domestic product per head in the United Kingdom (at constant 1913 prices) doubled in the three decades after the mid-1930s, when it was £52. By the mid-1950s it had reached £82, and by mid-1960s was £98.[1] At the same time the proportion of gross national product represented by building and construction increased from 4.1% in mid-1930s to 5.7% in mid-1950s. The results of decisions to build which underlay this expansion, from shadow factories to tower blocks and from factory farms to filling stations, appeared in almost every landscape and townscape.

The second theme was concentration, by which is meant the expansion and grouping of sponsors into large organizations which were once small and dispersed. Emergence of large public authorities and multi-national firms was echoed by less obvious growth among smaller organizations. Wherever power or capital was concentrated, sponsorship was further transformed from small, intermittent concern with building into continuous involvement, 'sophisticated' sponsors replacing 'naive' ones.[2]

Sponsorship: convergence, directedness

The third theme was convergence, a drawing together of private and public sponsors and approximate equalization in their respective spending powers following absorption of some private interests by the public side. Old differences diminished, with nationalized industries continuing to exercise predominantly commercial criteria and some private firms increasingly taking into account social considerations. On occasions there were sponsoring partnerships between private developers and public authorities and, elsewhere, old distinctions were blurred further by new quasi-autonomous agencies of government, such as the Housing Corporation.

The fourth theme among sponsors was directedness, or a greatly enhanced capacity of the State to influence decisions to build. Government regulated the proportion of national resources available for building, influenced the balance between different building types, and controlled building location. Motives which underlay government involvement included ones arising from exigencies of war and, later, the redemption of electoral promises and manipulation of the national economy. Sponsors could find themselves subject to official direction regarding what, where and whether they might build, for how much and in what form. Public sponsors could be controlled directly by government policy and decision while private sponsors were influenced mostly by planning control, rates of interest, subsidies, loans and taxation. Adjustment to these much affected the cost of borrowing to build and the demand for goods and services which a new building would make possible. When government helped to bring about a favourable financial climate, sponsors were stimulated into action; when government policies led to an unfavourable climate, projects were deferred. In all, government involvement appeared to increase the total amount of sponsorship while reducing the freedom of action of many sponsors.

Public sponsorship

The rise of public sponsorship was most evident when the government was pitchforked into action by the outbreak of war. Urgent building demand of strategic importance sprang from a variety of branches of government, of which the Ministry of Works (formerly the Office of Works) under Lord Reith was prominent as co-ordinator. Departments such as the armed services, Home Office, and Ministries of Aircraft Production, Supply and War Transport[3,4] competed intensely for scarce resources, and private sponsorship was virtually suspended except where it coincided with war aims. The coming of peace again profoundly changed the priorities assigned to departments, as the national economy was redirected towards revenue-earning exports and deferred social provision. This was the turn of the Ministries of Health (later succeeded in housing work by the Ministry of Housing and Local Government) and Education. Fluctuations in spending power and influence of departments reflected successive transitions from wartime command economy to welfare state planned economy and then to a mixed economy. The effects of policy changes were visible in increased housing, education and health provision, in the advance of social services in leisure and recreation, and in specialized fields like the Atomic Energy Authority.

Some public sponsorship came directly from central government departments, largely the Ministry of Works and its successors, but responsibility for many other public buildings was decentralized at local authority level. The established wide variety of local authorities became more evident, ranging in size from the LCC serving a population of over 3m, to district councils in some cases serving not many more than 3,000. Identities included over fifty county councils, rather more county boroughs, numerous non-county boroughs, urban and rural district councils, and the metropolitan boroughs and new town development corporations.[5] Authorities of different status had different powers of sponsorship and overlapping geographical areas which had accumulated haphazardly over many years. The picture was complex and made all the more so by increasing sponsorship activity, and reorganization such as that creating the GLC and London boroughs in 1965.

Equally complex, because priorities changed almost continuously, were the relationships between central and local government. The main aim of central government regarding sponsorship was to scrutinize local authority proposals to ensure good value and fairness between authorities. Central government, often working through regional branches, influenced local authorities over the size of their programmes and standards of accommodation, and checked project costs. Yet local authorities were more than instruments of central government, being popularly elected legally independent bodies able to interpret building need in their own individual ways. Potential for independent action was considerable, although close relationships with central government generally prevailed, backed by the ultimate power of the latter to withhold loan sanction for projects.

In early postwar years local authority sponsorship was circumscribed by systems of allocation laid down by central authority. Later these were replaced by rather more interventionist approaches[6] by central government, aided at the level of design by new techniques of project cost planning and control and explicit cost limits such as the housing cost yardstick introduced in 1967. House building was a responsibility of about 1,400 local authorities, of which only 250 had annual building programmes exceeding 100 dwellings. The customary sponsorship procedure was for elected members under the general guidance of the Ministry of Housing and Local Government (part of the Department of the Environment from 1970) to determine need, settle priorities and programmes and call up financial resources enabling chief officers to implement policy. Building costs usually were divided between local and central authorities with the latter making an annual grant for a number of years towards repayment of capital borrowed by local authorities. The local contribution came partly from rents and partly through local rates and other income. Main sources of capital were the Public Works Loan Board, long and short term mortgages, public issues on the stock exchange and temporary loans and bank overdrafts.[7]

Sponsorship of new schools by local authorities and the Ministry of Education (Department of Education and Science after 1964) differed in that the far smaller number of education authorities, less than 150, made for closer administrative relations. The Ministry of Education was regarded as one of the most progressive government sponsors, being helped by the consistently high priority accorded by both main political parties to school building, and by well-informed local education authorities. School building programmes were planned well in advance, unlike those of most other comparable building types, which were tied to the dictates of annual national budgeting[8] and hence prone to damaging reversals in size of commitment from one year to the next. Responsibility for public sponsorship generally was somewhat elusive, lying along an attenuated administrative chain stretching from Treasury and central government departments at one extreme, to chief officers and politicians of district councils at the other. In extent and complexity, public sponsorship was well beyond that which had existed previously, and must have exceeded the wildest dreams of nineteenth-century sponsors.

Private sponsorship

Private sponsorship differed from public because activity was relatively light for some of the time, and methods more direct, as well as less accessible to public view. Until the early 1950s private sponsorship was displaced from its former pre-eminent position by tight official control, together with nationalization of certain industries. Later, private sponsorship regained importance when industrial and commercial building gathered pace and private house building was resumed on an enlarged scale. However, a return to prewar conditions was not complete for, as well as continued heavy public spending, individual private sponsors appear to have been more rare than ever, and committee sponsors more common. Growth of organizations made responsibility for decisions to build in the private sector, like the public, more attenuated.

Prominent among methods of private sponsorship were those of developers who first busied themselves rebuilding bombed sites. When the supply of such sites approached exhaustion, it was observed wryly, developers resumed demolition where Hitler had left off. They did so in recognition of the opportunity offered by apparently insatiable demand for central urban commercial accommodation. Developers of great entrepreneurial zeal, combined with local authorities seeking prestige and gain, soon produced striking results. A few risk-taking developers, such as Jack Cotton, made immense profits (and attracted matching publicity) from speculative provision of offices and shops. Later came domination by more impersonal departmentalized property development companies. Their initial approach to comprehensive central area redevelopment was by raising short term loans of up to three years from clearing banks and, particularly later, merchant and secondary banks, the issue of stocks and shares, and use of income from earlier projects. Sums involved in purchase of a jig-saw of existing ownerships, legal and design work, demolition and rebuilding were very large and in the longer term frequently involved capital from insurance companies, pension funds, and property unit trusts. The credit market became progressively more sophisticated, at times involving sale and leaseback[9] and a profusion of consortia, nominees, subsidiary companies and agents. The financial success of developers encouraged local authorities and institutes working jointly with developers to press ever harder partnership terms in order to share in the considerable gains to be had. Traditional roles of developer, short term financier and long term financier merged with one another as they adapted in a fast-moving world to pressures of inflation and desire to secure better yields.[10]

Private sponsors were active also in suburban speculative housing estates, hotels, factories, warehouses and so on. The open market for accommodation expanded, so it would appear that occupiers increasingly sought to buy or rent 'off-the-peg' rather than purpose-built premises. It was estimated[11] that by the late 1960s not more than one fifth of new offices were built by their intending occupiers, the remainder being supplied by developers through the open market. Here was an instance of the move away from 'naive' sponsors commissioning their own premises, and towards 'sophisticated' sponsors building speculatively for the market, in a manner long common for low cost housing. Frequently a compromise was reached between speculative and custom building in which a basic building shell was erected speculatively, for subsequent fitting out when the identity and needs of the occupier were known. An example was that of shops initially consisting of a basic shell, for later addition of internal surface finishes, some services and shop front; many factories were provided in a similar way. This enabled the advantages of an open market in accommodation, such as sensitivity to and rapidity of response to demand, economies of scale, and specialization of those who provided the buildings, to be combined with the advantages of meeting the specific wants of occupiers for interiors.

ASPECTS OF DEMAND

Location: mobility and planning

The geographical location of new buildings was affected profoundly by planning policy and increased mobility. While greater mobility of goods and many people widened the choice of sites, planning policy often operated in the reverse way by restricting and directing that choice. Greater mobility came from an immense increase in the number of motor vehicles (nearly four-fold between 1948 and 1968), although offset in part by associated decline in public transport and cycling. The significance of growing motor traffic for building location lay in a change in the utility of sites, in which those assailed by traffic congestion, noise and fumes lost appeal while others became more accessible and attractive. Old constraints favouring central urban sites diminished, while many suburban and rural locations took on new potential. Decentralization, begun over half a century before by railways and tramways, was greatly intensified by motor transport so that the future built environment looked as if it would come to resemble a low-density and car-dependent American pattern.

The development of town and country planning from a rudimentary influence on location between the wars, to a very strong one, began with a wartime transformation of attitudes. This found expression in a release of purposefulness and egalitarian sentiment during early postwar years, when long-debated planning measures formed part of an attempt to make far-reaching changes in society. Established public health safeguards affecting building form were linked with new attempts to promote efficiency and prosperity, relieve unemployment and congestion and preserve amenity, largely by means of planned building location. Comprehensive planning control was established by the Town and Country Planning Act of 1947,[12] derived from the findings of the Barlow, Scott and Uthwatt Reports. The new system was based on land use plans compiled by the local authorities which also dealt with applications for permission to build. Further legislation subsequently adjusted and elaborated the system in the light of experience, and official commitment remained unwavering. The scope of planning in its national, regional and local aspects was extensive,[13] and among many aspects were financial incentives for development in poorer regions, Board of Trade control of industrial development, and dramatically sudden interventions like the 1964 'Brown ban' imposed on office building, mainly in London. By such means choice of building site and form, so long determined only by sponsors' internal economies and preferences, in addition were influenced by broader community interests.

Effects of planning control

An effect of planning policy at regional level was the introduction of new factories in formerly depressed heavy industrial areas of the north east, South Wales and elsewhere, which began afresh to experience economic growth. Planning policy in the south was intended to deal more with congestion and the threatened breakdown of overstretched public services stemming from prosperity. Instruments by which overheated regional economies might be cooled and ailing ones strengthened were the designation of new towns and planned town expansion schemes. Yet such planned schemes were quantitatively insignificant in total compared with the sum of building which took place on cleared sites and on the edges of towns. Outward expansion of major towns was constrained by green belts so that growth, where it was permitted, was more orderly than hitherto. Infilling and carefully considered urban extensions were the aims although, where pressure for new development was intense, there could be problems such as the leapfrogging of green belts.

Urban renewal

Numerous forces favoured urban renewal, including the effects of economic growth in raising consumer spending and white collar employment, hence demand for shops and offices respectively; rising expectations regarding the efficiency, convenience and appearance of buildings; desire for civic improvement, particularly among elected representatives aided by their officials; advancing average age of the building stock, requiring rehabilitation or renewal; increased traffic requiring larger road access; government slum clearance policies; greatly increased land values, especially in business districts, such that some sites became more valuable than the buildings on them, inviting replacement with larger buildings; and finally, the easing in the 1950s of acute accommodation shortage, making replacement feasible for the first time for fifteen years. Continued piecemeal redevelopment of sites was increasingly overshadowed by comprehensive schemes in which developers' capital and expertise were linked with the compulsory purchase and land-use zoning powers of local authorities. Activity spread from central London by stages to smaller town centres, in some cases giving rise to symbols of municipal status and prosperity, but in others leading to over-provision and some decidedly mixed feelings. Neither was renewal confined to commercial buildings, for great tracts of old housing also fell in front of an onslaught on the slums, releasing land for rebuilding purposes at a rate at times exceeding the sponsors' capacity to reuse.[14] Many other old houses benefited from improvements rather than clearance, for between 1965 and 1968 alone nearly ½m dwellings were the subject of local authority improvement grant approvals worth over £50m; the amount of private time and money lavished in such ways is not recorded.

Rural activity

Rural building activity was slight in comparison with the immensity of what took place in and around the towns. The only major exception was during a few war years, when the urban building stock suffered loss, and there were frantic endeavours deep in the countryside to provide camps, depots, stores and well over 400 airfields. This activity soon died away, leaving mainly agricultural provision, village expansion and scattered houses for the mobile who worked in, or had retired from, the towns.

Problems in assessing building quantity

From the location of building activity we move to questions connected with its quantity. An understanding of building quantity, in postwar years more than earlier ones, is beset by problems arising from the diminishing value of money on the one hand, and the changing nature of buildings on the other. Effects of inflation are familiar enough, but further explanation of the second problem of comparability is needed since there is no recognized unit volume of output in building. For example, a typical house of, say, 1946 was unlike that of 1973, having differences of floor area, garage, services and so on which affected quality and cost, making direct comparison difficult. Similarly, typical factories, offices, schools and other building types changed in allied ways. Being mindful of the changes among buildings of like purpose, the trend in total volume of building activity may be examined, as expressed in price of building output near the beginning and end of the period.

Between 1954, when wartime disruption had receded, and 1970 the total price of United Kingdom construction output more than doubled, at constant prices, from an index of 64 to one of 132 (1963 = 100). A further indication of growth over the same interval was that construction output at *current* prices increased from 5.7% of gross domestic product to 6.3%. At the same time, however, construction output at *constant* prices, as a percentage of gross domestic product, showed a slight fall from 5.5 to 5.3. This discrepancy, Sugden[15] has pointed out, was caused by a relatively faster rate of price increase in construction than in other industrial fields. The effect was of a price rise in construction, relative to the rate of price increase for all goods and services, of about 16% accompanied by a relative fall of about 3% in volume of construction output. In general terms sponsors were having to pay progressively more for buildings compared with other categories of expenditure, and this appeared to slightly diminish the volume of building relative to other aspects of the growing national economy. The higher cost of buildings was attributable in part to higher quality products, particularly in respect of services. Also there was a tendency for productivity in building to lag behind that in many other industries. A result was that larger cost reductions, or at least slower price rises, occurred outside building than in it, hence there were widening price differentials between the building and non-building fields.

Influences on building quantity

Some of the various influences on levels of building activity are already familiar but others took new forms. Economic growth raised real incomes, thereby stimulating demand for a growing range and quantity of buildings. The birthrate was higher than before the war, although well below nineteenth-century levels, lifting the population of England and Wales by 5m between 1951 and 1971. More significant in respect of housing need was an increase in the number of separate households which was proportionately greater than the population growth. Regional and local migration also continued to be a source of building demand, with the 'drift to the south east' and loss of people from old town centres to new suburbs continuing a prewar movement, though often at a faster pace. Replacement of outworn or unsuitable buildings, as requirements changed and fabrics ceased to be capable of repair, stimulated replacement demand to new levels. A much enlarged source of investment demand came from domestic owner-occupiers borrowing from building societies, insurance companies and local authorities. Owner-occupation increased from about a quarter of all dwellings in 1945 to over half by 1973, while private landlords escaped in growing numbers from a less and less attractive form of investment, due to rent and other controls. Further investment demand stemmed from institutions such as insurance companies channelling money into large commercial buildings, usually producing income from rents.

Many of these influences on building activity themselves were much affected by government policy, felt in two ways, the first being direct sponsorship of buildings. The second was through side-effects of policy, developing late in the period into explicit use of building by government as an instrument for manipulating investment in the economy as a whole, to promote general stability and growth. Intended and unintended impacts of government policy on building activity were crucially important, at times (perhaps at all times) being the strongest single influence of all.

Fluctuations

Demand for new buildings passed through four main phases beginning with the war when control over civilian building, initially unsure, was effectively asserted in 1940. A system of licensing of work exceeding £500 (later much less) was enforced[16] to prohibit non-essential work, although there appears to have been a good deal of evasion. Systems of allocation and priority were hastily improvised by government in order to prevent the building industry being overwhelmed by crushing demand for war work. Trial and error led by 1943 to a building programme which was centrally planned and co-ordinated far beyond any other in this country, before or since. By that time the gross value of building and civil engineering work, which exceeded 1938 levels in 1941, already was falling[17] and plans were being drawn up in anticipation of peace.

When this came, bringing the second phase of activity, demand changed in nature rather than intensity. Resources remained inadequate for the task and, amid deepening concern with costs, government retained rigid control over the amount and type of new buildings. Priority was given to war damage repair, local authority housing and schools, although the few private sponsors permitted to proceed, such as industrialists in development areas, were helped by the low cost of borrowing. Gradually the austere economic climate moderated, bringing the third phase in the early 1950s, associated with brightening prospects, shorter and less severe business cycles, full employment, more diversified economy, and expanded social and welfare provisions. Building restrictions were relaxed in 1953 and abolished the following year, activity expanded, a free market in the provision, if not location, of buildings was reestablished and accumulated arrears of demand were worked off. Keynesian economic policies brought gains in prosperity, at least of a superficial kind, with an alternating cycle of boom and credit squeeze. Building was much affected by these 'stop-go' sequences, being vulnerable to credit restrictions which cut more deeply into capital than current expenditure. Some building types, such as factories for consumer goods manufacture, were especially prone while others, such as local authority housing, enjoyed a degree of immunity.

The fourth and final phase of activity was a hectic time of property boom, accelerating inflation and uncertainty with which the period concluded in the early 1970s. Deep-seated economic problems, increasingly evident from unfavourable international comparisons and exacerbated by the OPEC oil crisis, brought the outlook for building and the economy as a whole to a deeply unsettled position.

HOUSING

Numbers

From generalities about building provision we move to a brief review of each major building type, beginning with housing which remained, by a diminishing margin, the largest single category. The value of housing output as a percentage of all building and construction was slightly over thirty in the later 1950s, falling to a little under that figure by the early 1970s.[18,19] About 7.4m dwellings were built between 1940 and 1973, divided fairly equally between public and private sectors. In wartime only a trickle of 5–10,000 dwellings per year were built, mostly to serve new camps and factories, but as early as 1941 preparatory discussions began about future peacetime activity.

When peace came, housing received the same high priority as had been given in similar circumstances in 1919. Early legislation included the Housing (Financial and Miscellaneous Provisions) Act of 1946 which granted a Treasury subsidy of £16–10s per house for sixty years, subject to local authority contribution of a much smaller sum. Much further legislation followed, sometimes reflecting political reversals, so that there were eleven major Acts in the following twenty-five years. Tightly stretched house building resources after 1945 were channelled mainly through the local authorities, with housing expenditure in the late 1940s more than five times that on all other local authority buildings combined. House completions exceeded

200,000 per year in 1948, a time when private house building was restricted to a maximum of one fifth of local authority allocation, although this was soon eased and then freed entirely in 1954.[20] Meanwhile the Housing Act of 1952 raised the level of subsidies to public authorities and two years later the Housing Repairs and Rents Act began to shift local authority provision from general housing needs towards slum replacement. Annual output reached a new postwar peak of just over 300,000 in 1954, and, in the ensuing fall to about 240,000 in 1958, private completions passed those of local authorities for the first time since the war to hold the leading position thereafter.

Important housing measures of the 1960s included the re-introduction of a general needs subsidy, an over-ambitious (and in the event unattained) output target, and an alteration of the basis of Exchequer grants to that of low interest loans in 1967. House completions[21] picked up gradually from the early 1960s to an all-time peak of 372,000 in 1968, still not so very far above the prewar peak. By 1973 completions had fallen to 264,000, of which 174,000 were private, 72,000 were local authority and fewer than 10,000 each were by new town corporations and housing associations.[22] Set against this decline in new work was growth in rehabilitation.

Quality and cost, 1940s and 1950s

The range of quality and cost of new houses in the 1940s narrowed with the disappearance of high quality examples and improvement in the lowest standards. New permanent houses, having an average floor area in 1947 of 1,029 sq ft, were larger than most prewar equivalents. They were also larger than the startlingly unorthodox 600 sq ft 'prefab' temporary bungalows of the time, considered in the following chapter. Improvement in permanent houses came from recommendations in the Dudley Report[23] and the ensuing *Housing Manual 1944*,[24] which suggested for five-person three-bedroom houses an area of 900 sq ft, and generally improved standards. This size was often exceeded in practice in early years but from the late 1940s need for economy brought reductions. Average floor areas fell from a peak of 1,055 sq ft in 1949 to 897 sq ft ten years later. The fall in quality was accompanied first by larger numbers of completions (more meant worse) and then by the policy change from general needs to slum replacement, implying a need for cheaper houses.

Reduced standards of new suburban local authority terraces

were balanced partly by greater effort and spending on schemes containing high flats. Earlier postwar flats were few and generally designed along prewar lines, but from the early 1950s 'mixed development' gained acceptance. This consisted of flats sited among family houses to give fairly high densities, as propounded in the 1943 County of London Plan.[25] Novel point and slab blocks of flats and maisonettes were not cheap, and around 1958 when two-storey houses typically cost 33/6d per sq ft, twelve-storey flats often cost double that amount.[26] Yet the extra cost of building high, incurred by additional complexity of structure, services and building operations, did little to deter the advance of the new fashion.

The private sector, by contrast, built few flats and hardly any high blocks, instead relying on a well-tried range of low and medium density single and two-storey detached, semi-detached and occasional short terraced houses. In this field little fundamental change took place, except (as rueful mortgagees might reflect) the price, although there were obvious superficial differences. Resumption of large scale private house building may be typified by examples built by Taylor Woodrow, of which three-bedroom types of 910 sq ft area put up in Kidlington in 1953 were priced at £1,655 each, presumably including land cost. The following year similar houses at Old Windsor were priced at £1,950 and superior versions were offered at £2,750.[27]

Quality and cost, 1960s

Houses of this sort appeared in large numbers in the 1960s, but it was local authority products which attained greater prominence in the form of high-rise flat building. This reached a peak in 1966 when one quarter of all new local authority dwellings were in blocks of five or more storeys. Soaring and potentially cloud-capped towers, it was noted,[28] might confer prestige, catch votes and be a visible sign that the council was doing its job, so an architectural ideal was taken up by various public interests and proprietors of building systems. Before long, social shortcomings began to be recognized and reinforced by economic arguments that land savings quite failed to compensate for inherently high costs. In 1966, the average cost of flats in blocks of five or more storeys exceeded 100/- per sq ft, compared with less than 60/- for houses. Government enthusiasm waned and the disastrous collapse of a block at Ronan Point in the East End in 1968 merely underlined what was already obvious (if not always to the news media), that in future high-density housing was more likely to be low-rise than high. Not all official housing provision of the 1960s deserved the opprobrium directed towards high flats, for the shrinkage of individual dwellings was reversed under the recommendations of the 1961 Parker Morris Report.[29] Among higher standards proposed were better heating and minimum floor areas of 960 sq ft (898 sq ft was the current average) for a five-person house. This was hardly a transformation in standards since the heady but short-lived days of Tudor Walters, but it was an improvement on the standards of the mid-1930s and 1950s.

Standards of private provision did not differ conspicuously from public although the range was somewhat wider. The cheapest private examples appear to have been inferior to local authority equivalents, but no doubt the most costly private houses had no public rivals. The size of most private provision was above 750 and below 1,000 sq ft, limits which included almost two-thirds of new houses mortgaged in 1962 by the Co-operative Permanent Building Society. Only 3% of that sample exceeded 1,499 sq ft and within a few years a peak appeared to have been reached, followed by a small fall except among the most expensive houses.[30] The latter are likely to have been fewer in number, size for size, than before the war, and another indication of the relative leanness in quality of private provision was that in the early 1970s only about one in five new private houses exceeded Parker Morris standards.[31] By then about a quarter of all building work by value was private housing and a seventh was public authority housing. The next largest category of building was public non-housing work, to which attention is directed now.

PUBLIC AND SOCIAL BUILDINGS

Schools

Public and social building activity increased during the period, from minimal levels in wartime to about one fifth of all building activity in 1957 and over a quarter by 1972. Schools were particularly prominent, largely because of their widely acclaimed reputation in design and construction. Although some classroom extensions and provision for school meals was built during the war, there was severe postwar accommodation shortage. The reasons included implications of the 1944 Education Act, bomb damage, insufficient wartime building, population growth and the construction of new estates requiring new facilities.

Spending on education buildings as a proportion of all local authority building increased fairly steadily from about a twelfth in 1948 to well over a quarter in 1958. Nearly 600 new schools were completed in that year, about the same figure as in 1970,[32] although there were intervening fluctuations. Private school building activity was small in comparison with public, about one fifth measured by value of new orders in 1973. School design developed intensively, new methods of construction were tried and circulation space was drastically reduced, apparently without detriment to useful teaching area.[33]

Some manufacturers developed proprietary systems of construction, such as Intergrid, and slightly later consortia of local authorities devised systems such as CLASP. The success of the consortia encouraged many authorities to join them in search of low price bulk purchase agreements, to pool experience and spread development costs. The good value for money widely believed to come from schools was largely attributable to the Ministry of Education development group and one or two local authorities, notably Hertfordshire and Nottinghamshire. An indication of the variety of schools in the late 1960s comes from a sample of seven discussed by Ward[34] which ranged from 10,000 sq ft each costing £62,000 upwards to over twelve times that cost and area.

Higher education buildings

Building for higher education initially received far lower priority than school building, but growth came eventually, in keeping with other aspects of public spending. By the mid-1950s the number of full-time students in higher education in Great Britain reached 122,000 compared with 69,000 in 1938–1939.[35] Colleges of Advanced Technology were designated in the later 1950s and new universities followed in the 1960s in response to population pressure, considerations of local and national prestige, and desire on the part of more and more school leavers to go on to higher education. Impetus for expansion reached a peak in 1963 with the publication of the Robbins Report, by which time seven new universities were already in hand. The University of Sussex, for example, planned £2.8m value of building in its first four year period, amounting to about 360,000 sq ft of accommodation.[36] Between 1960 and 1970 the number of all university students more than doubled to reach 220,000. Many non-university institutions were reordered in name and status so that by 1971 there were thirty polytechnics and over 600 art, agricultural and other major establishments of further education. In 1969, typical arts buildings cost slightly more than secondary schools, at about £6-15s per sq ft, and laboratories cost several pounds more.[37]

Health buildings

As with higher education provision, so with health, where activity was light in the early part of the period, but expanded later under attempts to catch up arrears. The establishment of the National Health Service in 1948 did not bring a heavy building programme and hospital building, which was the concern of Regional Boards, remained below prewar levels. Annual capital expenditure on hospitals in 1949–50 was £9m, and local authority expenditure on clinics, ambulance stations, provision for the handicapped and so on did not rise above a third of that figure. This somnolent scene began to stir in the 1960s when efforts were made to modernize the decidedly elderly hospital stock. Annual expenditure of £26m in 1960–61 almost quadrupled by 1967–68. Typical buildings were costly and, at about £9-10s per sq ft in 1969, equivalent to about two-and-a-half times the unit cost of houses. The difference was explained by the exceedingly complicated nature of hospitals, evident from the great time taken to formulate design briefs, and their deeply involved plans, structures and services. Some complications extended in lesser degree to quite humble group practice surgeries and similar buildings.

Miscellaneous public and social buildings

Of the miscellaneous public and social buildings which remain to review, growth in numbers and size perhaps are more apparent than widening variety. Library provision apparently was fairly typical, being light in the 1940s, but picking up in the early 1950s and, with growing national prosperity, continuing to appear in the following years. Projects in 1969 typically cost £8-10s per sq ft and could range from about the size of a house up to 50,000 sq ft or so.[38,39] In the same category of public and social building was accommodation for purposes of law, order and public safety. If military construction is admitted to this group, then wartime provision of airfields, camps and training establishments, but excluding industrial facilities, exceeded £120m value each year from 1940 to 1943. Later, levels more appropriate to peacetime prevailed, with activity being carried on by the Ministry of Public Building and Works and its successor the Department of the Environment.

On the civilian side, building provision for police and fire services commonly was less than one tenth of wartime military spending. In the 1960s there was limited activity in the field of town halls, museums and art galleries, representing the summit of public prestige building. Costs were set at an appropriate level, with civic suites (about £12-15s per sq ft in 1969) being triple that of low cost houses, although departmental offices cost about the same as good quality private offices. Numerous building types remain which public authorities provided, or were partly instrumental in providing, among them leisure and sports facilities, markets, depots, crematoria, old people's accommodation and community centres. Places of worship[40] often were associated with community centres, in physical proximity if not necessarily in source of funds. The cost per sq ft of churches in 1969 was about £8-5s and chapels were rather less, but both were comfortably below specialized provision for secular uses. There remains space only for passing reference to other building types such as the ARP shelters of war, and provision stemming from notably different circumstances, like bathing huts, youth centres and nurseries.

INDUSTRIAL BUILDINGS

Sponsors

Industrial buildings formed the next largest category and one more architecturally uniform than the last, although not altogether lacking variety. During the war great efforts were made to expand strategically important industries and after it there was diversification in the field of consumer goods. In the late 1950s, when the value of new industrial work was about 15% of building and construction output, those industries having the highest capital expenditure on new buildings were, in descending order, chemicals and allied industries, engineering and electrical goods, food, drink and tobacco, and metal manufacture. Other prominent industries were: vehicles, including aircraft, paper, printing and publishing, shipbuilding and marine engineering, and textiles.[41] Despite an upward trend, by 1972 the value of industrial building had slipped relatively to almost 10% of building and construction output, below the level of commercial building.

Nature and cost

The nature of factories and warehouses ranged from large utilitarian sheds, such as Ministry of Supply stores, to small groups of rented municipal 'nursery' workshop units, each only about the size of a pair of houses. In contrast to both were large developments, in some cases one site including facilities for processing, producing, storing and despatching, as well as researching and administering all aspects of groups of products. Agricultural buildings, for an industry greatly stimulated by the effects of war and which remained prosperous afterwards, increasingly converged in design with manufacturing accommodation. Various standard buildings appeared, in their most extreme form stark and repetitive factory farm installations for poultry and pigs.[42]

Despite a national record of generally indifferent manufacturing performance, some building groups were large: in 1964 £383m invested in new work for private industry produced 1,200 buildings with a total floor area of 33m sq ft.[43] Here was a field, perhaps more than others, where unit costs of large projects were demonstrably lower than those of small projects. Costs depended on the need of the particular industry concerned so that in the late 1940s, when heavy factories of several storeys cost the same as, or slightly more than, cheap houses per unit of floor area, light sheds and barns cost only half that amount. Light single-storey factories of the type often built speculatively and which probably made up the bulk of industrial floorspace, cost something midway between the foregoing extremes. In the late 1960s similar accommodation, together with an allowance for some associated office space, cost about £3-15s per sq ft. This was much the same as warehouses, but heavy industrial buildings having long spans, or bearing heavy loads, cost about half as much again.

COMMERCIAL BUILDINGS

Offices

New commercial buildings were quite few until relaxation of official controls and growth of consumer spending around the mid-1950s. Then the expanding white collar activities of administration, control and provision of services required new office accommodation; related but often less routine activities sprang up in new research centres, laboratories and studios; retail trading expanded in new shops, stores, garages and supermarkets; and much leisure and entertainment migrated from private houses to the specialized commercial surroundings of hotels, public houses, halls and clubs. In the late 1950s commercial building amounted to one tenth of the total value of building and construction output, advancing several per cent further by 1972. In that year offices were by far the most important commercial building type, followed by shops worth about half their value, and entertainment buildings worth about one third.

Office building began to make an impact from about 1954 in central London, while in Croydon, perhaps the most spectacular manifestation outside the City, between 1957 and 1964 over 5m sq ft of floor space was built or approved. At the same time other developments were getting under way in major cities, and in central London the pace accelerated to a peak in 1962.[44] Planning restrictions then were imposed, but demand for space had already begun to slacken, not to return to former levels for a decade. By 1973 activity was again fuelled by spiralling office rents, recovering so strongly that further restrictions were brought in. During the 1960s peak the average size of office buildings in central London appears to have been about 40,000 sq ft, frequently subdivided for rental purposes into units of about a quarter of that size.[45] Costs per sq ft in the late 1960s ranged from about £6 up to £7-10s for higher quality owner-occupied premises.

Shops and leisure buildings

Many comprehensive redevelopment schemes incorporated a range of shops beneath offices, while in suburbs and small towns, new shops, some with flats over them, replaced many older high street buildings. Early postwar shop building activity was light,[46] generally being confined to bomb damage replacements or bringing essential amenities to new estates. Activity appears to have accelerated during the later 1950s and intensified around the mid-1960s, when large developers were active in many town centres. Multiple retailers increased their market share, largely at the expense of independent owners and co-operative societies. One example, Marks and Spencer, built 1.5m sq ft of floor space between 1954 and 1968, quite apart from rebuildings and modernization.[47] Among important leisure and entertainment building was hotel provision, stimulated by increasing tourism and a government subsidy late in the period, and akin to shop building in that most took place from the 1960s. In 1969, banks were one of the most costly commercial building types per sq ft at £11-5s (still cheaper than a small number of projects such as theatres) while department stores were £7-5s, public houses £6-15s, and, among the cheapest commercial buildings, service stations with showrooms were £5, and shops with flats above them £4.

LOSSES FROM STOCK

Causes

The likelihood is that losses from the stock of buildings occurred at a faster rate than hitherto, certainly on a larger scale, and with a tendency for the economic life of buildings to shorten. Houses were said, in the 1960s, to be subject to clearance at an annual rate of something less than half, and probably less than quarter, of one per cent of stock,[48] probably slower than the rate for industrial and commercial buildings. The most effective agents of demolition were large urban local authorities keen to eliminate houses built before about the time of the 1875 Public Health Act. Other agents were private interests, and some public ones unconnected with slum clearance, which perceived that the benefits of retaining some old buildings were outweighed by those to be realized by clearing and rebuilding. Potential benefits included financial gain, improved service to customers, enhanced reputation and heightened satisfaction to the owner. Pressures favouring demolition were much the same as those above respecting urban renewal, with the addition of unpredictable changes in technology, taste and fashion, which condemned many buildings as diverse as cinemas (of the 4,800 in 1939, less than half were open by 1966), country houses, gasworks and churches. Physical decay, in many cases hastened by deferment of maintenance in war, was more likely to be an effect than a cause of obsolescence. The origins of obsolescence were less physical than economic and social, for these were the factors which first led to neglect and hence deterioration.

Extent, building types

The chronological course of building loss opened with the violent intensity of arbitrary devastation by the Luftwaffe. In London about 58m sq ft of commercial and industrial floor space, including over a tenth of all office space, was destroyed or damaged.[49] The number of houses in England and Wales destroyed or made permanently uninhabitable by bombing was 475,000. A long respite followed the war, while losses were replaced and accumulated demand was met before slum clearance was resumed effectively in the mid-1950s. It proceeded at about 20,000 to 35,000 dwellings per year, accelerating to about 65,000 in the 1960s.[50] Far smaller losses took place by reason of commercial expansion, natural calamities like fire and flood, or artificial calamities (in the opinion of occupants) like road widening. Among other building types were certain vulnerable categories: buildings such as corner shops, meeting halls and workshops in slum clearance areas, demolished to simplify comprehensive redevelopment; redundant specialized buildings defying adaptation or obstructing re-development, such as railway buildings after the Beeching closures; and certain public buildings looking increasingly anachronistic in an age which boasted of its affluence. Among the latter group were hospitals and schools of which in 1962 almost half were built prior to 1902.

With a larger and faster-growing stock of buildings than ever, it was to be expected that demolition would be correspondingly heavy. Yet attitudes towards clearance, which began favourably associated with ideas of progress, were redefined as needless violence wrought upon that which was pleasant, and greeted with growing hostility. The case for rehabilitation and conservation rather than destruction, even of the commonplace, was pressed more and more by individuals and amenity groups, and taken up by local authorities late in the period.

BUILDING FORM

Grouping of buildings

In some respects the physical form of new buildings continued to develop along lines evident before the war. The size of the largest projects continued to increase in volume and height (sometimes overwhelmingly so) and internally the provision of universal space expanded from the prewar extent. New features included a rigid segregation of building types of like function according to planning policy, here an industrial area, there a housing estate and elsewhere a shopping centre. Such land use patterns usually prevailed, but the antithesis appeared occasionally in the form of large complex centres combining in a single structure a varied mixture of building types. Town centre examples combined shops, offices, multi-storey car parks and perhaps a library and public house, while new universities might bring together teaching and laboratory space, lecture halls, a cafe, shops and a bank. Such centres made intensive use of sites, something also encouraged on many other projects by the fast growing value of land. One view was that agricultural land increased from an average of £25 per acre in 1939 to £662 in 1972[51], while in Greater London, where values were highest, some sites increased over 200-fold in a similar period.[52] Effects on building form included higher housing densities with smaller gardens, some return to terraced instead of semi-detached forms, extra storeys, and infill buildings on vacant sites; the sprawling open character of much interwar development became more compact, if not by very much. A reason for high land values was the restriction of supply by planning policy and another, lesser, reason may have been the apparently insatiable demand for land for motor traffic. Outside old centres many new buildings were arranged in loose groups separated from each other by the considerable open spaces necessary for traffic in motion and at rest; an age in which mobility was so highly prized created places which suggested that it was better, or at least more important, to travel hopefully than to arrive.

Standardization Many buildings were more standardized than hitherto (much low cost housing always had been), either in part, as with the interchangeable components of system-built schools and repetitive bays of industrial and commercial blocks, or in their entirety as with 'off-the-peg' home extensions, industrial and agricultural buildings, system-built high flats and demountable 'instant' accommodation. During the war the economies in design and production, possible through standardization, were exploited vigorously. Standard ordnance factory units, stores and other buildings appeared and development work was undertaken at all levels from construction details and specifications to the design of whole buildings. Prefabrication went hand in hand with standardization and was officially fostered at times when resources for building were most stretched. The main purposes of standardization were to save costs and labour by reducing the number of trivial differences among components, said by some to be possible without prejudicing quality or real design choice.

Convergence Yet it was arguable that variety in appearance did diminish in some respects, partly as a consequence of standardization, partly of growing constraints from building regulations and allied controls and partly of more obscure influences. The plurality of styles evident in, say, Edwardian architecture was no longer to be found and universal design solutions appeared in the ascendant. Convergence seemed to be taking place in the appearance of such buildings as primary schools and branch libraries, supermarkets and warehouses, private and local authority houses. If visual uniformity was growing, its origins remained unclear, whether among designers' intentions, economics of production, or the growing preponderance of corporate over individual sponsors, leading to reduced individuality. If old boundaries and differences in the appearance of buildings were losing earlier clarity, if old stereotypes were weakening, new replacements were not yet overwhelmingly obvious. It is possible that the differences between some types of buildings, based on function and symbolism, were beginning to follow extinct regional differences based on materials, down the path of decline.

Modern Movement

Such issues cannot be pursued further here, but instead must serve to introduce the topic of the Modern Movement and its eventual dominance of postwar architecture. After slow interwar progress, acceptance of many of the superficial characteristics of the Modern Movement was rapid, reaching a strong position by the time of the Festival of Britain in 1951. This acceptance was balanced by rejection of much that was traditional, especially in buildings above the scale of housing: framed structures in many cases superseded loadbearing walls, even for single-storey buildings of small roof span, frequently giving rise to grid pattern walls of exposed frames and infill panels; structural frames brought more large horizontally proportioned windows, light claddings, and flat roofs. The latter made possible deeper and more complicated plans, with projecting wings, recesses and courtyards, than were possible with pitched roofs. Another aspect of the Modern Movement evident to casual observers was increasing use of synthetic materials such as aluminium, plate glass, concrete and plastics. Most interiors contained ready reminders of rising material standards in the shape of more fittings, furnishings, lighting and heating.

Lighter, brighter buildings, arising from an alliance between Modern Movement principles and advancing technology, was accompanied by several developments unforeseen by early protagonists of the movement. One was the sponsors' growing concern with value for money from their buildings: the rejection of ornament, branded by designers as old-fashioned meaningless clutter, seemed to open the way for pressure to cut costs by eliminating all spaces and features which were not demonstrably functional. In some cases such as schools, avoidance of redundant space in the interests of economy was said to be entirely beneficial, and elsewhere it might be only designers' mere flights of fancy which suffered. However, in other cases undue zeal in minimizing expenditure must have led to duller if not worse buildings: examples were officially declared minimum standards such as Parker Morris observed in practice as maxima; large spaces in which ceiling heights were brought down to a uniform minimum; circulation spaces so reduced as to enforce dark, narrow corridors or movement through rooms containing other activities; spending on external walls and windows so mean as to make certain high maintenance costs and a shabby appearance. Some such manifestations drew attention to conflict between different levels in the sponsors' hierarchies, such that the capital saving of one department reappeared as the increased running costs of another. Not that cost limits and their inhibiting effects were new; rather it was the extension of those limits to restrain spending on nearly all higher quality, as well as cheaper, buildings.

Another development which accompanied the Modern Movement was an increase in the number of artificially controlled interior environments, very deep rooms relying on artificial lighting, windowless rooms dependent on mechanical ventilation, and air-conditioned buildings. Some of these features appeared in high density housing from the 1950s, and others were used increasingly to meet needs of complicated planning, prestige and high performance, for example in computer rooms and auditoria. Artificial environments, relying on heavy energy consumption, made it possible to provide accommodation of standards, and in places otherwise impossible; they also conveyed a forward-looking image of technological confidence. In 1973, difficult questions about the energy costs of such buildings, posed by the oil crisis and ensuing depression, had barely begun to be asked.

8

Workhorse Learns to Canter: The Industry 1940-73

'Builders are pleasant people, but their completed work is commonly preferable to their company.'

(*N. Harvey,* A History of Farm Buildings in England and Wales, *1970*)

THE INDUSTRY IN CONTEXT

Government intervention

The upheaval of the Second World War, which shattered inter-war patterns of building activity, led before long to peacetime prosperity. Almost continuously thereafter, demand for new buildings matched or exceeded capacity to provide them, and the problems of the industry became less ones of shortage of work than of resources. Old uncertainties of future workload and employment, which had plagued building since time immemorial, now were mitigated by the effects of government intervention in the national economy. Productive capacity, we saw in the previous chapter, expanded strongly to bring a degree of security not known before.

Yet there was a price, for instead of being prey to the blind impersonal forces of the trade cycle, the building industry now was influenced by government planning and sudden changes of programme. For many, resentment towards the governmental cause of variations in workload replaced fear of slack trade, despite fluctuations being less violent than in the past. The industry felt the effect of government direction most during the war when unprecedented powers of planning were assumed and peace time 'normality' was disrupted even more than during the First World War. The industry was required to work as quickly as possible, often without regard to costs, amid measures including compulsory registration of firms, control of materials and licensing of work.[1] Controls were maintained for six or more years after the war, while problems of overloading, inefficiency and low productivity persisted[2] and unexpected changes in official programmes from time to time upset attempts to plan ahead. Many in the industry thought expectations of efficiency to be unrealistic, at least while building was treated by government as a tap which could be turned on and off at will. After a false dawn, when licensing restrictions were eased only to be reimposed, lasting relaxation came in the early 1950s and was followed by expansion of activity. Nevertheless complaints continued through the 1960s and after that successive governments failed to take account of the harmful consequences of their policies on the industry.[3]

Government economic manipulation was such that when cuts were imposed or lifted there were long lags before change was evident, by which time the reverse influence was possibly what was required. Because new orders, rather than work in hand, were affected many months might elapse before impact was felt, calling into question the wisdom of government measures. While the effectiveness of economic management might be doubted, the consequent disruption to long-term building programmes could not. At worst there was a damaged capacity to face eventual expansion, with experienced men leaving the industry, confidence undermined, materials overproduced and bunching of demand when recovery occurred. Yet the building industry was not unique in facing these problems (for example, so did the motor industry) and seen in an historical perspective, perhaps their severity was exaggerated. Indeed, it was not until 1969 that 'stop-go' policy caused an absolute, rather than a merely relative, fall in building output. Fluctuations were far from new, but the building industry had found, in the shape of government, a scapegoat for one of its major problems.

DESIGNERS AND ADVISERS

Internal relations

In addition to the hardy perennial of workload, a number of other issues existed in the industry and associated professions, some connected with internal procedures and practices. There was a belief, fostered by comparisons with technically more advanced industries, that more could be done in building to move with the times and that changes were overdue. For example, the characteristic division of responsibility between design and production was noted[4] as one which damagingly isolated the two sides, leading to failures of understanding. Communications were said to be poor in an industry characterized by interdependence of the parts harmfully mixed with uncertainty.[5] Individuals and firms were inclined, perhaps forced, to accept independent but ill-defined responsibility for their work, despite dependence on others for information. The uncertainty which arose over timing and quality of information created a fertile breeding ground for dispute, delay and financial claims leading to calls for better co-ordination, and more serious consequences for some victims of circumstance.

External relations

Another issue, this time connected with the external relations of the industry, was that of overall efficiency, noted by observers and sponsors doubtful about the quality of service which they received. Those whom they criticized were quick to point out that many sponsors had unrealistic expectations about the time scale of building, and no grasp of disruptions to schedules and impact on costs caused by inadequate briefing and subsequent changes of mind.

Other issues arose from the means by which demand for building was brought in touch with agencies of supply, in other words the methods of tendering and placing contracts for non-speculative work. In lengthy debate about the relative merits of different ways of selecting contractors, traditional open tendering lost favour. Although it assisted unfettered competition by being open to any firm to submit a price, it had the disadvantages of wasting unsuccessful tenderers' time and sometimes leading to inadequate contractors winning projects. Selective tendering, in which only an approved list of contractors were invited to compete, reduced these problems and was successfully advocated by many, including the authors of the Banwell Report.[6] Negotiated contracts also found favour due to opportunities to save time and allow firms to offer their own constructional systems. This approach could be used when sponsors initially commissioned consultant designers in the customary way and also in cases in which sponsors initially commissioned building firms which then employed their own designers. The latter case of a package deal, or design and construct, in which larger building firms provided both design and production services, acquired a fair record for completion of projects on time. On the other hand, without independent specialist supervision, the reputation for rectifying faults and keeping to original cost estimates was poor.[7] For most non-speculative projects an independent design team continued to be commissioned initially by the sponsor, or was already in his direct employment, but by the close of the period package deals were used for about one third of all new factories, rather fewer offices and nearly a tenth of local authority housing contracts.

Architects

Many of the foregoing issues concerned the growing architectural profession which occupied a leading position in the building team. Private practice maintained its central place in the profession, but a typical postwar architect was more likely to be salaried than self-employed, and to have experienced more full-time higher education than his prewar predecessor. In the early 1970s the 3,600 practices in the United Kingdom between them employed about half of the profession, much as they had done a decade or more previously. A survey[8] of 1962 showed that 13% of private practices had more than ten staff (and carried out over half of all work certified, including most big projects), while 69% of practices had fewer than six staff. Local government architects made a notable climb to positions of power in the early postwar years, with the number of RIBA members in local authorities increasing by a quarter between 1939 and 1948. There were 135 local authority architects' departments by 1957, many quite large, employing over a quarter of RIBA membership. Architects were strongest in county authorities and weakest in non-county boroughs, where engineers and surveyors continued to hold sway. The existence of an architects' department in a local authority did not prevent some commissions being placed with private consultants in order to draw on special experience for important schemes, meet peaks in workload and give stimulus.[9]

Architects also obtained salaried employment in government departments, hospital boards and nationalized industries, where altogether about 10% of RIBA membership was to be found in 1957. A further 6% were employed directly by industrial and commercial firms, including contractors, where a strict code of professional conduct barred architects from direct participation in top level management. The highest and the lowest incomes in the profession were among principals in private practice, while local authority architects received middle range incomes avoiding both extremes. Overall, the earnings of the profession were not as high as those of some of the leading professions outside building, although a few architects with the very highest earnings seem to have been well off by almost any standards.

Professional leadership, mainly through the RIBA to which a majority belonged, soon reflected the rise of architects in the public sector. A spell of fervour for reform in the 1960s diminished in the 1970s, when the profession found itself in an uncomfortable position between the upper and nether millstones of contractor and client, not an easy place in which to sustain disinterestedness or uphold the values of the community. A day-to-day problem was shortage of architectural staff, leading to rapid turnover and difficulty in meeting commitments on time. Growing numbers of technicians and unqualified assistants were taken on and the Society of Architectural and Associated Technicians was set up in 1965 with the blessing of the RIBA. A less tangible problem than staff shortage was the view, increasingly questioned later, that the artistic side of architectural skills was obsolescent in a scientific age[10] and that new and more functional skills were needed. The origins of this view seemed to lie in the demands of technology and criticism from builders that lack of progress was due to the 'inefficiency and folly'[11] of architects. Their practical understanding was compared unfavourably with that of engineers, and the lack of incentive for economy in design implicit in the fee structure was pointed out.[12] If such criticisms were justified it was equally true that the work of a minority of architects, at least, gained highest international acclaim, and that some led the industry in the field of technical developments. It was also true that measures were taken readily to correct shortcomings which came to light, for example in management, though it must remain open whether any human agency could ever reconcile interests as disparate as those with whom architects worked. They included practical men, like builders' foremen and clerks of works assisting with site supervision; officials with powers of veto, like building inspectors; critics, such as civic societies; and not least, clients ranging from property tycoons to converters of holiday cottages.

Quantity surveyors

If architects occasionally appeared under pressure from events,[13] how did their co-professionals fare? There were about 6,000 quantity surveyors at work by the mid-1960s (less than a third of the number of architects), most in the 700 practices in the United Kingdom, but some employed in public authorities. A large proportion of quantity surveyors engaged on the design side of the industry were members of the Royal Institution of Chartered Surveyors (proclaimed a Royal Institution in 1946), while many others employed by builders belonged to the Institute of Quantity Surveyors, about 2,000 strong in the mid-1960s.

The traditional skills of quantity surveyors were close to practical aspects of building and the profession hitherto had not sought much direct involvement in early design decisions. Main functions had been to compile bills of quantities, price and agree the progress of works, and settle final accounts. More experienced sponsors, and general cost consciousness, caused new functions to be added gradually: preliminary estimates in order to advise on costs from an early stage of design; cost planning and cost control in order to obtain balanced spending in design and during construction, and to find from a number of design alternatives that which would give best value for money. New concern to predict costs as well as account for them, together with direct appointment of quantity surveyors by sponsors, brought the profession closer to initial decisions about projects, and in doing so enhanced its professional influence.

Engineers

Structural engineers, slightly fewer in number than quantity surveyors, continued to be engaged for virtually all large projects and many smaller ones. They either acted as consultants nominated by the architect and paid by the sponsor, or were employed direct by firms of contractors or manufacturers. A small minority, along with architects and others, joined forces to form multi-disciplinary practices offering all necessary services for the design of large schemes. Engineers' skills were employed mainly in designing foundations and frames so that, unlike architects whose interests often leaned towards the sponsor and society at large, they retained strong links with technology and the industry.

A growing number and variety of engineers possessed other design responsibilities which were useful on large projects, namely mechanical, electrical and other services work. Again, some acted as consultants, like many quantity surveyors, while others were employed by engineering firms supplying goods to the sites. The pace of technical change in the field of services appears from time to time to have outrun the quality of advice provided to the remainder of the design team, happily something which did not apply in the structural field.

Research and development

The work of design professions was underpinned by a growing mass of regulations and recommendations which emanated from various bodies concerned with research, development and dissemination.[14,15] Their activities reflected, just as building activity reflected, economic and social priorities of the times, in the way in which directions changed and activity rose and fell. In the war, there were government inspired attempts to secure speedier construction, economy of manpower and materials and substitution of new resources for scarce traditional ones. New Directorates of Post-War Building and Building Materials under the Minister of Works were created and studies were pressed forward on Codes of Practice, Standardization and non-traditional construction.[16] After the war, continued efforts were made to introduce more efficient methods (the Building Research Station alone employed well over 300 in 1947) but growth appears to have slackened in the 1950s. Work quietly proceeded in public bodies such as Forest Products Research Laboratory (later Princes Risborough Laboratory) and Fire Research Station but, in comparison with other large industries, privately conducted research and development remained light.

A new phase of expansion came in the 1960s, when research effort in construction stood at only about a tenth of that in all industries, relative to value of output. The importance of disseminating information was recognized increasingly and took place through a variety of channels including the technical press and Building Centres. A Directorate of Research and Development was set up in the reorganized Ministry of Public Building and Works and growing activity in other ministry development groups was augmented in 1964 by the establishment of the National Building Agency, to promote mainly housing development. Two years later the Agrément Board was created with the function of assessing new building products and, elsewhere, an increasing quantity of theoretical and practical work was promoted by such bodies as the Timber Research and Development Association, Construction Industry Research and Information Association, institutes of higher education and trade associations.

BUILDING FIRMS

Size and number

The number of building firms, although large throughout, fell somewhat during the war, recovered, and then declined gradually from the late 1940s to a total of about 70,000 in Great Britain in 1973. Very small firms continued to exist in large though declining numbers with the proportion of one-man businesses diminishing from over a third of all firms in 1943 to about a quarter in 1973. In that year about 90% of all firms employed twenty-five or fewer people and rather under 2% of firms employed 115 or more.[17] The long-established pattern of easy entry and short life for many firms persisted due, as ever, to easily available credit and an unwavering supply of people keen to begin their own businesses. The efficiency of firms varied widely, with particularly heavy casualties among a postwar glut of small ones and a rate of bankruptcy which, at the close of the period, amounted to a quarter of all in the country. Profits in the late 1950s were said to be somewhat below the average for industry as a whole, and in the buoyant 1960s typically reached 8½ to 9% which was similar to, or higher than, manufacturing industry, but less than non-manufacturing industry.[18]

Large firms

An emerging dominance of large firms amid persistence of many small ones is visible in a comparison between the amounts of work carried out by each group in the early 1970s. The largest 0.1% of firms were found to carry out the same proportion of work, almost a quarter, as that carried out by the smallest 90% of firms. Yet large firms appear still not to have benefited overwhelmingly from the economies of scale which more and more came their way.[19] Among them were superior ability to raise finance, attract high quality staff, spread risks of unfavourable projects, procure goods in bulk at cheap rates, make full use of indivisible resources such as specialist manpower, and survive extremes of workload. Some of these advantages helped to give larger firms higher output per man than smaller firms, but this also in part was a consequence of their avoidance of labour-intensive maintenance work.

Set against these advantages were two disadvantages which had the effect, in the short term at least, of allowing smaller firms to compete on equal terms, despite their lower resistance to ill fortune. The first handicap of large firms was a danger of outgrowing their capacity for management, and the second was their higher overheads. In the latter respect the proportion of office workers relative to site workers increased with time and size of firm. Altogether about a fifth of employees held administrative, professional, technical and clerical jobs but, amid wide variations, most small firms had a much smaller proportion.

At the other extreme of scale the firm of Wimpey, latterly with a staff of 9,000, illustrates a general trend in which overheads crept up, in that case from 4% of turnover in 1944 to 5½% in 1969. The structure of such large firms was complex, often with associated property, materials-producing and subcontracting companies and simultaneous involvement with many separate projects. Typical larger building firms had sections devoted to plant and transport, joinery making, planning, work study, design services, bonus surveying and site safety.[20] Key figures in addition to top management included estimators, buyers, planning engineers, contracts managers and surveyors, and on site on the largest projects were project manager, site manager, site agent, section foremen and general foremen. Smooth running of projects depended on them, but people of the right calibre were scarce, occasionally leading to so-called 'management by crisis'.

Typical development of the largest firms began with a wartime shift from speculative house building to large contracts, including civil engineering, which freed them from problems of dispersed management and from having capital tied up in land stocks. In the 1950s and 1960s many moved into property development, among them John Laing which formed, in 1954, the first of a series of fifty or more companies for that purpose. Expansion of the largest firms was considerable during the 1960s when, for example, the same firm tripled its turnover in seven years. In 1970, the 'big six' were Wimpey, with a turnover of £225m, Laing, Sir Robert McAlpine and Sons, and Richard Costain, all with turnovers exceeding £100m, and slightly smaller, Taylor Woodrow and Wates.[21]

Medium and small firms

Medium-sized firms, many with a family controlling interest and reputation for good quality work, were the ones worst affected by workload fluctuations. They were too large to survive on maintenance work alone, but too small to undertake the biggest contracts which would have smoothed out troughs in workload. Another handicap was the vulnerability to recession of speculative house building to which many were heavily committed. Small firms such as that portrayed by Foster,[22] shared some of the same problems when they engaged in speculative building, small contracts and conversion jobs. The smallest firms of all continued to be simple partnerships or one-man businesses rather than limited liability companies, with activities restricted to light repairs and maintenance work, in extreme cases probably enlivened with window cleaning. Small firms were represented at the national level by the Federation of Master Builders, while the NFBTE continued to represent larger firms. Increasing awareness of public image could be seen in some promotion of professionalism, for instance by the Institute of Builders.

Direct labour A minority of projects and much maintenance were carried out by building departments attached directly to local authorities, public utilities and large factories. Some of the strongest support for such direct labour organizations came from large urban local authorities, particularly around London, which undertook a considerably increased volume of work after the war. In the mid-1950s about 4% of new work, mostly housing, was handled by direct labour organizations, but the proportion fell subsequently.[23] In the 1960s about 15% of local authorities carried out at least some new work by direct labour,[24] a few entirely so, and virtually all carried out maintenance by that means. Political controversy which shrouded the subject of direct labour made comparisons with private contractors difficult but, on balance, direct labour quality appears to have been quite high, while operations sometimes were planned poorly and suffered from weak incentive to control costs.[25]

Sub-contractors Amid the labyrinthine complexity of the 'untidy and shambling giant',[26] which was the building industry, most observers agreed about the changing importance of sub-contractors. Increasing numbers of firms, the proportion of work entrusted to them, and degree of specialization, represented growth of trends evident before the war. By the early 1970s more than half of the firms which appeared in the construction census were specialists of one sort or another whether, in order of descending magnitude, painters, plumbers, joiners and carpenters, electricians, plasterers, heating and ventilating engineers, plant hirers or roofers. This list was extended by smaller numbers of specialists in suspended ceilings, insulation, flooring, reinforced concreting and many other fields.[27] About one third of all work in a typical project was sub-contracted, but on some large schemes a total of fifty or more sub-contracting firms might account for 70% of the work. Larger sub-contractors typically obtained most of their work by tendering, while smaller firms relied rather more on architects' nominations.

Specialization aided productivity so that sub-contractors compared well in this respect with general contractors, although usually smaller than the latter in size of firm. Apart from productivity, there were various reasons for growth of sub-contracting, including increased technical complexity, the contractors' desire to avoid liability in slack times, and the inability of contractors to find continuous employment for specialists. Among the consequences of increased sub-contracting were a heavier burden of co-ordination on general contractors, sometimes leading to stress, and growth of controversy surrounding the 'lump', otherwise known as labour-only sub-contracting. This involved gangs of self-employed operatives engaged as sub-contractors for their labour (but not materials or much equipment), mainly on private house building in the south, and often at high rates of pay for piece-work. Self-employment opened the way for tax evasion by the men and saved the general contractor selective employment tax, holiday pay and so on. High general labour turnover and site management of doubtful quality were thought to have assisted in the growth of the 'lump' to something approaching 200,000 men by the late 1960s.[28]

Builders' merchants

Builders' merchants continued to provide the necessary link between sites and the producers of goods used on them. Merchants maintained stocks, absorbed shocks when demand fluctuated, collected and delivered goods, helped manufacturers by dealing in small lots when necessary, possessed knowledge of sources of supply, and provided technical advice and credit. There were of the order of 4,000 merchants in Great Britain, with a trend among them towards some concentration. They handled the majority of all materials and components with the exception of goods, such as bricks, which some large customers preferred to buy direct from the makers. Merchants varied widely in size, with some of the larger supplying the smaller, and some specialization between firms handling heavy goods and those dealing in light ones and the retail do-it-yourself market.

DO-IT-YOURSELF ACTIVITY

Origins and growth

So far the field of building activity on the part of amateurs has not been considered. Yet some handymen had long plied their craft, for had not Charles Pooter made a brave but streaky showing with red paint in his suburban home in the 1890s?[29] Such well-intentioned endeavours probably increased between the wars, and certainly they became sufficiently widespread not long after 1945 to justify inclusion here. Home maintenance and decoration cannot be quantified, but growing popularity (or at any rate volume) may be traced through the rise of publications serving the do-it-yourself market. In 1951, the monthly *Popular Handicrafts* began to include a do-it-yourself section and three years later *Handyman* appeared, followed in 1957 by *Do-It-Yourself* magazine.[30] The appeal of the pastime, assisted by television coverage, broadened into a mass one (annual wallpaper sales tripled in the ten years before 1958) and deepened into specialisms among the most dedicated, so that retailers multiplied to become a familiar high street sight. Interior painting and decorating skills were acquired (more or less) in nearly every household, while a minority learned to deal with services, rehabilitation and whole extensions.

A 1973 survey[31] found that do-it-yourself ranked fourth in estimated frequency of participation, behind gardening, needlework and knitting, and games of skill. Here were growing numbers of people who, as sponsors, designers, contractors and operatives all rolled into one, looked to be a species of economic anachronism. This singular growth may be attributed variously to greater availability of money, lesisure time and goods, and a growing desire to combat anonymity by 'personalizing' the home. What seems certain is that much work was undertaken because the building industry in effect had priced itself out of the small jobs market. While increased family income directed householders' thoughts to ways of improving their homes, such improvements had become almost prohibitively expensive when executed by builders, owing in part to higher wages in the building industry. The solution was obvious, that householders should pay only for materials and use their own free labour. Apparent overall gains in national prosperity and income, therefore, were compensated by demands on householders' time, skill and patience with paintbrush and screwdriver.

LABOUR

Size of labour force

From the unpaid we turn to those who worked on site for their livelihood. It will be recalled that between the wars their number was large and unemployment endemic, but this soon changed. Conscription quickly reduced the size of the labour force and the remaining 'poor remnant'[32] got as much to do as they could manage, and more. Official plans were drawn up early to meet the anticipated return of ex-servicemen to the industry and, after initial shortages, the labour force approached prewar size by 1948. In that year manpower in building and contracting in Great Britain was 1.45m, fluctuating thereafter to reach 1.8m in 1968, and declining to about 1.6m in 1973. By that time employment in construction amounted to over 7% of the national labour force, of which about 907,000 were employed by private contractors and 242,000 by public authorities. In addition, there were estimated to be 117,000 working proprietors who were self-employed owners, managers and partners, and 367,000 administrative, technical and clerical staff, few of whom worked near sites. With very approximate allowance for statistically elusive self-employed workers, and also certain small categories not covered above, the grand total for the industry was said to amount to some 1.9m,[33] although completely reliable data remained wanting.

Full employment

Transformation from prewar insecurity to postwar security through near-full employment probably represented the largest improvement in operatives' experience since the early nineteenth century. Full employment (shared with most other industries) was sustained more or less continuously after the war by government policy, to the extent of severe and, at times, desperate shortages of some craftsmen. At the same time it was true that unemployment in building was higher than the national average, due partly to the practice of men out of work from other industries registering as building labour, just as they had before the war. Another reason for higher unemployment than in other fields remained the casual and transitory nature of the work, with job opportunities appearing and disappearing as projects started and finished. Labour turnover was particularly high among younger men who were relatively numerous in building, and among the unskilled and those employed by larger firms; one fifth of a 1965 sample of operatives had been employed by their current firm for less than a year.[34] The consequences of full employment, and with it the strengthened bargaining position of labour, amounted to more than lifting of insecurity for wages and general conditions also were improved. Men were spared the need to drive themselves as hard as they once had for fear of losing their jobs, leading to lower productivity which persisted after recovery from wartime disruptions. When output per man increased by 3% or more per year from the late 1950s, improvement was won partly by working longer hours.[35]

Recruitment, training, conditions

Almost all operatives were recruited to the industry direct from school at fifteen or sixteen years of age and educationally were not readily distinguishable from other manual workers. Doubts about their performance were expressed from time to time, perhaps because an unattractive public image of building deterred many of the more able school leavers. Recruits increasingly were trained through apprenticeships and systems of day release to technical colleges, but such training was by no means universal. About half of a sample taken in the 1960s had never begun an apprenticeship, nearly one third had completed one, and the remainder were serving one or had begun but not completed one. About 1963 the length of apprenticeships was reduced from five years to four and shortly afterwards the Construction Industry Training Board began to make levies on firms in order to pass on grants for approved training courses. At about the same time some two-fifths of all operatives worked in smaller firms employing less than fifty, where a relatively high proportion were skilled. Over a third of operatives worked in larger firms employing between that number and 500, and the remainder were in the largest firms each employing over 500.

A decade or more earlier, work on site was depicted[36] in terms which suggested that typical labourers followed the employment patterns of their fathers and led semi-nomadic lives, moving from site to site and town to town. They were said to owe more loyalty to their foremen than their employers and to appreciate working on varied, lightly supervised and outdoor tasks. Later, in a largely unchanged scene, job satisfaction remained reasonably high, probably helped by improved site amenities which softened the effects of bad weather and the rough and ready nature of much of the work. A dark side of site work was the poor safety record, there being at times in the

1960s over 250 fatalities annually and innumerable less serious accidents.

Size of trades

Traditional craft trades gradually assumed a less important position than hitherto, declining relative to new skills (but seldom absolutely) such as those of frame erectors, fixings specialists and plant operators. Greater fluidity between the tasks of skilled and unskilled men became apparent in wartime and old boundaries between the crafts generally became less distinct.[37] By the late 1960s slightly over half of all adult male operatives were craftsmen, one fifth were general labourers and the remainder, roughly equal proportions of foremen and miscellaneous grades.[38] Trades which expanded in the late 1950s and early 1960s, relative to the total labour force, were carpenters and joiners, electricians and, most of all, heating and ventilating engineers. Those which lost strength, but not by much, were bricklayers, plasterers and painters.[39] In 1973, the largest trade group (excluding the self-employed) with 13% of all operatives, was carpenters and joiners, just as it had been before the war. Painters with 9% and bricklayers with 7% followed, and then electricians, plumbers and gas fitters, and plant operators each with over 5%, and finally the other crafts, none of which exceeded 3%.[40]

Wages and hours

The income of operatives began to increase in real terms during the war, a time when wages generally went up by almost half, and earnings even more, while the cost of living rose by 29%. Building craftsmen's rates increased rather less than those of labourers, to begin a narrowing of differentials which continued in peacetime. War conditions also brought improvements other than wages increases in the form of holidays with pay from 1943, and extended notice of dismissal. From 1945 employers guaranteed half-pay for time lost due to bad weather, with a minimum guaranteed payment for the week, later extended to cover stoppages arising from other causes. In 1947, incentive payments for a minority of operatives were formally introduced in the face of some opposition and these, together with other bonus payments and overtime, increased most earnings well above rates agreed in the National Joint Council for the Building Industry. Various payments in addition to basic rates continued to be made widely, especially to younger men and employees of the largest firms, in order to stimulate recruitment and productivity.

Just as actual earnings exceeded basic pay, so actual hours worked usually exceeded the figure agreed nationally between employers and operatives. In 1948 the average weekly earnings (as opposed to wage rates) for a 46.6-hour week were £6-8-4d, almost exactly double that of 1938 when average hours worked were fractionally less. By 1958 averages had reached about £12-1-4d for 48.2 hours.[41] There were some differences between trades, despite theoretical parity, but far more significant were changes in the cost of living. From an index of 100 in 1937, this moved to 170 in 1948, and 265 in 1958. Overtime payments enabled operatives, whose basic rates were several pence per hour less than the average for manufacturing and other industries, to bring up their earnings to the national average. In 1968, when the cost of living index was 357, the basic weekly pay of craftsmen was £16-18-1d for a 40-hour week, made up by overtime and other extras to £22-14-7d, just ahead of labourers' earnings of £20-12-10d. Rising inflation thereafter was such that, after an average annual retail price increase of 3.3% between 1953 and 1969, a figure of 6.4% was recorded in 1970. In 1973, retail prices increased 9.2% and average weekly earnings of adult manual workers in construction were £41-41p, that is eleven new pence less than those in manufacturing industry.[42,43]

Organization

Pay and conditions remained a foremost concern of trades unions which found conditions, early in the period, in their favour. Internal reorganization in wartime took place alongside an increase in membership and greater recognition given by government in exchange for relaxation of rules inhibiting efficiency. Decline followed in the 1950s and 1960s when membership tailed away to about one third of all those in the industry. In the mid-1960s the larger of the twenty unions affiliated to the NFBTO were the woodworkers with 122,000 members, the Amalgamated Union of Building Trade Workers with 80,000, the painters and decorators and the Transport and General Workers each with about 60,000. Other unions with quite large memberships included those of plumbers, general and municipal workers, and plasterers which, with the remainder, brought total membership of affiliated unions to over 400,000, although many unions (for example T & GWU) had other members outside building who were not affiliated.[44] A number of union mergers took place in the 1960s, such as the one between the electricians and plumbers, and there was the emergence of the Union of Construction, Allied Trades and Technicians. Union membership was highest among larger firms and direct labour organizations, but low in comparison with that in manufacturing industry. From an economic standpoint, some restrictive practices hindered innovations in production and wasted resources,[45] but they appear not to have been unduly widespread. Negotiations between employers and operatives did not often degenerate into acrimony nor was there great loss of working days through disputes: the two largest were in 1963 (356,000 working days lost in a week) and in 1972; most strikes were unofficial and negotiating machinery was adequate, if slow moving.

METHODS, MATERIALS AND COMPONENTS

Prices

Building costs, like wage levels, were profoundly affected by the changing value of money, and the added complication of changing standards and quality of building should also be recalled. In general terms materials prices probably increased by about two-thirds between 1938 and 1946, and again by about the same amount between 1946 and 1955. From 1938 to 1955 the nominal price of labour seems not to have risen more than that of materials.[46] From the late 1950s the official index of new construction costs (1970 = 100) went up from 70 in 1958 to 88 in 1968, almost the same increase as that of the retail price index. By 1973 the construction cost index had reached 147, having increased rather more than retail prices.[47] The overall trend, if anything, was for materials prices to rise less quickly than labour, although increases in world commodity prices sometimes operated in the reverse direction in respect of imported materials such as timber. Near the close of the period a typical project was likely to embody labour costs of more than half, and materials costs of less than half, of the total cost.[48]

Responsibility for methods

The relative proportions of cost of labour and materials in a project depended largely on the methods of construction chosen by designers well in advance of the contractors' decisions about organization, programme and equipment. If an architect or engineer decided at the design stage on, say, precast concrete floors, it was unusual for the contractor, once he had been appointed, to propose an alternative, even where it would have suited him to do so. Contractors' freedom regarding building method generally was limited to minor alterations agreed in the light of changing circumstances as the project proceeded. Occasionally contractors decided what methods to use prior to winning a contract, but such a sequence was limited mostly to package deals and industrialized system building.

Progressive methods

Building methods may be imagined to have occupied places along a scale or continuum, with the most traditional methods at one extreme and the most recent innovations at the other. Methods introduced at the progressive end of the continuum may be conceived as having moved gradually towards the traditional end, displacing some of the oldest traditional methods as they did so. Diffusion of new methods among designers and contractors often was erratic and protracted, needing to pass through the four stages of information availability, awareness of those who would implement the idea, consideration by them, and finally adoption. Experience elsewhere suggests that the progress of a successful new method may be likened to an elongated 'S' shaped curve of slow initial take-up, acceleration as acceptance increased, and deceleration as the most resistant minority finally were won over.[49]

At the progressive end of the continuum were innovations encouraged both by rational arguments and by faith in the efficacy of technological and scientific problem solving. Among the promises held out by advocates of change in building were cost savings, higher performance and greater precision. It was argued that these qualities would spring from greater mechanization, specialization and economies of scale, probably involving transfer of more site operations to the factory. There, controlled conditions would avoid delays due to bad weather, and increased productivity would follow the application of mass production methods, allowing site operations to be reduced to rapid assembly of ready-finished components. Had not, it was asked, materials suppliers such as cement and glass makers, as well as non-building industries, already benefited enormously from such changes?

These ideas were not novel when the government took them up in an 'immense but rather heterogeneous effort'[50] to meet wartime scarcity and heavy demand, in part with prefabricated

EFM (emergency factory made) temporary bungalows. About 160,000 were made, largely by the aero-industry attempting to adjust to peacetime conditions, between 1945 when they cost £600 each and 1948 when they cost £1,300. The effort foundered on over-optimism, especially regarding costs, while builders looked on with characteristic scepticism.[51] A related government drive involving less-novel products was the construction of various permanent non-traditional house types, which amounted altogether to 16% of new dwellings between 1945 and 1955. Better known proprietary systems were Airey, Cornish Unit and Wates (pre-cast concrete); Laing Easiform and Wimpey No-Fines (in-situ concrete); and BISF and Unity (steel frame). Most of these systems failed to compete with traditional construction on cost and once official support ceased they were quietly dropped. In the smaller programme of school building the position of progressive methods was better sustained with 'closed' proprietary systems (such as one of aluminium) later giving ground to more 'open' ones devised by public authorities.

Impetus for change in house building methods returned in the 1960s, with renewed doubts whether the traditional industry would be able to meet demand, particularly in respect of skilled labour. Again the government stimulated private interests to take up the challenge of industrialization by developing and adapting numerous systems, some from abroad. Concrete panels were favoured for high-rise flats and, in smaller numbers, timber frames for houses, although many other alternatives were tried. The proportion of public sector housing starts by industrialized methods doubled between 1964 and 1967, when it reached 40% (the same proportion as for schools), and as output climbed so prices fell. But all was to little avail, for deep cuts in high-rise and other building programmes soon returned system house building and its proponents to the doldrums, and subsequent events have cast doubt on many of the products.

Problems of industrialized methods

What circumstances led to the failure or, at most, limited success of industrialized methods, despite heavy investment of money and effort? Certainly the problems were formidable and perhaps most intractable was the familiar one of fluctuations in demand. Heavy capital investment in factory and plant making prefabricated buildings meant high fixed costs and economical operation only when production was near full capacity. For example, one firm having invested £300,000 in a factory in the

1960s needed a yearly output of 2,500 dwellings to make their enterprise worthwhile. Manufacturers required large sustained markets in order to justify investment, and when government assurances proved ill-founded (as they did), plants lost money and were closed. Other problems included the co-ordination of large numbers of small contracts; the limit placed on markets by heavy transport costs; high overheads of factory work compared with site work, giving severe cost competition from traditional methods; and a mixed response from design professions regarding the quality of finished products, amply vindicated by events at Ronan Point. In addition, there were difficulties in standardizing products in order to secure long unbroken production runs, due to the early variety of controls on building and lack of dimensional co-ordination, both of which eventually received official attention.

Underlying many of these problems was a lack of unity of decision by sponsors, designers and producers in agreeing the aims and nature of fundamental changes in methods and products. Where agreement appeared to exist it often dissolved before long, a victim of changing demand for building. In all, industrialized methods were only resorted to when demand was high; they were dropped when demand fell, thereby discriminating against progressive ideas. Only the caravan and mobile home makers (outside our scope) were able to provide some sort of accommodation from the factory, at a price people were prepared to pay, and cope successfully with fluctuations in demand.

Traditional methods

From the problems associated with progressive methods we move to the opposite pole, to consider traditional methods. Here, among that which was well-tried, were small changes due indirectly to the efforts of progressives. Innovations, though not always themselves lastingly successful, helped to put traditional methods in new perspective, giving a basis of comparison and creating a pool of new ideas which could be applied in traditional contexts. For example, the traditional part of the industry was quick to extend greatly the use of plant on site so that heavy machines replaced initially scarce, and later expensive, labour for earth moving, materials handling and concreting. Tractor-diggers, hoists, cranes, and concrete mixers became commonplace, and increasingly hired from specialists rather than bought outright. As the value of speeding work without increasing labour became better appreciated, so light equipment such as tubular scaffolding, formwork and power tools became more plentiful. Investment in plant increased although fixed capital able to be employed per worker remained much lower than the level in manufacturing industry.[52] Increased mechanization and use of small prefabricated components in traditional building, without fundamentally altering finished products, compounded the influence of full employment and higher wages in drawing attention to site management. Flexibility regarding delays and disorganization diminished from that in earlier labour-intensive times and the cost of easy-going inefficiency increased as rapidly as tolerance of it lessened. In these ways new ideas and approaches were absorbed piecemeal into traditional practice, with the result that building methods, with their complicated interrelations, remained far more the subject of gradual evolution than of revolution.

Materials: composite goods

Space permits only a brief survey of materials and components used in building, and scope for generalization is limited by the growing number of goods made of diverse combinations of different materials. The picture also was complicated by the very great variety of goods available and the apparently accelerating rate at which they were altered or replaced. At the same time traditional materials such as brick, timber and cement were still used in enormous quantities in similar forms to those of the past. Instances of composite goods were the appearance on site of cement, not in bags for mixing on the spot but in, say, factory cast, pre-finished concrete units containing steel reinforcement, fixings and perhaps a sandwich of plastic foam insulation and some pipe ducts; some timber was delivered, not rough sawn, but precisely dimensioned and factory assembled into roof trusses complete with metal connectors; again, some prefabricated partitions were made of combinations of steel-faced plywood or plastic-faced particle board framed in metal; these examples could be multiplied to include systems of walling, windows, ceilings, roof deckings and so on. A result of diverse materials used in different combinations was that competition intensified between firms making dissimilar products for like purposes. To take one illustration from many possible examples, the makers of precast concrete claddings competed against makers of asbestos-cement sheets and metal claddings.

Cement products

In a short review of developments on a material-by-material basis, leaving aside composite goods, one of the major examples was concrete. In its various forms this was the material which moved most conspicuously to the centre of accepted practice. Cement-based products increased in number and variety, just as cement production became concentrated in fewer but larger firms. Concrete was used in place of clay, when blocks and in-situ or precast units were substituted for brick; in place of timber, when concrete floor slabs were substituted for timber joists and boards; and in place of steel, when reinforced concrete frames were substituted for rolled steel members. Developments, most of them assisted by wartime steel scarcity, included improved precasting techniques, pre-stressing and ready-mixed deliveries. Cement production, not too badly affected by war, increased and price changes relative to many other materials were favourable. Post, pile, beam, block, screed and slab, cement products all; little wonder the demand for concrete increased, whether for goods which were poured, craned or shovelled into place.

Bricks and timber

Brick usage was less buoyant than that of concrete, with production much reduced in war, and common bricks, in particular, losing markets in competition with other materials. Fletton brick production was helped by relatively low price rises and facing bricks retained an important place, especially in house building. Brickmaking became concentrated mainly in the hands of large firms of which London Brick in 1973 produced about 43% of British output. Timber supplies also were profoundly affected by war since imports were curtailed drastically and stocks used very frugally indeed, both then and in the early years of peace. More economical use of the material followed technical advance in structural applications based on stress-grading and new methods of jointing. Similarly, a more and more widely used cost-saving substitute for solid timber was sheet material of reconstituted and composite type such as blockboard and chipboard.

Metals and plastics

Use of steelwork for building, although widespread for structural purposes, was hindered by periods of shortage (this sometimes also applied to brick) and price rises in excess of those of the rival concrete. Innovations appeared in the form of welded joints and light structural frames of hollow sections and lattices, as used in school building. Aluminium showed great postwar promise which was not entirely fulfilled when later price rises operated against it. Structural applications of the metal fell away in favour of such uses as claddings, window frames, roof coverings and trims. No doubt the use of metals generally widened, but also there were losses as, for example, in the cases of galvanized sheeting displaced by asbestos cement, and cast iron displaced by plastics for rainwater and other goods. Plastics appeared in a variety of new and developed forms and soon claimed a substantial market in such varied applications as floor finishes, damp-proof membranes, plumbing goods, laminated surface finishes, thermal insulation, rooflights, door furniture and inflatable temporary buildings.

Miscellaneous other goods

Familiar goods, now produced by monopolies, which continued to hold their own were plasterboard which progressed relative to traditional plastering, and glass, use of which was augmented by architectural fashion. Other traditional goods included quarry tiles and glazed tiles; clay and stoneware goods; concrete roof tiles, now dominating their competitors; and asphalt and bituminous felt, used on increasing numbers of flat roofs. The field of services remained one of rapid change with metal, asbestos-cement and pitch fibre pipes and fittings in addition to plastic. Electric, gas and oil heat sources largely superseded solid fuel, being used to power a variety of radiant, convected, underfloor, waterborne and ducted air systems. The development of such systems began to move space and water heating from the realm of hit-or-miss empiricism to that of technology and engineering, and a similar change began also in the fields of lighting and ventilation for large buildings. In the extreme cases of laboratories, air-conditioned offices and hospitals, services installations became very extensive and complicated, so that costs amounted at times to well over half of the total costs of construction.

Change in building methods

Such buildings, with their characteristically complex structures and construction, make an appropriate point at which to stop and reflect on the extent of changes which had occurred in building methods since the early nineteenth century. So diverse had the range of skills and products of the building industry become, that those who wished to point to a technological and organizational revolution over the century-and-a-half might well find evidence to do so. Yet so large and diffuse was the industry, so gradually evolving in respect of that which was typical rather than exceptional, that those who wished to point instead to a picture of continuity and comparative changelessness also might well do so, perhaps with greater conviction.

9

Epilogue

'... the whole "new frontiers" show is over, and deep down we know it.'
(Christopher Booker, Spectator, *21 July 1979)*

BUILDING ACTIVITY AFTER 1973

Change wrought in 1973

It remains only to complete the narrative of events of more than a century-and-a-half by bringing it up to date, and to draw attention to some general themes which have emerged. In several respects 1973 has the appearance of a turning point which marked the beginning of a change of attitudes and activity in building. As with many watersheds, hindsight makes it possible to see that there were earlier signs of impending change. Nevertheless, it was not until 1973 that a crisis in oil supply, repercussing throughout the economy, had the effect of calling into question much about building activity which previously had been accepted without thought. Henceforward different ideas and expectations began to emerge respecting the prospects and desirability of economic growth. Pessimism began to replace optimism as inflation replaced relative stability; building demand retreated as energy costs, and all that they implied, escalated; the modern environment was viewed with increasing disfavour and retention of that which was old was regarded as more desirable. The future appeared to hold the prospect of only low building activity, with a sufficiency rather than a scarcity of stock, and demand depressed by weakness in the national economy.

Building stock

Among diminishing numbers of sponsors prepared to commit themselves in an uncertain climate were private interests in retailing and warehousing, and housing associations straddling the old division between public and private sectors. Private developers in speculative markets, on the other hand, withdrew as demand fell back and the cost of borrowing went up. Similarly, with a weak national economy, there was little enough to spend on new public or social building by public authorities. Public opinion, soured by the 1960s excesses of local authority tower blocks and developers' insensitive maltreatment of town centres, favoured small unobtrusive buildings and rehabilitation. Where large buildings were needed, bulk sometimes began to be disguised and concealed rather than celebrated, and overtly modern external appearances sometimes gave way to the 'neo-vernacular' revival of earlier commonplace forms.

Building industry

Not surprisingly, the building industry was depressed, although output remained high by the standards of the nineteenth century, and the hardships of those times, of course, were nowhere to be found. The problems were those of low demand relative to capacity, and of inflation (building costs doubled between 1973 and 1978). Many firms found survival difficult and people left the industry in search of employment which was less dependent on economic growth. Among the professions some relief, at least, was to be had from work on projects in the Middle East, where economic conditions were the obverse of those at home. A ray of light was the progress, perhaps only temporary, in making government more aware of the damage to the industry caused by cuts in capital expenditure. However, this was of little help to those who wrestled with what was regarded more and more as a stiflingly bureaucratic system of planning and building control. Such circumstances were unpropitious for technical innovations, which did not make much obvious headway. Yet even amid depression and uncertainty there were shortages of certain craftsmen, maybe an augury of renewed attempts at prefabrication, when circumstances change once more.

GENERAL THEMES: BUILDING STOCK

Aim

With the completion of the historical narrative, some general themes which have emerged during its course are noted. The pitfalls associated with doing so are numerous and well known; the aim here is not to attempt comprehensive conclusions, but rather to identify some general features relevant to the period as a whole, beginning with descriptive points about the physical form of the building stock.

Evolution of stock

The long-term development of the building stock may be regarded from the viewpoint of evolution, in which buildings of the present day are seen to have evolved from 'lower' and earlier forms. A process of selection took place continually among the stock, as a main but not exclusive means of modification. Evolution depended firstly on variations being introduced among buildings of nominally similar function. Secondly, it depended on differential survival, or the early elimination of disadvantageous variations and perpetuation of variations which conferred advantage. The vast majority of variations may have been harmful and therefore doomed to early disappearance; it may be said that the building industry proposed and society disposed. Unlike the pattern of biological evolution, fundamentally novel variations might be introduced at once in their entirety (although in practice very seldom were) as well as accumulating over long periods from series of small variations.

Capacity for survival

The capacity of building forms for survival appears to have been related to the flow of value which they produced to the benefit of the sponsor, occupier and community. In general terms the flow of value was derived from three qualities: exchange, meaning that the building might be transferred for something else; utility, or usefulness; and merit, or the power to satisfy. Concepts of value differed, but it was always the case that some buildings were perceived as more useful, better and valuable than others; they worked, met needs, were sought after, priced and prized. An illustration of the effects of selection at work comes from the housing stock in 1972.[1] Different parts of the stock dating from different periods, may be characterized broadly as yielding different amounts and types of value. The 0.4% of stock which survived from before 1800 was highly valued since only meritorious examples had been retained; the 3.5% of stock which survived from the first half of the nineteenth century was mixed, one part being valued for merit, but another part being lowly valued and facing imminent destruction due to obsolescence; most of the 31% of stock built between 1851 and 1918 was of low value in respect of utility (merit went largely unrecognized), being obsolescent and subject to attrition; the 24% of stock built between the wars was beginning to be regarded in a similar way, but still remained highly valued; and the 41% of stock built since 1945, possessing both utility and merit, was certainly highly valued.

Evolutionary change in entire stock

Examples of evolutionary change in the stock since 1815 tentatively may be set down, the foremost being growth. The *number of buildings* and *total floor area* show an immense increase in absolute terms, and almost certainly in relation to population. Individual buildings too, show a related evolutionary trend, having progressively larger *average sizes*. A third change is in the physical (and financial) resources which were absorbed by *services* in individual buildings, increasing from a small to a large proportion of the total, to give ever higher performance.

Evolutionary change in parts of stock

Other evolutionary changes, of which six examples are given below, appear to have affected only limited parts of the stock. First is change of *location*, with early clustering of stock in towns succeeded by less dense growth around their edges. Associated with this change is one in the relative size of regional stocks. Second is change of building *lifespan*, which must have increased among lowest quality buildings, crude hovels being replaced by superior construction, and perhaps decreased among high quality buildings. The pattern appears to be one of convergence from both extremes, as in the case of the third evolutionary change. This is the extent of *regional and local differences* between buildings intended for similar purposes. Regional differences diminished and nationally occurring patterns appeared more and more, even among cheap simple buildings which were slower to change in this respect than more costly examples. The fourth evolutionary change is *differentiation* between buildings according to intended function and purpose. There was proliferation among Victorian industrial, commercial and social buildings, for example new forms of railway station, hotel, town hall and school. In the twentieth century the list was extended by new forms of factory, garage, office, hospital and so on. Recently other new types have appeared, but it may be the case that the growing provision of universal space checked the trend, at least in part. New functions developed, such as hypermarkets, sports halls and automated warehouses, but often the resulting forms were fairly similar to one another.

The fifth evolutionary change concerns the range and distribution of building *quality* as expressed in cost and performance. The broad trend was upward, being readily visible in the cases of schools and low cost housing. At the same time there appears to have been convergence between extremes of quality, exemplified by extinction of new hovels and major country houses. In the last seventy years or so, and perhaps longer, the amplitude between upper and lower quality buildings in respect of unit costs appears to have been fairly steady, with high quality buildings between four and five times more costly than low. Within this range high quality commercial examples remained near the top, high quality houses fell and welfare buildings climbed, while low cost housing remained consistently near the bottom, above cheap industrial buildings.[2]

The sixth and final evolutionary change mentioned here is that of *materials content* of buildings where, again, there was convergence. Low quality examples increased in bulk, range and complexity, while higher quality buildings were reduced in bulk and had some redundant materials eliminated.

GENERAL THEMES: BUILDING INDUSTRY

Responses of industry: productive capacity

How did the building professions and industry respond to changing demand from society? A commonly held view of the industry is that it was backward and an exception to many of the general rules applicable to other industries. The view here is that continuity and recurring cycles were prominent, often conveying a sense of repetition, but that some noteworthy changes also took place. Five of them are noted below, the first of which is one of degree rather than nature, being the increase in *productive capacity*, both absolutely and per person in the industry. Output, we have seen, proceeded in a cyclic pattern about a rising trend, while most productivity increase occurred late in the period.

Division of the parts

The second response of the industry is connected with its subdivision into different *specialisms* and firms. One specialism after another emerged from the industry to become distinct in its own right; division between designers and constructors clarified early on, sub-contractors multiplied, and materials suppliers became differentiated from site operations. At the same time, some hitherto separate responsibilities were united: general contractors supplanted single trade master craftsmen; combined design and build organizations latterly gained ground;

and speculative provision of building shells sometimes was united with custom provision of interiors. In all, a tension is evident between fragmentive pressures for further division giving advantages of specialization, and integrative pressures for unity between the parts, in order to improve control.

A different aspect of subdivision was an increase in the *size* of the largest business units of general contractors, sub-contractors, and professions. Alongside this, the conditions which favoured small firms and practices operating in their own markets persisted quite strongly. This left medium-sized units in the most vulnerable position, maybe heralding a new division within the hierarchy of size.

Another aspect of subdivision was the decline of *self-build* in the nineteenth century, under the twin effects of economic growth and by-laws, and its eventual return in the guise of modern do-it-yourself. In a sense, as the carpet of increased specialization in the industry was unrolled before us by the foot, so do-it-yourself activity began to roll it up behind us by the yard.

External relations

Other responses of the industry to changing demand were connected with its external relations, firstly with *sponsors*. The picture was of progressively larger and more experienced sponsors, with fewer individual and more corporate examples. This probably attenuated the decision to build, prolonged relations with the building professions, and influenced built form. Many large sponsors with continuous building programmes became more integrated with the industry by permanently employing their own specialist building advisers. By doing so, they effectively extended the influence of the building industry back into sponsor organizations. The external relations of building professions and industry also changed with respect to society at large. Here the industry was brought progressively into more formal positions, regulated by legal *controls*. Building and planning legislation and codification, intended to protect the public, increasingly circumscribed the decisions and activities of those who provided buildings.

Technical change

The final response of the industry considered here is that of technical change among building products and processes. Here the pace was only moderate, with relatively low levels of capital investment. Technical innovations typically involved only parts of buildings, and a recurrent cycle of official attempts at more sweeping change was not conspicuously successful. Innovations, even where effective, long co-existed alongside orthodoxies, suggesting the inevitability of gradualness.

SOCIETY AND BUILDING ACTIVITY

Building activity as reflection of society

The relationship between building activity on the one hand, and the society which gave rise to it on the other, forms a fitting topic with which to conclude. That building activity reflected many aspects of a changing society seems beyond dispute, although a question which remains is the extent to which the reflection was an accurate one. Does building activity provide us with a distorting mirror or a true one, albeit of limited extent, through which to regard society past and present? Views about this may be clarified by drawing attention to some very general phenomena in society which appear to have been reflected strongly in building activity. The reflections were connected both with quantities of activity at different times, and with its innumerable qualities, respecting what was built and how. Relationships are apparent between the phenomena which follow, and the general themes about stock and industry set out above. However, direct attribution of causes to effects should be made only with caution, in view of the nature and complexity of the subject.

Demographic influences

Eight phenomena will be mentioned, but the list is far from exhaustive and neither is significance intended in the order in which they appear. The first two are primarily demographic in nature, being *population size and number of families* and *migration*, at times all acting as powerful stimulants to the volume of building activity.

Political and social influences

The next three phenomena are political and social in nature. The first is the *effect of war* as a catalyst of social and technical change. Impact on building activity was to be seen in the appearance of new, centrally controlled and redirected sponsors in new fields, and also in technical development in materials and methods. The second is the gradual *redistribution of wealth* which was associated with changing relative proportions of highest and lowest quality buildings in the stock. The third is the growth of *state responsibility for welfare* of the population, associated with increased public sector sponsorship and official direction of activity.

Economic influences

The final group of three phenomena is primarily economic in nature. The first is the *division of labour*, involving the splitting of tasks into component parts for execution by specialists. This may be seen, as it were, crystallized in the increased differentiation of building types by function. In a different manifestation, it could be seen in increased specialization within building professions and industry. The second is the *growth of the economic system* from local to national scales and beyond. The death of local near-self-sufficiency was associated with the decline of local characteristics in buildings and also with the rise of large firms. The third and final economic phenomenon and one which we cannot fail to observe, is *economic growth* in several aspects. Sustained and reasonably fast increase in income per person greatly increased the volume of building activity in comparison with that in times of depression and the pre-industrial period when growth was slow. Also growth made possible a rising trend in average building quality, for a rich society may afford numerous high quality buildings, but a poor society may not. Further, economic growth is associated with rapid change frequently accompanied by the breaking down of boundaries, overthrow of rules and convergence of practices hitherto separate. Various relationships, such as those between private and public sectors, within the industry, and between industry and sponsor, all reflected this. More tangibly, so did buildings having universal interior space and provision for flexibility in use. Lastly, in addition to stimulating activity and challenging accepted practices, economic growth posed something of a threat to building activity. It did so by creating rival outlets for spending, so that as early as 1914 there were complaints that money was spent on cars instead of house decoration and maintenance. From interwar years onwards building was challenged increasingly by expenditure on new ways in which to obtain more comfort and pleasure.

Building competes with other spending

Competition between building and non-building outlets for spending seems seldom to have been explicit or obvious. In part, competition was disguised by the fact that spending on building was sustained by larger price rises than those which applied in other fields. Substitutes for new buildings were few, where they existed at all, so sponsors were forced to pay progressively larger real sums for similar buildings. On the other hand, spending in non-building fields benefited from lower, or only slow-rising, prices. From this, and the increasing range of non-building goods and services, building as an outlet for spending probably appeared to offer declining value for money. As building looked relatively less attractive it would have lost ground qualitatively, if not in terms of actual expenditure. Wealth spent instead on vehicles and mobility was wealth unavailable, for the most part, for building; convenience foodstuffs and drink, kitchen and electrical equipment, and other consumer durables, vied with building as means of display and of demonstrating conspicuous expenditure. Consequently it was possible that surplus funds were less likely than in the past to be invested in order to derive pleasure and meaning from architecture. Instead they were used to derive pleasure and meaning from movement, material convenience and stimulus. If this were so, the public face of new architecture (as distinct from private interiors) was in decline as a source of satisfaction. Buildings perhaps were losing symbolic significance and any tendency towards being ends in themselves and becoming, more than ever, only means to other ends.

Appendix:

Some General Economic and Demographic Trends

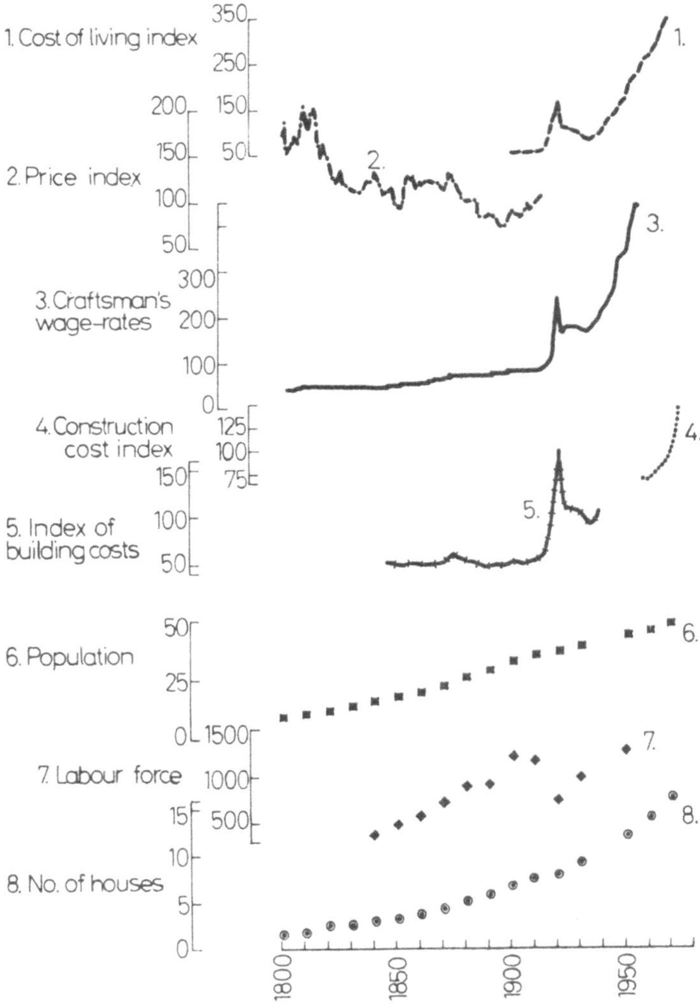

EXPLANATORY NOTES AND SOURCES

1. Cost of living index. UK, 1900–1968 (1930 = 100). From: Halsey, A. H. *Trends in British Society Since 1900*. Macmillan, 1972, p. 122.

2. Price index. Rousseaux, 1800–1913 (average of 1865 & 1885 = 100). From: Mitchell, B. R. & Deane, P. *Abstract of British Historical Statistics*. Cambridge University Press, 1962. p. 471–473.

3. Craftsman's wage-rates, 1802–1954 (pence per day). From: Brown, E. H. P. & Hopkins, S. V. 'Seven Centuries of Building Wages.' *Economica* New Series, Vol. XXII, No. 87, 1955.

4. Construction cost index. New construction, 1958–1973 (1970 = 100). From: Department of the Environment *Housing and Construction Statistics*. HMSO, various dates.

5. Index of building costs. 1845–1938 (1930 = 100). From: Maiwald, K. 'An Index of Building Costs in the United Kingdom, 1845–1938.' *Economic History Review* 2nd Series, Vol. VII, No. 2, 1954.

6. Population. England & Wales, 1801–1971 (millions). From: Mitchell, B. R. & Deane, P. op cit. p. 6; Central Statistical Office *Annual Abstract of Statistics 1973*. HMSO.

7. Labour force. Building and construction, Gt. Britain, 1841–1951 (thousands). From: Mitchell, B. R. & Deane, P. op cit. p. 60–61.

8. Number of houses. At census, England & Wales, 1801–1971 (millions). From: Robinson, H. W. *Economics of Building*. King, 1939. p. 109; Mitchell, B. R. & Deane, P. op cit. p. 239; *Census Report*. HMSO, various dates.

Notes

1 BUILDINGS IN COKETOWN: 1815–50

[1]Dyos, H. J. & Wolff, M. *The Victorian City: Images and Realities.* Routledge & Kegan Paul, 1973. Contains Olsen, D. J.
[2]Cleary, E. J. *The Building Society Movement.* Elek, 1965. p. 44.
[3]Price, S. J. *Building Societies. Their Origin and History.* Franey 1959.
[4]Mitchell, B. R. & Deane, P. *Abstract of British Historical Statistics.* Cambridge University Press, 1962. p. 20, 24, 26.
[5]Burnett, J. *A Social History of Housing 1815–1970.* David & Charles, 1978; Methuen, 1980. p. 14.
[6]Harvey, N. *A History of Farm Buildings in England and Wales.* David & Charles, 1970. p. 66 et seq.
[7]Chapman, S. D. 'The Transition to the Factory System in the Midlands Cotton-Spinning Industry.' *Economic History Review* 2nd series, Vol. 18, No. 3, 1965.
[8]Chalklin, C. W. *The Provincial Towns of Georgian England. A Study of the Building Process 1740–1820.* Arnold, 1974. p. 311.
[9]Brunskill, R. W. *Illustrated Handbook of Vernacular Architecture.* Faber, 1971. p. 27.
[10]Flinn, M. W. (ed.) *Report on the Sanitary Condition of the Labouring Population of Gt. Britain by Edwin Chadwick 1842.* Edinburgh University Press, 1965. p. 83.
[11]Aspin, C. *Lancashire. The First Industrial Society.* Helmshore Local History Society, 1969. p. 94–95.
[12]Mitchell, B. R. & Deane, P. op cit. p. 20, 24, 26.
[13]Deane, P. & Cole, W. A. *British Economic Growth 1688–1959.* Cambridge University Press, 1967. p. 271.
[14]e.g. Carus-Wilson, E. M. *Essays in Economic History.* Vol. 3. Arnold, 1966. Contains Shannon, H. A.
[15]Lewis, J. P. *Building Cycles and Britain's Growth.* Macmillan, 1965. p. 192.

[16]Carus-Wilson, E. M. op cit. Contains Cairncross, A. K. & Weber, B.

[17]Chapman, S. D. *The History of Working-Class Housing. A Symposium*. David & Charles, 1971. Contains Treble, J. H.

[18]Aspin, C. op cit. p. 93.

[19]Olsen, D. J. *The Growth of Victorian London*. Batsford, 1976. p. 191.

[20]Chapman, S. D. (1971) op cit. p. 228.

[21]Burnett, J. op cit. p. 51.

[22]Pollard, S. *A History of Labour in Sheffield*. Liverpool University Press, 1959. p. 18–20.

[23]Rubinstein, D. *Victorian Homes*. David & Charles, 1974. p. 260–262.

[24]Smith, L. D. W. 'Textile Factory Settlements in the Early Industrial Revolution.' Unpubl. PhD Thesis, University of Aston in Birmingham, 1976. p. 137–138, 140.

[25]Hitchcock, H.-R. *Early Victorian Architecture in Britain*. Vol. 2. Trewin Copplestone, 1972. XIII, 17, 18, 22.

[26]Flinn, M. W. op cit. p. 5.

[27]Deane, P. & Cole, W. A. op cit. p. 213.

[28]Tann, J. *The Development of the Factory*. Cornmarket, 1970. p. 147.

[29]Mathias, P. *The First Industrial Nation*. Methuen, 1972. p. 283.

[30]Maggs, C. *The Bristol and Gloucester Railway*. Oakwood, 1969. p. 16.

[31]*The Builder*. 29 July 1843.

[32]Howell, P. *Victorian Churches*. Country Life, 1968.

[33]Hughes, A. M. D. *Cobbett Selections*. Oxford University Press, 1923. p. 110.

[34]Hitchcock, H.-R. op cit. Vol. 1. p. 97 et seq.

[35]Seaborne, M. *The English School. Its Architecture and Organization 1370–1870*. Routledge & Kegan Paul, 1971. p. 131 et seq.

[36]Ibid. p. 140.

[37]Nicholson, P. *New Practical Builder and Workman's Companion* . . . Kelly, 1823. p. 576 et seq.

[38]Dixon, R. & Muthesius, S. *Victorian Architecture*. Thames & Hudson, 1978. p. 110.

[39]Engels, F. *The Condition of the Working Class in England*. Panther, 1969. p. 91.

[40]Kellett, J. R. *The Impact of Railways on Victorian Cities*. Routledge & Kegan Paul, 1969. p. 7.

[41]Sheppard, F. *London 1808–1870: The Infernal Wen*. Secker & Warburg, 1971. p. 134.
[42]Mumford, L. *The City in History*. Secker & Warburg, 1961. p. 449.
[43]Girouard, M. *The Victorian Country House*. Clarendon, 1971. p. 19–20.
[44]Pevsner, N. *A History of Building Types*. Thames & Hudson, 1976. p. 289.
[45]Hitchcock, H.-R. op cit. Vol. 1. p. 431.
[46]Herbert, G. *Pioneers of Prefabrication. The British Contribution in the Nineteenth Century*. John Hopkins University Press, 1978.

2 MASTERBUILDERS AND JERRYBUILDERS: 1815–50

[1]Aston, M. A. *Stonesfield Slate*. Oxfordshire County Council, Dept. of Museum Services, 1974. p. 32.
[2]Clapham, J. H. *An Economic History of Modern Britain. The Early Railway Age 1820–1850*. Cambridge University Press, 1950. p. 72.
[3]Mitchell, B. R. & Deane, P. op cit. p. 60.
[4]Elsam, R. *The Practical Builder's Perpetual Price Book* . . . Kelly, 1826. p. vii.
[5]Cooney, E. W. 'The Origins of the Victorian Master Builders.' *Economic History Review* 2nd series, Vol. 8, No. 2, 1955–1956.
[6]Port, M. H. 'The Office of Works and Building Contracts in Early Nineteenth Century England.' *Economic History Review* 2nd series, Vol. 20, No. 1, 1967.
[7]Bowyer, J. *History of Building*. Crosby Lockwood Staples, 1973. p. 240.
[8]Nisbet, J. 'Quantity Surveying in London during the Nineteenth Century.' *J. of the Royal Institution of Chartered Surveyors* Vol. 31, 1951–1952.
[9]Thompson, F. M. L. *Chartered Surveyors. The Growth of a Profession*. Routledge & Kegan Paul, 1968. p. 88–91.
[10]Sigsworth, E. M. *Black Dyke Mills. A History*. Liverpool University Press, 1958. p. 169–171.
[11]Sheppard, F. op cit. p. 101.
[12]Olsen, D. J. op cit. p. 265–266.
[13]Hobhouse, H. *Thomas Cubitt, Master Builder*. Macmillan, 1971.
[14]Coleman, T. *The Railway Navvies*. Penguin, 1968.
[15]Brown, E. H. P. & Hopkins, S. V. 'Seven Centuries of Building Wages.' *Economica* New Series, Vol. XXII, No. 87, 1955.
[16]Elsam, R. op cit. from which numerous prices have been taken.

[17]Postgate, R. W. *The Builders' History*. Nat. Fed. of Building Trade Operatives, 1923. Appendix I.
[18]Hobsbawm, E. J. *Labouring Men. Studies in the History of Labour.* Weidenfeld & Nicolson, 1964. p. 81.
[19]Burnett, J. (ed.) *Useful Toil.* Penguin, 1977. p. 267.
[20]Ibid. p. 274–275, 312 et seq.
[21]Thompson, E. P. *The Making of the English Working Class.* Penguin, 1968. p. 285–286.
[22]Brockman, H. A. N. *The British Architect in Industry 1841–1940.* Allen & Unwin, 1974. p. 21.
[23]Crook, J. M. & Port, M. H. *The History of the King's Works.* Vol. VI. HMSO, 1973. p. 129.
[24]Hilton, W. S. *Foes to Tyranny. A History of the Amalgamated Union of Building Trade Workers.* AUBTW, 1963. p. 34–49, 74–85.
[25]Postgate, R. W. op cit. p. 26 et seq.
[26]Gayer, A. D., Rostow, W. W. & Schwarz, A. J. *The Growth and Fluctuations of the British Economy 1790–1850.* Oxford University Press, 1953. p. 417.
[27]Chalklin, C. W. op cit. p. 192–193.
[28]Bowley, M. *Innovations in Building Materials.* Duckworth, 1960. p. 62. et seq. Upon which this section relies extensively.
[29]Clifton-Taylor, A. *The Pattern of English Building.* Batsford, 1962.
[30]Mitchell, B. R. & Deane, P. op cit. p. 291.
[31]Potter, J. 'British Timber Duties 1815–60.' *Economica* Vol. 22, 1955.
[32]Davey, N. *A History of Building Materials.* Phoenix, 1961. p. 98 et seq.
[33]Hudson, K. *Building Materials.* Longman, 1972. p. 49.
[34]Smeaton, A. C. *The Builder's Pocket Manual . . .* Taylor, 1835. p. 122.
[35]Sheppard, R. *Cast Iron in Building.* Allen & Unwin, 1945.

3 BUILDINGS UPWARD AND OUTWARD: 1851–1914

[1]Daunton, M. J. *Coal Metropolis, Cardiff 1870–1914.* Leicester University Press, 1977. p. 75–118.
[2]Jenkins, S. *Landlords to London. The Story of a Capital and its Growth.* Constable, 1975. p. 99.
[3]Bell, C. & Bell, R. *City Fathers.* Penguin, 1972. p. 262.
[4]Dyos, H. J. 'The Speculative Builders and Developers of Victorian London.' *Victorian Studies* Vol. XI, Summer 1968, Supplement.

[5]Cleary, E. J. op cit. p. 45–152.
[6]Marriott, O. *The Property Boom*. Hamilton, 1967. p. 19.
[7]Mitchell, B. R. & Deane, P. op cit. p. 19 et seq.
[8]Ashworth, W. *The Genesis of Modern British Town Planning*. Routledge & Kegan Paul, 1972. p. 8 quotes Local Government Board *Statistical Memoranda and Charts Relating to Public Health and Social Conditions*. B.P.P. 1909, CIII.
[9]Mitchell, B. R. & Deane, P. op cit. p. 6.
[10]Glynn, S. & Oxborrow, J. *Interwar Britain. A Social and Economic History*. Allen & Unwin, 1976. p. 16 quotes Feinstein, C. H. *National Income, Expenditure and Output of the United Kingdom 1855–1965*. Cambridge University Press, 1972.
[11]Deane, P. & Cole, W. A. op cit. p. 274.
[12]Cooney, E. W. 'Long Waves in Building in the British Economy of the Nineteenth Century.' *Economic History Review* 2nd series, Vol. 13, No. 2, 1960–1961.
[13]Mackay, D. I. 'Growth and Fluctuations in the British Building Industry.' *Scottish J. of Political Economy* Vol. 14, 1967.
[14]Aldcroft, D. H. & Richardson, H. W. *The British Economy 1870–1939*. Macmillan, 1969. p. 45.
[15]Lewis, J. P. op cit. p. 301 et seq.
[16]Saul, S. B. 'House Building in England 1890–1914.' *Economic History Review* 2nd series, Vol. 15, No. 1, 1962.
[17]e.g. Kenwood, A. G. 'Residential Building Activity in North Eastern England, 1853–1913.' *Manchester School of Economic and Social Studies* Vol. XXXI, 1963.
[18]Cairncross, A. K. *Home and Foreign Investment 1870–1913*. Cambridge University Press, 1953. p. 110.
[19]Glynn, S. & Oxborrow, J. op cit. p. 227.
[20]Lowe, J. B. *Welsh Industrial Workers Housing 1775–1875*. National Museum of Wales, 1977.
[21]Tarn, J. *Five Per Cent Philanthropy. An Account of Housing in Urban Areas between 1840 and 1914*. Cambridge University Press, 1973. p. 43 et seq.
[22]Chapman, S. D. 1971. op cit. Contains Wohl, A. S.
[23]Sutcliffe, A. (ed.) *Multi-Storey Living*. Croom Helm, 1974. Contains Taylor, I. C.
[24]Gauldie, E. *Cruel Habitations*. Allen & Unwin, 1974. p. 172.
[25]Hole, J. *The Homes of the Working Classes with Suggestions for their Improvement*. Longmans Green, 1866. p. 71.
[26]Webb, C. A. *Valuation of Real Property*. Crosby Lockwood, 1913. p. 42 et seq.

[27]Rubinstein, D. op cit. p. 203.
[28]Wohl, A. S. *The Eternal Slum. Housing and Social Policy in Victorian London*. Arnold, 1977. p. 294.
[29]Birch, J. *Examples of Labourers' Cottages &c*. Blackwood, 1892.
[30]Weaver, L. *The 'Country Life' Book of Cottages Costing from £150 to £600*. Country Life, 1913. p. 38–46.
[31]Osborne, W. H. 'England's First Rural Council Houses.' *Country Life* May 20 1976.
[32]Girouard, M. op cit. p. 5–6.
[33]Rubinstein, D. op cit. p. 50–52.
[34]Service, A. *Edwardian Architecture. A Handbook to Building Design in Britain 1890–1914*. Thames & Hudson, 1977. p. 128 et seq.
[35]Winter, J. *Industrial Architecture. A Survey of Factory Building*. Studio Vista, 1970.
[36]*The Architect*, *Architect* & *Building News*, *The Builder* & *Building News* & *Engineering J*. Upon which this and certain other sections rely extensively.
[37]Jeffreys, J. B. *Retail Trading in Britain 1850--1950*. Cambridge University Press, 1954. p. 19–22.
[38]Glasstone, V. *Victorian and Edwardian Theatres. An Architectural and Social Survey*. Thames & Hudson, 1975. p. 48.
[39]Sachs, E. O. & Woodrow, E. A. E. *Modern Opera Houses and Theatres*. Blom, 1968. Vol. I p. 37–46, Vol. II p. 35–45.
[40]Briggs, A. *Victorian Cities*. Penguin, 1971.
[41]Bell, Lady *At the Works*. David & Charles, 1969. p. 8.
[42]Deane, P. & Cole, W. A. op cit. p. 266.
[43]Pinker, R. *English Hospital Statistics 1861--1938*. Heinemann, 1966. p. 56.
[44]Seaborne, M. op cit. p. 215.
[45]Robson, E. R. *School Architecture*. Leicester University Press. 1972. p. 2, 291–350.
[46]Robins, E. C. *Technical School and College Building*. Whittaker, 1887. p. 75 & Appendix.
[47]Clarke, B. F. L. *Church Builders of the Nineteenth Century*. SPCK, 1938. p. 223.
[48]Micklethwaite, J. T. *Modern Parish Churches*. King, 1874. p. 339.
[49]Ashburner, E. H. *Modern Public Libraries. Their Planning and Design*. Grafton, 1946. p. 20.
[50]Hudson, K. *Industrial Archaeology*. Baker, 1963. p. 151.
[51]*First Report of Her Maiesty's Commissioners for Inquiring into the Housing of the Working Classes*. HMSO, 1889. p. 33.

[52]Cowan, P. et al *The Office. A Facet of Urban Growth.* Heinemann, 1969. p. 157.
[53]Kellett, J. R. op cit. p. 327.
[54]Fremantle, F. E. *The Housing of the Nation.* Allan, 1927. p. 16–17.
[55]Knowles, C. C. & Pitt, P. H. *The History of Building Regulations in London 1189–1972.* Architectural Press, 1972. p. 60–64.
[56]Examples examined were: Bristol 1840, 1847, 1871, 1896; Canton (Cardiff) 1872; Cardiff 1859, 1900; Liverpool 1875; Ystradyfodwg (Rhondda) 1879; Model By-laws 1880.
[57]Harper, R. 'The Conflict between English Building Regulations and Architectural Design 1890–1918.' *J. of Architectural Research* Vol. 6, No. 1, March 1977. Also informative correspondence with the author.
[58]Vaughan, A. *A Pictorial Record of Great Western Architecture.* Oxford Publishing, 1977. p. 8, 9, 192, 334, 376.
[59]*Kelly's Directory of the Building Trades.* Kelly, 1886.
[60]Hamilton, S. B. *A Note on the History of Reinforced Concrete in Buildings.* HMSO, 1956, & *A Short History of the Structural Fire Protection of Buildings.* HMSO, 1958.
[61]Banham, R. *The Architecture of the Well-Tempered Environment.* Architectural Press, 1969. p. 39, 45–46.
[62]Middleton, G. A. T. *Modern Buildings. Their Planning, Construction and Equipment.* Caxton, n.d. (c. 1905). p. 119 et seq.
[63]Derry, T. K. & Williams, T. I. *A Short History of Technology from the Earliest Time to AD 1900.* Clarendon, 1960. p. 508–513.
[64]Banham, R. *Mechanical Services. History of Architecture and Design 1890–1939.* Open University Press, 1975.
[65]Wright, L. *Clean and Decent. The Fascinating History of the Bathroom and the Water Closet.* Routledge & Kegan Paul, 1960.

4 RAGGED TROUSERED PHILANTHROPY: THE INDUSTRY 1851–1914

[1]After Mitchell, B. R. & Deane, P. op cit. p. 60.
[2]Richardson, H. W. & Aldcroft, D. H. *Building in the British Economy between the Wars.* Allen & Unwin, 1968. p. 276.
[3]Aldcroft, D. H. & Richardson, H. W. op cit. p. 45.
[4]Gotch, J. A. *The Growth and Work of the Royal Institute of British Architects.* RIBA, 1934. p. 121–123.
[5]Kaye, B. *The Development of the Architectural Profession in Britain.* Allen & Unwin, 1960. p. 64.
[6]Micklethwaite, J. T. op cit. p. 236.
[7]Kaye, B. op cit. p. 173–174.

[8]Summerson, J. *The London Building World of the Eighteeen-Sixties.* Thames & Hudson, 1973. p. 20.
[9]Nisbet, J. op cit.
[10]*Kelly's Directory* . . . op cit.
[11]Dyos, H. J. *Victorian Suburb. A Study of the Growth of Camberwell.* Leicester University Press, 1966. p. 122 et seq.
[12]Crossick, G. *An Artisan Elite in Victorian Society. Kentish London 1840–1880.* Croom Helm, 1978. p. 54.
[13]Dyos, H. J. 1968. op cit.
[14]Sheppard, F. H. W. (ed.) *Survey of London. Vol. XXXVII Northern Kensington.* Athlone, 1973. p. 8.
[15]Summerson, J. op cit. p. 13.
[16]Bowley, M. *The British Building Industry. Four Studies in Response and Resistance to Change.* Cambridge University Press, 1966. p. 339.
[17]Sheppard, F. H. W. (ed.) op cit. p. 9.
[18]Dyos, H. J. 1968. op cit.
[19]Tressell, R. *The Ragged Trousered Philanthropists.* Panther, 1965.
[20]Clapham, J. *An Economic History of Modern Britain. Free Trade and Steel 1850–1886.* Cambridge University Press, 1963. p. 120.
[21]Samuel, R. (ed.) *Village Life and Labour.* Routledge & Kegan Paul, 1975. p. 164, 175, 230.
[22]Jones, G. T. *Increasing Return.* Cambridge University Press, 1933. p. 270.
[23]Maiwald, K. 'An Index of Building Costs in the United Kingdom, 1845–1938.' *Economic History Review* 2nd series, Vol. VII, No. 2, 1954.
[24]Brown, E. H. P. & Hopkins, S. V. op cit.
[25]Levi, L. *Wages and Earnings of the Working Classes* . . . Murray 1867. p. 65.
[26]Usill, G. W. (ed.) *The Builders' and Contractors' Price Book and Guide to Estimating.* Scientific Publishing, 1885.
[27]Routh, G. *Occupation and Pay in Great Britain 1906–1960.* Cambridge University Press, 1965. p. 88.
[28]Postgate, R. W. op cit. p. 181.
[29]Kingsford, P. W. *Builders and Building Workers.* Arnold, 1973. p. 122–123.
[30]Hilton, W. S. op cit. p. 165.
[31]Maiwald, K. op cit.
[32]Barker, T. C. & Savage, C. I. *An Economic History of Transport in Britain.* Hutchinson, 1974. p. 105, 141.
[33]Woodforde, J. *Bricks to Build a House.* Routledge & Kegan Paul, 1976. p. 146–154.

[34]Laxton, W. *Laxton's Builders' Price Book.* Kelly, 1894.
[35]Mitchell, B. R. & Deane, P. op cit. p. 298–300.
[36]Jones, G. T. op cit. p. 66, 83, 94.
[37]Skyring, W. H. *Skyring's Builders' Prices.* Skyring, 1856.
[38]Bowley, M. 1960. op cit. p. 90.
[39]Slater, E. A. *Structural Economy.* St. Bride's Press, 1912. p. 21, 23, 32.
[40]Maiwald, K. op cit.
[41]Laxton, W. op cit.
[42]Dobson, E. *Foundations and Concrete Works.* Crosby Lockwood, 1891. p. iv.

5 BUILDINGS IN RIBBONS AND SUBURBS: 1915–39

[1]Richardson, H. W. & Aldcroft, D. H. op cit. p. 43.
[2]Bowley, M. 1966. op cit. p. 368–369.
[3]Jackson, A. A. *Semi-Detached London.* Allen & Unwin, 1973. p. 121–122.
[4]Robinson, H. W. *The Economics of Building.* King, 1939. p. 9–10.
[5]Young, G. M. *Country and Town. A Summary of the Scott and Uthwatt Reports.* Penguin, 1943. p. 35–36.
[6]Priestley, J. B. *English Journey.* Heinemann, 1934. p. 398–399, 401.
[7]Richardson, H. W. & Aldcroft, D. H. op cit.
[8]Bowley, M. 'Some Regional Aspects of the Building Boom, 1924–36.' *Review of Economic Studies* 5, 1937–1938.
[9]Burnett, J. 1978. op cit. p. 246. Upon which this section relies extensively.
[10]Thomas, P. E. (ed.) *Modern Building Practice.* Newnes, n.d. (c. 1938). p. 244–245.
[11]Burnett, J. 1978. op cit. p. 247.
[12]Young, C. (ed.) *Spons' Architects' and Builders' Pocket Price Book.* Spon, various years. Upon which this section relies extensively.
[13]Jackson, A. A. op cit. p. 359.
[14]Wright, H. M. *Small Houses £500–£2500.* Architectural Press, 1946.
[15]Bowley, M. 1960. op cit. p. 132.
[16]Bowley, M. *Housing and the State 1919–1944.* Allen & Unwin, 1947.
[17]Pepper, S. & Swenarton, M. 'Home Front: Garden Suburbs for Munition Workers.' *Architectural Review* Vol. CLXIII, June 1978.

[18]Marriner, S. 'Cash and Concrete. Liquidity Problems in the Mass-Production of "Homes for Heroes".' *Business History* Vol. XVIII, No. 2, 1976.
[19]Local Government Board R*eport of the Committee . . . to Consider Questions of Building Construction in Connection with the Provision of Dwellings for the Working Classes* . . . (Tudor Walters Report) HMSO, 1918.
[20]Powell, C. 'Fifty Years of Progress. The Influence of the Tudor Walters Report on British Public Authority Housing Examined and Compared with Present Day Standards.' *Built Environment* Vol. 3, No. 10, 1974.
[21]Sayle, A. *The Houses of the Workers*. Unwin, 1924. p. 153.
[22]Hole, W. V. & Attenburrow, J. J. *Houses and People*. HMSO, 1966. p. 49.
[23]Sutcliffe, A. (ed.) op cit. Contains Ravetz, A.
[24]Richardson, H. W. & Aldcroft, D. H. op cit. p. 35–36.
[25]*Architects' Journal* 16 July 1930.
[26]Kahn, M. *The Design and Construction of Industrial Buildings*. Technical Journals, 1917. p. 11.
[27]Swift, G. A. *Steel Framed Works Buildings*. Draughtsman Publishing, 1930. p. 5–6.
[28]Brockman, H. A. N. op cit. p. 118 et seq.
[29]Kohan, C. M. *History of the Second World War. Works and Buildings*. HMSO, 1952. p. 278.
[30]Harvey, N. op cit. p. 170–171.
[31]Richardson, H. W. & Aldcroft, D. H. op cit. p. 43.
[32]Jeffreys, J. B. op cit. p. 59.
[33]Halsey, A. H. (ed.) *Trends in British Society Since 1900*. Macmillan, 1972. p. 558.
[34]Sharp, D. *The Picture Palace and Other Buildings for the Movies*. Evelyn, 1969. p. 120, 125–126.
[35]Yorke, F. W. B. *Planning and Equipment of Public Houses*. Architectural Press, 1949. p. 204.
[36]Richardson, H. W. & Aldcroft, D. H. op cit. p. 62.
[37]Stevenson, J. *Social Conditions in Britain Between the Wars*. Penguin, 1977. p. 11.
[38]Wright, H. M. & Gardner-Medwin, R. *The Design of Nursery and Elementary Schools*. Architectural Press, 1938. p. 16.
[39]Halsey, A. H. (ed.) op cit. p. 206.
[40]Pinker, R. op cit. p. 56.
[41]Orwell, G. *The Road to Wigan Pier*. Penguin, 1963. p. 58.
[42]Ashburner, E. H. op cit.

[43]Thompson, A. *Library Buildings of Britain and Europe*. Butterworths, 1963. p. 106 et seq.
[44]Cross, K. M. B. *Modern Public Baths*. Simpkin Marshall, 1938. p. 8.
[45]Richardson, H. W. & Aldcroft, D. H. op cit. p. 105–106.
[46]White, R. B. *Prefabrication. A History of its Development in Great Britain*. HMSO, 1965. p. 103.
[47]Nuffield Foundation, Division for Architectural Studies. *The Design of Research Laboratories*. Oxford University Press, 1961. p. 19.
[48]Thomas, P. E. op cit. p. 49, 531.
[49]Stillman, C. G. & Cleary, R. C. *The Modern School*. Architectural Press, 1949. p. 17, 23.
[50]Seaborne, M. & Lowe, R. *The English School, Its Architecture and Organization. Vol. II 1870–1970*. Routledge & Kegan Paul, 1977. p. 132.

6 MEN OF SPRAWL: THE INDUSTRY 1915–39

[1]Richardson, H. W. & Aldcroft, D. H. op cit. p. 269.
[2]Ibid. p. 271 quotes Lomax, K. S. 'Production and Productivity Movements in the U.K. since 1900.' *J. of Royal Statistical Soc.* A122, 1959.
[3]Robinson, H. W. op cit. p. 5–6.
[4]Richardson, H. W. & Aldcroft, D. H. op cit. p. 154 quotes Ministry of Works *Working Party Report on Building*. HMSO, 1950, p. 80.
[5]Gotch, J. A. op cit. p. 121–123.
[6]*Architects' Journal* 27 July 1939.
[7]Rowntree, B. S. *Portrait of a City's Housing*. Faber, 1945. p. 19.
[8]Times, The *British Homes. The Building Society Movement*. The Times, 1938. p. 68.
[9]Kaye, B. op cit. p. 151–156, 174.
[10]Gotch, J. A. op cit. p. 119.
[11]Creswell, H. B. *The Honeywood File. An Adventure in Building*. Faber, 1972.
[12]Kaye, B. op cit. p. 165.
[13]Bowley, M. 1966. op cit. p. 78 et seq.
[14]Davey, N. *Building in Britain*. Evans, 1964. p. 101.
[15]British Standards Institution *Fifty Years of British Standards 1901–1951*. BSI, 1951.
[16]Marriner, S. 'Sir Alfred Mond's Octopus: a Nationalised

House-Building Business.' *Business History* Vol. XXI, No. 1, 1979.
[17]White, R. B. op cit. p. 64–65.
[18]Robinson, H. W. op cit. p. 12.
[19]Richardson, H. W. & Aldcroft, D. H. op cit. p. 157–158.
[20]Bowley, M. 1966. op cit. p. 374.
[21]Robinson, H. W. op cit. p. 15.
[22]Burnett, J. 1978. op cit. p. 257.
[23]Bowley, M. 1966. op cit. p. 382.
[24]Richardson, H. W. & Aldcroft, D. H. op cit. p. 48, 70.
[25]Postgate, R. W. op cit. Appendix I.
[26]Young, C. (ed.) 1924. op cit.
[27]Maiwald, K. op cit.
[28]Chapman, A. L. & Knight, R. *Wages and Salaries in the U.K. 1920–1938*. Cambridge University Press, 1953. p. 27.
[29]Kingsford, P. W. op cit. p. 175.
[30]Hilton, W. S. *Industrial Relations in Construction*. Pergamon, 1968. p. 161–162.
[31]Maiwald, K. op cit.
[32]Ibid.
[33]White, R. B. op cit. p. 73–74.
[34]Jackson, A. A. op cit. p. 152–153.
[35]Bowley, M. 1960. op cit. p. 133.
[36]Gunn, E. *Economy in House Design*. Architectural Press, 1932. p. 36.
[37]Woodforde, J. op cit. p. 155.
[38]Young, C. (ed.) various years. op cit. Upon which this section relies extensively.
[39]Stobart, T. J. *Timber Trade of the United Kingdom*. Crosby Lockwood, 1927. Vol. I Table facing p. 1, 1–2, 91. Vol II Table facing p. 2.
[40]Bowley, M. 1960. op cit. p. 133, 151, 263–265.
[41]Bowley, M. 1966. op cit. p. 108.
[42]Gunn, E. op cit. p. 65.
[43]Bowley, M. 1960. op cit. p. 279–285.

7 BUILDINGS IN AUSTERITY AND AFFLUENCE: 1940–73

[1]Glynn, S. & Oxborrow, J. op cit. p. 16 quotes Feinstein, C. H. *National Income, Expenditure and Output of the United Kingdom 1855–1965*. Cambridge University Press, 1972.
[2]Higgin, G. & Jessop, N. *Communications in the Building Industry*.

The Report of a Pilot Study. Tavistock, 1965. p. 16.

[3]Emmerson, H. *The Ministry of Works*. Allen & Unwin, 1956. p. 20.

[4]Kohan, C. M. op cit. p. 353 et seq.

[5]Cullingworth, J. B. *Housing and Local Government in England and Wales*. Allen & Unwin, 1966. p. 67.

[6]Sharp, E. *The Ministry of Housing and Local Government*. Allen & Unwin, 1969. p. 26.

[7]Needleman, L. *The Economics of Housing*. Staples, 1965. p. 135, 138.

[8]Layton, E. *Building by Local Authorities*. Allen & Unwin, 1961. p. 72.

[9]Balchin, P. N. & Kieve ,J. L. *Urban Land Economics*. Macmillan, 1977. p. 91.

[10]Cadman, D. & Austin-Crowe, L. *Property Development*. Spon, 1978. p. 174, 176–177.

[11]Cowan, P. et al. op cit. p. 127.

[12]Ashworth, W. op cit. p. 233.

[13]Cullingworth, J. B. *Town and Country Planning in England and Wales. The Changing Scene*. Allen & Unwin, 1970.

[14]English, J. et al *Slum Clearance. The Social and Administrative Context in England and Wales*. Croom Helm, 1976. p. 36–37.

[15]Turin, D. A. *Aspects of the Economics of Construction*. Godwin, 1975. contains Sugden, J. D.

[16]Hancock, W. K. & Gowing, M. M. *History of the Second World War. British War Economy*. HMSO, 1949. p. 174–175, 321.

[17]Kohan, C. M. op cit. p. 137, 488.

[18]Allen, G. C. *British Industries and their Organization*. Longmans, 1964. p. 298.

[19]Central Statistical Office *Annual Abstract of Statistics 1973*. HMSO, 1973. p. 191.

[20]Donnison, D. V. *The Government of Housing*. Penguin, 1967. p. 167.

[21]Vipond, M. J. 'Fluctuations in Private Housebuilding in Great Britain, 1950–1966.' *Scottish J. of Political Economy* Vol. 16, 1969.

[22]Ministry of Housing & Local Government *Housing Statistics. Great Britain*. HMSO, various dates, succeeded by Department of the Environment *Housing and Construction Statistics*. HMSO, various dates.

[23]Central Housing Advisory Committee *Design of Dwellings*. HMSO, 1944.

[24]Ministry of Health & Ministry of Works *Housing Manual 1944*.

HMSO, 1944.
[25]Forshaw, J. H. & Abercrombie, P. *County of London Plan*. Macmillan, 1943, p. 78.
[26]Barr, A. W. C. *Public Authority Housing*. Batsford, 1958. p. 132.
[27]Burnett, J. 1978. op cit. p. 299–300.
[28]Jephcott, P. with Robinson, H. *Homes in High Flats*. Oliver & Boyd, 1971. p. 7.
[29]Ministry of Housing & Local Government *Homes for Today and Tomorrow*. (Parker Morris Report) HMSO, 1961.
[30]Burnett, J. 1978. op cit. p. 302–303.
[31]Stone, P. A. *The Structure, Size and Costs of Urban Settlements*. Cambridge University Press, 1973. p. 104.
[32]Seaborne, M. & Lowe, R. op cit. p. 155.
[33]Pilkington Research Unit; Manning, P. (ed.) *The Primary School: an Environment for Education*. Dept. of Building Science, University of Liverpool, 1967. p. 135.
[34]Ward, C. (ed.) *British School Buildings. Designs and Appraisals 1964–74*. Architectural Press, 1976.
[35]Halsey, A. H. (ed.) op cit. p. 206.
[36]Brawne, M. (ed.) *University Planning and Design. Architectural Association Paper No. 3*. Lund Humphries, 1967. p. 24.
[37]Davis, Belfield & Everest (eds.) *Spons' Architects' and Builders' Price Book*. Spon, 1948 & 1969. From which various prices have been taken.
[38]Berriman, S. G. & Harrison, K. C. *British Public Library Buildings*. Deutsch, 1966.
[39]Reynolds, J. D. (ed.) *Library Buildings 1965*. Library Association, 1966. p. 28–92.
[40]Incorporated Church Building Society *Sixty Post-War Churches*. ICBS, n.d. (c. 1956). p. 11.
[41]Builder Ltd. & Roskill, O. W. *The Building Industry –1962 Onwards*. Builder, 1962. p. 126 quotes Census of Production for 1958.
[42]Harvey, N. op cit. p. 212–248.
[43]Colclough, J. R. *The Construction Industry of Great Britain*. Butterworths, 1965. p. 10.
[44]Marriott, O. op cit. p. 5.
[45]Cowan, P. et al. op cit. p. 112, 181.
[46]Jeffreys, J. B. op cit. p. 101.
[47]Rees, G. *St. Michael. A History of Marks and Spencer*. Weidenfeld & Nicolson, 1969. p. 230.
[48]Needleman, L. op cit. p. 149.

[49]Cowan, P. et al. op cit. p. 162.
[50]Burnett, J. 1978. op cit. p. 277, 279.
[51]National Economic Development Office *How Flexible is Construction? A Study of Resources and Participants in the Construction Process*. HMSO, 1978. p. 75.
[52]Thomas, R. & Peacock, R. *Housing. Statistical Sources Unit 4*. Open University Press, 1975. p. 41–42.

8 WORKHORSE LEARNS TO CANTER: THE INDUSTRY 1940–73

[1]Dow, J. C. R. *Management of the British Economy 1945–1960*. Cambridge University Press, 1965. p. 149–151.
[2]Rosenberg, N. *Economic Planning in the British Building Industry 1945–49*. University of Pennsylvania Press & Oxford University Press, 1960.
[3]Emmerson, H. *Survey of Problems Before the Construction Industries*. HMSO, 1962.
[4]Bowley, M. 1966. op cit. p. 441.
[5]Higgin, G. & Jessop, N. op cit.
[6]Ministry of Public Building and Works *The Placing and Management of Contracts for Building and Civil Engineering Work*. HMSO, 1964.
[7]National Economic Development Office *Before You Build. What a Client Needs to Know About the Construction Industry*. HMSO, 1974. p. 26–27.
[8]Royal Institute of British Architects *The Architect and His Office*. RIBA, 1962. p. 26.
[9]Layton, E. op cit. p. 168.
[10]Jenkins, F. *Architect and Patron. A Survey of Professional Relations and Practice in England from the Sixteenth Century to the Present Day*. Oxford University Press, 1961. p. 236.
[11]Burn, D. (ed.) *The Structure of British Industry. A Symposium*. Cambridge University Press, 1958. Contains Carter, C. F.
[12]Bowley, M. 1966. op cit. p. 279.
[13]MacEwen, M. *Crisis in Architecture*. RIBA, 1974.
[14]Cheetham, J. H. (ed.) *House's Guide to the Building Industry 1970*. House.
[15]Parlett, D. S. (ed.) *Construction Industry UK*. House, 1976.
[16]White, R. B. op cit. p. 123, 137, 152 et seq.
[17]Balchin, P. N. & Kieve, J. L. op cit. p. 233.
[18]Hillebrandt, P. M. *Economic Theory and the Construction Industry*. Macmillan, 1974. p. 157.

[19]Allen, G. C. op cit. p. 299–300.
[20]Forster, G. *Building Organisation and Procedures*. Longman, 1978. p. 72–77.
[21]Turner, G. *Business in Britain*. Penguin, 1971. p. 292, 296–300.
[22]Foster, C. *Building With Men*. Tavistock, 1969.
[23]National Economic Development Office. 1978. op cit. p. 21.
[24]Gray, H. *The Cost of Council Housing*. Institute of Economic Affairs, 1968. p. 65.
[25]Colclough, J. R. op cit. p. 35.
[26]Burn, D. (ed.) op cit. contains Carter, C. F.
[27]Department of the Environment, op cit.
[28]*Report of the Committee of Inquiry under Professor E. H. Phelps Brown into Certain Matters Concerning Labour in Building and Civil Engineering*. Cd. 3714. HMSO, 1968.
[29]Grossmith, G. & Grossmith, W. *The Diary of a Nobody*. Dent, 1964. p. 57 et seq.
[30]Design Council *Leisure in the Twentieth Century*. Design Council, 1977. Contains Johnson, D.
[31]Office of Population Censuses and Surveys, Social Survey Division *General Household Survey 1973*. HMSO, 1976. p. 80.
[32]Bowley, M. 1960. op cit. p. 135.
[33]Department of the Environment. op cit.
[34]Thomas, G. *Operatives in the Building Industry*. HMSO, 1968. p. 2, 5–6, 42.
[35]Stone, P. A. *Urban Development in Britain: Standards, Costs and Resources, 1964–2004*. Cambridge University Press, 1970. p. 231.
[36]Zweig, F. *The British Worker*. Penguin, 1952. p. 35–36.
[37]Wallis, L. *The Building Industry: Its Work and Organisation*. Dent, 1945. p. 17.
[38]National Board for Prices and Incomes *Report No. 92. Pay and Conditions in the Building Industry*. Cd. 3837. HMSO, 1968. p. 8, 39–40.
[39]Royal Institute of British Architects *The Industrialisation of Building*. RIBA, 1965. p. 36.
[40]National Economic Development Office. 1978. op cit. p. 27.
[41]Hilton, W. S. 1968. op cit. p. 143–144.
[42]Prest, A. R. & Coppock, D. J. *The U.K. Economy. A Manual of Applied Economics*. Weidenfeld & Nicolson, 1976. p. 38, 44.
[43]Central Statistical Office *Monthly Digest of Statistics*. No. 349, Jan. 1975. p. 146–147.
[44]Hilton, W. S. 1968. op cit. p. 47–48, 71–72.
[45]Stone, P. A. *Building Economy*. Pergamon, 1966. p. 158.

[46]Bowley, M. 1960. op cit. p. 140.
[47]Department of the Environment. op cit.
[48]Stone, P. A. 1966. op cit. p. 167.
[49]Nabseth, L. & Ray, G. F. *The Diffusion of New Industrial Processes. An International Study*. Cambridge University Press, 1974. p. 299.
[50]White, R. B. op cit. p. 138–149.
[51]Barham, H. *Building Industry. A Criticism and a Plan for the Future*. St. Botolph, 1947. p. 6.
[52]Turin, D. A. op cit. Contains Sugden, J. D.

9 EPILOGUE

[1]Riley, K. M. 'An Estimate of the Age Distribution of the Dwelling Stock in Great Britain.' *Urban Studies* Vol. 10, 1973.
[2]Webb, C. A. op cit; Young, C. (ed.) op cit; & Davis, Belfield & Everest (eds.) op cit.

Index

For Product Safety Concerns and Information please contact our EU representative GPSR@taylorandfrancis.com Taylor & Francis Verlag GmbH, Kaufingerstraße 24, 80331 München, Germany